GW01325893

THE FIRST EMSWORTH COOKBOOK SOLD OUT IN TWO WEEKS

Emsworth Seasons Cookbook & Pictorial Souvenir

This book is dedicated to our granddaughter, Emma Jacqueline Dawson born April 2004.

Following the overwhelming response to 'The Emsworth Cookbook and Pictorial Souvenir' published in 2003, we decided that rather than re-print the original book to meet demand we would produce a new limited edition book.

As a result, we have been able to include much more, with new recipes from those who contributed to the last book as well as from others wishing to be a part of this celebration of our village. The general history, information and photographs, covering Emsworth and surrounding areas are all new to this book.

Yet again our thanks go to all those who have contributed to the production of this book, whether preparing their recipes or writing articles and sourcing old photographs. Without this willingness to participate, the book could not exist. There are too many individuals and organisations to list here, however their names are included at the end of the book.

We do hope that you, the reader, enjoy this new book as much as you so obviously did the first, and see it as we do, a tribute to our beautiful village and its people.

Elaine Connolly & John Tweddell
CTComms, Emsworth

The publishers have made every effort to gain permission for publication from the respective originators of the historical photographs included in this book. The copyright for all photographs remains with the originator or the person to whom ownership has been passed. If you should be able to identify any photographer whose work has been used, but not contacted, we would welcome this information.

Emsworth Seasons Cookbook & Pictorial Souvenir

Recipes from Emsworth

Copyright © 2004 CTComms, Emsworth

First published in 2004
By CTComms

10987654321

All rights reserved. No part of this publication may be reproduced, stored in a retrieval system, or transmitted in any form or by any means without the prior permission of the publisher, nor be otherwise circulated in any form of binding or cover other than that in which it is published without a similar condition being imposed on the subsequent purchaser.

ISBN 0-9545751-1-3

Edited by Elaine Connolly
Designed by Ems Editorial & John Tweddell
Photography by John Tweddell

Printed and bound in Great Britain by BorcombeSP, Romsey, Hampshire
www.borcombesp.com

CTComms
Keswick House
48 Victoria Road
Emsworth
Hampshire
PO10 7NJ
t. 01243 374416
e. ctcomms@btconnect.com

www.emsworthcookbook.co.uk

The editor and publishers accept no responsibility for the content, accuracy or otherwise of the recipes and information contained in this publication. The recipes have been accepted in good faith, and have not been independently tested.

PHIL VICKERY, RATED AS ONE OF THE TOP 20 CHEFS IN BRITAIN, COOKS GREAT BRITISH FOOD AND IS RIGHTLY FAMOUS FOR HIS PUDDINGS.

BORN IN FOLKESTONE, KENT, PHIL TRAINED IN THE LAKE DISTRICT BEFORE WORKING AT GRAVETYE MANOR IN WEST SUSSEX AND RESTAURANT 74 IN CANTERBURY. HE THEN MOVED TO TAUNTON, BECOMING HEAD CHEF AT THE CASTLE HOTEL. DURING HIS NINE YEARS THERE, AMONG MANY AWARDS, HE WON MICHELIN AND EGON RONAY STARS FOUR YEARS IN A ROW.

HE APPEARS REGULARLY ON 'READY, STEADY, COOK' AND 'THIS MORNING' AS WELL AS MANY OTHER TV PROGRAMMES. PHIL ALSO WRITES FOR A NUMBER OF MAGAZINES, HAS PRODUCED A NUMBER OF HIS OWN COOKBOOKS AND IS MARRIED TO TV PRESENTER, FERN BRITTON.

During 2003 when I was asked to write the preface for the 'Emsworth Cookbook & Pictorial Souvenir', little did any of us realise what a huge success the book would be, selling out as it did so quickly.

So, I am really delighted that the many chefs of the village of Emsworth, and even more of them this year, have taken the time to help in the production of this new and even bigger 'Emsworth Seasons Cookbook & Pictorial Souvenir' by preparing and cooking some of their favourite recipes.

Knowing that others share my passion and interest in food is heart warming, and I commend all those who have contributed in whatever way to this book. It is again a source of inspiration, with its many different and varied recipes. And, it is always a pleasure to see children from the local schools showing such enthusiasm for cookery at an early age – perhaps some will become future chefs.

Yet again the book contains many wonderful photographs of all the food as well as the village and surrounding areas. My wife, Fern lived in the area for a number of years and the contents of the book have brought back happy memories of her time there with her family. We hope to be able to come and visit at some point in the future.

I do hope that this book proves to be as successful as the previous one, and extend my congratulations to all the residents and businesses of Emsworth who have made this possible.

Good Luck and Best Wishes,

CONTENTS

FOOD, AND NOTHING BUT THE FOOD
BY LINDA NEWELL, EMSWORTH

THIS ARTICLE IS DEDICATED TO MY HUSBAND, ERNIE NEWELL, WHO DIED 17TH APRIL 2004. HIS PATIENT RESEARCH WAS ALWAYS IMPECCABLE AND THOROUGH: A SOLID BASIS FOR ALL MY WORK. HIS LOVE AND SUPPORT WILL BE SO GREATLY MISSED BY ALL HIS FAMILY.

food *(n.)* substance(s) (to be) taken into the body to maintain life and growth. (Concise Oxford Dictionary)

food *(n.)* source of nutrients for living things. Material that provides living things with the nutrients they need for energy and growth. *Food for thought* (Old English *fōda*. Ultimately from an Indo-European word that is also the ancestor of English *feed, fodder,* and *pastor*.) (Encarta World English Dictionary)

This is a gentle ramble through the history of food, food management and household hints. It seems a secret subject; probably because it is so fundamental to the survival of the human race. There are quite a few books on household hints, but there is nothing to tell us who first decided to grind corn, or who thought it would be a good idea to boil and eat an egg! From time immemorial, in order to survive, man has had to eat, and in order to eat he has had to obtain food. He hunted it, fished for it, gathered it or grew it.

Food took up a phenomenal amount of time for our early ancestors. They did not have the convenience of supermarkets, fast food or microwaves. Implements for catching food had to be made or devised, tools for preparing food had to be fashioned. All food had to be prepared by the members of the household who were going to eat it. Wood had to be gathered to create the heat to cook the food. The catching of meat was a skill that needed years of training to perfect, and then those years of experience had to be passed on to the next generation. Any interruption in this line of skill and experience could mean the end of the group, because they would starve through an inability to catch enough meat.

Gathering wood sounds easy, but it was not just any wood. The right sort of wood was needed, and also the sort of wood that was suitable for the type of cooking that was being undertaken. Fires could be controlled to give a certain type of heat, by burning the correct wood. Oak would give a long intense fire, while pine and apple would give a fast fire, but the wood would spit because of the resin in it. Depending on how the fire was built would also affect the way it burned. All living wood has air in the channels where the sap runs up and down the trunk, and if the logs are stood upright to burn, they will burn hot and fast, because the air channels are operating the as little funnels to draw fire upwards. Wood laid horizontal in the fire would be a long, slower, steadier burn. Right throughout history wood has been the principal source of heat for cooking, and despite the fact that the majority of dwellings were made of flammable materials, there were comparatively few recorded incidents of serious fires, apart from 1666 in London. Another serious incident happened in Havant during the early 1700s. The fact that fires could be controlled so well was down to the respect that everyone had for the damage that fire could do. No housewife would ever leave her fire burning overnight. In the early 900s AD, a law was made that insisted that all fires were extinguished at sundown, and this in the early 11th century was continued. The word curfew comes from this period when people were required to "couvre le feu" - cover the fire. The fire was the centre of the household, in a similar way that today people gather in the kitchen. Then it was the centre of light and warmth, and songs and stories told around the fire in the evening were a way of passing on the traditions of hunting and living from the land.

Who decided that food should be cooked? We find it unpleasant to think of eating all our food raw, but it is almost certainly possible that this did happen. Then, someone accidentally dropped something edible into a fire and they found that the result was not a disaster, but that the food had been made more pleasant by being cooked. Not only did it taste nicer and look better, it was easier to eat, because the cooking process tenderised the fibres. All food that needed to be cooked was cooked over a wood fire, and to start with there were no pots or pans to hold the food. It sounds like a modern barbecue, with burnt outside and raw inside! However, the people soon learnt to improvise and design utensils. The first one may have been a skin held between a pyramid of sticks. The skin could not be used over the direct heat, but the water was heated by putting hot stones into the skin, and that heated the water, which heated the food in it. This was a slow system, but it was obviously effective. Gradually, as they applied their minds to the problem, utensils evolved. Fish and long thin cuts of meat could be coated in clay and cooked in the fire. As the clay hardened into a crust it conducted the heat, and sealed the flavour and juices in. Stones could be used for grilling and the husk or skin of the food was used as a container. Then pottery was introduced and this transformed the art of cooking, bringing the ability to boil, roast, fry and grill all being within grasp. The human race just had to develop the skills of cookery.

In order to eat this food, man had to catch it. If he did not catch it he would suffer great hardship during the winter months, and possibly not survive the cold weather. He had to eat well during the warm months to build up enough fat stores to survive the months when food was not plentiful. Man did not hibernate, but it might have been in his interests to develop this skill! The animals that he depended upon for food tended to move around the countryside in cycles. They would breed in one area, mate in another and graze in another. They would migrate with the seasons, and all these skills the early hunters had to be able to learn fast. If animals were creatures of habit, man would have to follow them, and once he had learned their patterns of behaviour he could

plan to trap and kill them. Deer were fast and could outrun a man, but if he could set a trap and then drive the deer into it, he would be able to catch them. The auroch was a wild cow, which was 6ft high at the shoulder, with horns as big as elephant tusks. It could gore a man as easily as tossing a leaf, so the men had to hunt in groups and track it carefully in order to bring it down. They would follow it and try to injure it with their spears and arrows. These were barbed, so that they would stick into the side of the animal and move when caught on branches, and eventually the wound would be serious enough that the animal would be weakened through loss of blood, and the men could close in and finish it off. It was a great prize and would keep a group of people well fed for some time, so it was worth the long, patient chase. Bear in those days were as dangerous as now, and there were wolves, elk, and various members of the cat family to add variety, but they were always dangerous. Geese, duck and various birds were also trapped for food. Obviously, these were easier because they were not so fast or so fierce. I imagine most of us would be quite happy to catch these, rather than risk everything for one big fantastic animal!

To add flavour and variety to their diet, and sometimes to stave off hunger, there would be berries, nuts and seeds to collect, such as are found in the hedgerows of our countryside today. Grasses and leaves could be used to stuff and wrap food in to preserve the juices and to protect them from the fierce heat of the fire. Evidence has shown that

early man was eating grass seeds and early forms of grain, fruits such as elderberries, raspberries, rose hips and hawthorn berries. Bog beans, knotweed and bull-rush roots were useful. The bull-rush roots were a form of starch which when cooked was fibrous and could be chewed and sucked to get the nourishment out of it. The sap of the birch tree was a form of sweet syrup, which they would have tapped straight from the tree.

If the encampment was near a river or the coastal inlets, then the variety increased with the addition of fish, shellfish and seaweeds.

Weapons had to be fashioned to assist early man with the tasks of hunting, killing and preparing the food. Obviously, the first weapons were stones, but it takes a brave man to hit a wild animal on the head with a stone! Flint was, and still is, a form of stone nodule that is found in the chalk downlands, where most early men lived, and when this stone is chipped or broken it makes a very sharp edge. This edge was found to be valuable for all sorts of tasks. It could be inserted into a length of twig to make a spear, harpoon or an arrow, and once the idea was thought of, then every man could make his own variations, and the sophisticated developments were endless. Spears could have a sharp point of flint in the end, but also little points of flint in the sides to give a barbed effect, so that the arrow would not be shaken off

easily, but could work its way into the animal and make capture easier. In heavily wooded areas bows could not be used, because they would catch on overhanging branches and the aim would be deflected, but spears and harpoons would fly through the trees easily.

Having caught the animal and taken it back to the encampment, the flints could be used as scraping tools to take the skin or hide from the meat, and also to take the hair from the hide, to use the skins for tents. Blades were made to cut the meat into joints, and also to remove the sinews from the meat, to be used as ties and ropes. Every part of the animal would be used, because it was such an effort to catch and kill it. The meat obviously was used for food, and what could not be eaten immediately was dried to be preserved and carried. The skin and fur were used for clothing and tents. Many of the bones could be used as tools or needles. In fact, the shoulder blade of a cow or deer was a very good flat shovel! The sinews were good strong ropes, or could be shredded to

make finer threads to sew hides together for tents or clothing. Very resourceful and efficient!

Early man was developing his skills during the time immediately after the last Ice Age. Northern Europe was still a cold and damp place, but between 10,000BC and about 6,000BC the sea level was rising due to the increase of water from the melting ice, and the north-western tip of the continent became detached, and formed the British Isles. The early British people were on their own!

Gradually by 4,000BC the idea of farming began to be introduced from the Middle East. Again, it is another major innovation, and who thought of putting a seed in the ground in a particular place and who thought of putting a cow in a field? We will never know, but it was a wonderful step forward. Wheat and barley were just wild grasses, but someone saw the potential of preparing the ground and growing it in a dedicated area. Then, by keeping the other plants away from it, cutting it when it was ripe and then grinding the seeds to make flour. It meant not fast food, but was definitely quicker than hunting the hedgerows. This offered not only food outside the door, but by letting the domestic animals roam, the soil could be kept fertilised. The land had to be cleared of woodland in order to make the space to lay out the fields.

The land was not covered with wonderful dense forests, but by a scrubby sort of woodland, remnants of which remain in some remote areas today. In order to clear the land, man had to be very innovative. He did not have chain saws and super sharp axes. All he had was flint axes, which

would take a month of Sundays and a lot of sharpening to get through old wood. The innovation was that man took a long-term view of the problem. He planned ahead and made a work schedule for several years. By damaging the bark, the tree died. Each year last year's trees could be stripped out and a new batch of trees could be scarred. Over a period of years the trees were removed and the land prepared for farming. Obviously, the land was fertile to start with, but as the amount of goodness being extracted by the crops was more than the fertilising of the animals, the land lost its ability to grow good crops. Therefore, early man was the first to use the now traditional third world method of slash and burn.

By 1500BC a lot of the woodland areas were cleared, farmers and villagers were cutting out their land along the sides of the valleys. The lower part of the valley was usually left as water meadows for the grazing of animals. It would flood during the winter, and that would replenish the nutrients for the grasses. The tops of the hills were harder to cultivate

because the soil would be thinner and more liable to be blown away by the winds whipping over the landscape. Field systems were being developed; hedges were being planted to prevent animals straying onto the crops where they were not wanted and the settlements were co-operating to raise crops for the community. Thus the landscape took the shape it was to retain until the enclosures of the 17th and 18th centuries, when land was divided up by large landowners.

Iron was being used to make cooking pots and farm implements by the 7th century BC. It was another of those great breaks in history, when the course of life would have been very different if someone had not decided that iron could be the wonder material of their times. It could be sharpened and it held its point for longer than the softer tin and bronze, so implements would last longer, and could be used harder. Tools were also easier to make, because iron was easier to work, and they were more efficient, so that farming became more efficient. Men could do more, or it took less men to do the same

tasks. Ground could be broken for crops more easily and therefore some of the less easily worked areas could be brought into cultivation. Every village at this time had their cows and goats for meat and also milk. Sheep gave mutton, lamb, milk and wool for clothing and keeping warm. There was also bread and beer from barley and wheat, and then there were fruits and vegetables. Horses and dogs were also eaten when their useful life was over. Obviously, without refrigeration, food did not keep very well, so it had to be dried or salted.

By 400BC the hill forts that we see dotted around the country were the equivalent of early towns and trading centres, which could be made defensive when the need arose. Coastal communities were developing their links across the sea, and trade was bringing in figs from the Mediterranean, spices from the Middle East and the East Indies and wine from Rome.

The overseas trade was in grain and foodstuffs that the villages and communities were so successful at producing and this is possibly one of the reasons the Romans decided to invade. If there was this amount of food in this strange country over the sea, it would be worth conquering to feed the Roman legions. British beer was exported to all parts of the Roman Empire, and was considered so superior that it was twice the price of beer from other countries. The Romans brought their own ways of eating, which were consid-

ered more refined and sophisticated, and like so many people keeping up with the Jones', the locals copied them. They no longer sat around the fire and helped themselves from the central pot. Each person was given a place at a table, although the tables were still arranged around the fire. In larger houses the food was cooked in a separate area, and the food was served in a dining room or hall.

Farming was now a lucrative form of income, and those people who rose to the top of the pile could afford to employ people to do the work for them, while they lived a more idle life, and spent part of their year living in the towns which were developing. This is the beginning of the pattern established right through to the great aristocratic families of the 17th and 18th centuries. Their estates were maintained by agents, and their tenants worked for them. Bignor at this time was one of these big estates, and consisted of 800 acres on the south side of The Downs. There were 200 sheep, 12 ploughing teams of oxen, 50 cattle bred for meat and dairy products, and they grew over 10,000 bushels of grain a year.

After the Romans left, the country was left open to all sorts of invasions from the east, which were prompted by lack of land and therefore lack of food. The Vikings and Danes were essentially farmers who had run out of land to expand into, and therefore had to turn into seafarers and warriors to find more food. The land of England was a wide fertile land, with relatively few people living in it. It was ideal for them to come and bring their ideas, which were assimilated into the local culture. 793AD was the first recorded raid by Vikings on Northumbria, and by 800AD they were arriving in force, and they were staying all year long, rather than returning to their homes in the winter. They built their own settlements, which contained a main hall where they all ate, slept and lived, and it appears that they may have brought these with them to assemble when they settled. Were they the first Ikea and did they flat pack all those beams?

By the year 1000AD the country was fairly stable and settled. Most of the people looked like us and were about the same height as us. It was not until the 18th and 19th century that people became malnourished and overworked so that they could not grow well. Anglo Saxons were well nourished and healthy and they lived in a green, unpolluted country and the majority of them lived in small communities in the countryside.

Houses in villages were clustered together, either around the village green, or along either side of the road. There would be about 90 to 100 people living in a village, and between them they would farm about 700 acres of corn and

beans, together with pasture for the animals (sheep and cows) and woodland for fuel, grazing for pigs and building materials. In addition each villager would have his own portion to tend, when not working for the Lord of the Manor, and from this he would be able to feed his family and have a surplus to pay to the Lord as his rent or tax. His plot would not be a square, but would be divided into strips in the communal fields, and everyone would join in to tend the land. Depending upon how wealthy a man was or how important he was in the village, he would be allocated his strips. The houses were sturdy wooden structures with wooden uprights supporting crossbeams, fastened together with wooden pegs. The frame would be covered with planks or branches,

which would be woven to make the walls and then be covered with daub. This was a paste made of clay and straw mixed with cow dung to hold it together. This was pressed by hand into the weave of the walls to make it wind and waterproof. A very smelly wall covering! In Emsworth evidence has been found that a small Saxon settlement used local red brick clay for their daub. Most of the houses were about 30ft by 15ft with a dividing wall in the middle between the living, eating and the inner sleeping chamber, although some poorer people would sleep on a platform in the rafters. There was no floor covering, and the bare earth was swept to keep it clean, and then covered with rushes or grasses to absorb anything that was spilled.

Life in general must have been very much smellier than today, because the domestic animals shared the family home during the winter. The floor was sloped down towards the end where the animals lived, so that the slurry they produced would not flow into the
family area, thank goodness! This would be cleared out into the yard when necessary and then used as fertiliser on the fields. It was always best to do this first thing in the morning, especially in winter when the frost made it more solid and less smelly! The toilets for the humans were not much better, being open cesspits that were fairly close to the door. These must have been a magnet for every fly in the area, and they would not have had far to fly to land on the food in the house, which was being prepared. However, archaeologists love investigating these cesspits and they have found that the diet of these people was very healthy and better than our own. They have found that villagers ate lots of vegetables, meat and fish as well as apples, plums and cherries. Most people

were totally unaware of the health hazards and put their trust in God to keep them well. The only people who seem to have sorted out their sanitary arrangements were the monks, who sited their toilets over a stream, so that it was always downstream, and away, from the kitchens and water extraction points, which were always sited further upstream.

Everything in a village was integrated. Nothing could happen if there was a break in the chain. The year was ruled by the weather, and the first important date was Plough Sunday. This was the first Sunday of January when the ploughs would be taken up to the fields and the first furrow would be cut. However, it could not be done without due ceremony, which entailed dragging the ploughs through the village and stopping at various

points for suitable liquid refreshment, and also at the church for a blessing. In later times, in order to get the first furrow absolutely straight, the Lord of the Manor would use the cross on the handle of his sword as the marker for the ploughman to aim for. The ploughman was an important man in the village, but he did not own the plough. The Lord of the Manor owned this, and the team of oxen, and the ploughman worked for him. He had to make sure that the Lord's land was ploughed first. Everyone else had to wait for this to be done before their land could be ploughed. The ploughman had a team of 10 oxen and he was responsible for caring for them. At this time the iron plough of England was one of the most advanced designs in the known world.

However, the ploughman could not have such an efficient plough if the blacksmith was not proficient in his craft. He would be based at the edge of the village, because he needed a supply of water to cool his work, as well as a forge. Plenty of room was allowed around his workshop because of the risk of fire with wooden buildings. Again, the Lord of the Manor owned the forge, but he would lease it to the craftsman, who would then be able to charge for items made for the village. He would make many household

items and nearly all the farming implements were iron shod, even if they were not made completely of iron.

Another important man in the village was the miller. Again, he did not own the mill, but rented it from the Lord, and had to grind the Lord's grain first. He became very busy at Lammas, which is Anglo Saxon for 'loaf mass'. This was the feast time when the harvest had been collected in and the first loaf made with that year's grain was blessed. Every village had a water or windmill, although water mills were more common.

By 1066 there were over 5,624 mills in the country, and the miller was a very skilled man. Mills tended to be made of wood. The water wheel would be made of oak, and the power was fed through an oak shaft, which was cased in iron to reinforce it. The gear-ing was usually made of elm, and the stones had to be transported over long distances to get really hard stone. These stones had to be shaped and dressed (cut in lines) to allow the corn to be ground properly. If they were cut incorrectly there would be extra pressure, which could cause heat to build up, and the grain could be incredibly flammable. Fire in the mill was a common occurrence, and they seemed to have to be rebuilt fairly frequently. The bread was round, flat and coarse, with the natural gluten in the wheat providing any raising agent. Everyone made their own bread, although they may have taken it to a central oven to be cooked. Very often the bread would be used as a platter at meal-times to hold stew or meat and then eaten at the end. This was one way of using stale bread, because the meat juices would soften the bread.

Life could be very precarious, because if the harvest failed there would be famine in the village, and it was at this time that the difference between rich and poor became obvious. The rich could afford to buy in extra supplies, while the poor could not, and then they would starve. Bad weather or plant diseases could cause havoc with the finely balanced economy and if the harvest failed there was the prospect of not eating and saving the grain to plant the next year, or eating and then hav-ing nothing to plant to grow. There were fam-ines in 975AD, 976AD, 986AD and 1005AD. These were in quick suc-cession, and it is possible that some communities did not recover from four famines in one generation.

The most dif-ficult time of the year was July. Many people think that the winter is the worst time, but apart from the cold and trying to keep healthy,

winter was a time when the barns and granaries were fairly full, and they were using supplies that had been laid down in August and September. These supplies had to last until the harvest was collected. Spring sown crops were not ready until August, and many of the hedgerow crops were not ready until the same time. July was known as the Hungry Month. All sorts of things were added to the flour to make it last until the harvest, such as acorns, beans, peas and tree bark. It was thought that lack of food caused mass hysteria. At the time it was attributed to religious fervour from pilgrimages in fine weather, but it has now been discovered that the

mould that collected on old grain stocks was a source of hallucinating drugs such as LSD. Hedgerow plants that were used as a stopgap could also help this state of mind, because they used poppies, hemp and other flowers in drinks and dried as flour. They might have been poor and starving, but they were happy!

The pig was the main source of protein for the villagers, and virtually every part of the animal could be used. The joints were hung in the rafters to be smoked and cured into bacon, while the intestines were used to make sausage skins and the stomach made tripe. All the other animals were more expensive to keep, but the pig was allowed to forage for its own food in the woodland. All farm animals were smaller than today's versions, and the only form of selective breeding was the culling of the oldest and weakest first, in the hope that the fitter ones would last through the winter to breed again.

Fruit trees were grown in all orchards, with the more exotic fruits being cultivated in the palace and monastery gardens. Every Lord of the Manor would make sure his skilled fruit experts knew how to graft his fruit trees, and also prune them correctly. They already knew that cultivated trees provided better fruit than the wild variety. Apples,

plums, pears, figs, quinces, peaches and mulberries were all common fruit, while chestnuts, almonds, hazelnuts and walnuts were cultivated. The kitchen garden was also well stocked with onions, leeks, celery, radish, carrot, garlic, shallot, parsnips, cabbage, parsley, dill, chervil, marigold, coriander, poppy, lettuce and peas. Again they were smaller than we are used to, but it is possible that they had a more intense flavour, because they were allowed to grow naturally and were harvested when they were ripe.

Those villages that developed along the coast and rivers were able to add fish to their diets. They could catch them with net, bait, hook or basket. The basket was a long woven cone that was placed in the river where the currents would sweep the fish into the basket and then trap them. These baskets would be strung across the rivers, and in 1060 King Edward the Confessor had to pass a law banning some of the baskets, because they were affecting the navigation on some of the main rivers. River fish were eel, pike, minor, burbot (a type of eel) and lamprey. Rowing boats were used off the coast and the selection of fish caught in the sea was greater. It included herring, salmon, porpoise, sturgeon, oysters, crabs, mussels, winkles, cockles, plaice, flounders and lobsters. It is reported that some fishermen ganged together to catch whales, but they were taking a very big risk, and not many of them were that brave!

Various exotic plants and foodstuffs were

introduced all through the Middle Ages, with the expansion of trade and the increase in English sea power and prestige throughout the known world. The Crusaders brought spices from the Middle East. Broccoli, cauliflower, runner beans and Brussels sprouts were brought into the country in the 15th and 16th centuries. Spinach arrived in the 17th century at about the same time that Sir Walter Raleigh brought his potatoes and tobacco from America. Tomatoes also arrived via the same route. One of the last major introductions was sugar. Honey had been the main sweetener for food, and sugar did not come into the country until the 15th century. However, it was so exotic and expensive that only the rich could afford it. It did not become a common commodity until the Caribbean plantations began growing sugar cane in the 17th century.

All through the Middle Ages life evolved. Ordinary people were very inventive and even in the home they were always looking to devise ways of making life easier to cope with or adapting ideas they had heard about. Cooking could only be done by heating the food either directly by threading it on a stick, or indirectly through heating water in a pot. For many centuries this fire was in the middle of the floor. The only safety feature, to stop the fire spreading into the rushes and straw on the floor, was that the fire would be lit on a stone slab. Depending on the size of the household, this determined how big the fire was, and therefore how big the slab, or slabs, were. A good cook would know how to keep her fire burning at the right temperature. Also, how to have it ready at the right time, and how to damp it down overnight, so that it did not burn the house down, but would not have to be lit from cold each morning. Very important, if you were the first person up in the morning! Being in the middle of the room, whether peasant's cottage or lord's large hall, the fire was the centre of the household and everyone gathered there for warmth, and also companionship. Even today we gather in the kitchen for a chat! With the fire in the centre of the room the smoke was allowed to waft around, hopefully going upwards, but usually settling down around everything. Luckily it was a wood fire, and did not produce the soot that a coal fire does. Even so, it was another smell to add to the assorted ones of toilets, poor personal hygiene and animals!

Anything that needed to be cooked in an oven, such as bread, had to be done in a pit in the ground, which was then sealed over to retain the heat, and this had to be done outside. Sometimes there was a separate building, sometimes it was just outside in the yard, and sometimes it was a cavity in the outside wall of the main building. From there, some bright soul thought that it would be interesting to make a flue up to the roof, which would cause a draught that would take the smoke upwards. Obviously, this could not be done with a wooden building, because this was one sure way of burning the house down!! However, ordinary people could not afford to build their dwellings in stone, so they cleverly thought of building a chimney in stone, but leaving the rest of the building in wood. Gradually, these little chimneys tacked on the outside of dwellings grew and grew until they became the great open fireplaces of the Tudors and Stuarts, where they were able to burn enormous tree trunks without having to split them.

Now there were sides to the fireplace the cook was able to devise all sorts of contraptions to fit in front, beside, on top and even under the heat of the fire. Therefore, no matter how big the household, lots of different types of cooking could be done all at the same time: some needing fierce heat, some simmering temperatures and others just warming through. The spit was devised to suspend joints of meat and poultry in the heat, so that it could be well cooked. An iron pole passed right through the joint meant that heat could be taken right into the heart of the meat to ensure even cooking. No more burnt outside and raw inside! However, if it just hung there it would cook one side and not the other. It needed turning, and a handle was attached at one end. No power to turn it, so the smallest boy in the kitchen was required to sit to the side of the fire and turn the spit, until he was told to stop. Obviously he would be scorched by the heat, so someone used a screen to protect him. It was possibly a disused archery target, which was a metal frame covered in straw. The straw could be damped down and the heat of the fire would not penetrate it. Again the continuation of this contraption can be seen in the fire screens which decorated the Victorian households, although they had sunk to mere decoration and an excuse to show off the skills in needlework.

As spits developed and became very sophisticated they added extra spits for different types of meat. Some were interchangeable, while others could be used altogether, and had claws welded along them to dig into the joint so that it would not swing around the spit, but move with it. Some were very fine to use with small birds, and could have a row of them all cooking at the same time, while others were very large and bulky to take the weight of a large joint of beef. Fish was cooked in this way, but had to have a frame-work attached to the outside, like a grid, to prevent it flaking off. Fire dogs were then needed to hold all the spits, and, because the poor little kitchen boy was not strong enough to turn all these spits, chains and pulley wheels were added and then gears to make the operation easier.

The fat falling from the meat would fall into a long shallow trough put just under the spits in front of the fire, because they found that fat and fire causes spitting and the fire getting out of control. Other food could be fried in the dripping pan. In very large households, the height of the banquet would be the parade of the main dish, left on its spit, and carried into the hall by two of the cooks and carved from the spit. Not only meat, but also sweet dishes such as fruit could be cooked this way, especially if they were battered and covered in sugar. This sounds like an early kebab to me!

When chimneys first came to prominence, the actual mechanics of draught and the upward lift of heat were not really understood. Also the effects of the build-up of soot were not recognised. The fire would be sluggish and cold if there was not a good up draught of air through the chimney, and the build up of soot could cut down on this draught. The secondary effect was that soot could catch fire, and cause the chimney to catch fire, thus causing the wooden building to be destroyed. At this time the chimneys were very wide and not very tall, so men could climb up a ladder and sweep the soot out. However, the trade of chimney sweep developed with the fashionably convoluted, tall, twisting chimneys of the Elizabethan age. They were very narrow and a man could not get into all the twists, but a chimney sweep would be able to employ pauper boys to be climbers, and they were able to get into all the nooks and crannies. If they were reluctant to climb into the chimney some of the more unscrupulous sweeps would light a fire in the grate to make them climb. Many chimneys were constructed with hand and foot holds built inside, and the practice of using little boys lasted until the laws of the late 19th century forbade it. It was only then that chimney-sweeps distinctive brushes were devised. However, during the Second World War when a building was destroyed in the Blitz, it very often came down in a cloud of soot, where these brushes were not as successful as boys.

In rural areas, people were very much more

inventive. Rather than employing someone to do the job for them, an iron ball with a brush attached could be lowered slowly down the chimney and swung around to get into all the nooks and crannies. However, it was quite an art, because if it was swung too much it could dislodge the mortar between the stones, and cause smoke to leak into the house. In some villages a holly bush was tied to a rope and either dropped down the chimney, or hoisted up from the grate. This was slower than the iron ball, but was a lot safer, and if enough sheets were used around the grate the people could collect the soot that fell, to use on the garden. No matter how many sheets were used, it still made a mess of the living area, and took ages to clear up. Everyone had to help. It was also reputed that in some small cottages a chicken was dropped down the chimney! As it flapped, it knocked the soot off the sides of the chimney. What mental and physical state the chicken was in when it got to the bottom is never revealed. Some miners and quarrymen used to bring back small quantities of explosive, illegally, that they had been working with in the quarries, and set them off in the fireplace. This had the effect of blasting the soot off the sides of the chimney, where it then flew up, down and out in all directions. The overseer could see who had done this, by the pall of soot hanging over a house!

The rules for dining in the upper levels of society were very rigid and had their own etiquette, which became more elaborate with time. During the 15th century the serving dishes were known as chargers and were made of wood or pewter. People sat in pairs, male with female, and they shared their plat-ters, although they had a bread plate each, with their own utensils. People did not bite their bread, but tore off as much as they needed, so the rest could be given to the poor. Everyone had to wait for the host to indicate when to start eating and there would be no talking while eating. People were not allowed to put too much food into their mouths at once, nor to blow on hot food, nor to leave a spoon in a cup or bowl. Knives should never be wiped on the table, nor used to put food into the mouth. They could not drink with food in their mouths and not put their fingers in the liquid. It was not allowed to blow the nose at the table, nor to put the elbows on the table. All of these rules are very familiar to us as they are the basis of polite table man-ners today.

The courses of a meal would be paraded around the hall as a sign of the host's wealth and generosity, and it would be a compli-cated procedure. Each course would consist of a mixture of savoury and sweet dishes, with meat, fish and game served at each course. All the dishes of a course were laid on the table at the same time and they were all removed before the next course was pre-sented. The variety of dishes was to cater for all sorts of people. The boar's head and all strong meats were thought to be suitable for strong men, while the ladies would prefer the poultry. Fish was served with every course, because there was likely to be a religious person who was on a special diet as a pen-ance. It was not expected that everyone would sample all the dishes, so if they chose one item from each course, they would have, similar to today, a four or five-course meal. These rules were obviously for the highest in the land.

In the lower classes and country farm-ing families, meals varied with the season. Everything was governed by what grew when and the seasons for hunting various types of meat. Summer meant fish, meat, poultry, fruit of all sorts and fresh puddings and creams. Some areas preferred wine, some mead and others cider and this could depend upon whether they could brew different sorts of drinks.

The single meal for all the family, eating in the hall with servants and workers, was a good solid meal. It was the main meal of the day and everyone sat together. All the food was shared throughout the hall, although the master and the top table would have first pick. By all dining together the head of the household was making sure that all his servants had a good meal, and the serv-ants could see that the master cared for all of them. One for all and all for one! It made for a sense of unity and good workers for the master. If a servant had done very well or performed a special service he could be rewarded with an extra helping, in front of all the others. As times changed and the mas-ters began to have separate dining areas and left the servants to eat in their own hall, this unity was lost, and some of the loyalty was eroded. It led eventually to the separate hier-archies of the great Victorian and Edwardian households.

During the early medieval times there were times when a servant, or official, had to miss the main meal of the day. He may have been on an errand to another place, or had to fin-ish his work. By all eating together, it would be noted if someone was absent, and they made arrangements for the absentee to be fed when he arrived. This was the develop-ment of the livery cupboard, which seems to have been the 11th to 16th century equiva-lent of the snack bar or fast food centre. It was a wooden cupboard, with an openwork lattice front and holes in the sides to allow the air to circulate. There would be a series of hooks and shelves inside to store the food and it would be stocked with easy to prepare foods. Usually it would be in the hall between the main dining area and the kitchen. One of the kitchen staff would be instructed to keep the cupboard stocked, and if the absen-tee was on official business he would be instructed to help himself when he returned. Food such as salt, vinegar, bread, cold meat and ham, cheese, pickles and preserves, together with ale would be kept there. Gradually the livery cupboard was adapted

for use in the private apartments, especially the bedrooms, in case the Lord or his family woke with hunger during the night. Small parties could be catered for, without having to have the servants intruding into the gossip, and it was useful if there was an invalid in the household. This was not the forerunner of the sideboard, but more the forerunner of the fridge. The sideboard was used to display the family wealth. It was covered with a white cloth and all the salvers, bowls and jugs would be placed there, so that everyone could see how wealthy they were! We now call it ostentatious display!

By the time of Queen Elizabeth I the farmer's wife or even the small artisan's wife was the lynchpin of the household and she had the bulk of the work in the house. Her husband dealt with all the work of maintaining the wealth of the family, but it was her lot to utilise the product of his labour, and also to utilise it in the most economic way. Her life was a lot harder than any housewife today and she had a lot of chores to be done before breakfast could be served. She always had to start the day with her prayers, otherwise things would not go well. Then she milked the cow or cows, fed the chickens and then prepared breakfast for her family. She was expected to preside over the table with them. Then she baked bread, brewed beer and arranged for the grain to be ground at the mill, for which a payment was made. This could be money or in kind. At least once a week she had to make butter and cheese, and every morning feed the pigs with the scraps from the table, collect the eggs from the hens, ducks and geese.

In the spring she would have to prepare her vegetable and herb garden, sow the seeds at the right time, and keep the plots weed free. Flax and hemp were her province; she had to make sure it grew well for cloth and rope, and she had to spin it ready for weaving. She always had her distaff at her side, which she could spin with one hand, while she was cooking and weeding. When she had time, she could work at her spinning wheel, and make thread quicker. She would use this

thread for finer work, than the distaff-spun thread. Flax made linen so was used for undergarments and fine babies clothing. She would also be able to have a fleece from her husband's flock to make woollen cloth for the main clothing of the family, as well as for bed covering. Sometimes she would be able to exchange some of her goods for someone else's. She may do good work with linen, while her neighbour was better with wool or preserves.

She would help with winnowing the grain from the chaff, to make malt for beer and help make hay, harvest the corn and feed the workers who were doing this. It was always important to keep everyone fed, so that they worked willingly. On top of all these chores, she had to keep her home clean, help her husband to fill the muck wagon (help to clear the animal manure, but also the human toilet area). Even her outings were business, such as going to market to sell her surplus butter, milk, eggs, chickens, pigs and geese and any corn and then buy anything she was unable to make. At the end of this she had to prepare dinner for everyone in the household and put her children to bed. Then she finished her working day by completing her accounts and presenting them to her husband for him to inspect. She finished her day with prayers before getting into bed. She got up with the lark and went to bed at sunset. That is multi-tasking!

With the growth of the British Empire and

the advances in technology in all areas of life, there were new influences coming into the country. The East India Company was formed to trade with India and the Far East, and many young men who went to work in India acquired a taste for their unique foods and traditions. They brought back stories and curiosities, so that Indian became the fashion for everything, and returning travellers brought turbans, muslins and cashmere. They also introduced lighter dishes that could be eaten with rice and fruits. Ginger had always been dried in order to bring it overland by the Silk Routes, but now the shipping routes had been opened it could be stored in jars in syrup and kept fresh. Curry was considered too hot for many people, and it did not come into everyday use until the 20th century, but discerning fashionable people would be tempted occasionally. The main import from India was tea.

Tea was brought into England from Holland in the late 16th century, but it did not appeal to people at first because they thought it was insipid. However when they experimented by leaving the leaves in boiling water to brew, they then found that the taste could be varied. It was another of those innovations that had lots of ceremonies attached to it, to show how wealthy and upper class the drinkers were. It was drunk from little china bowls, which were made in China, and although by 1700 it was considered the English drink, it was still very expensive, and would not grow in this country. The tea leaves were kept in elaborate locked chests, and the lady of the house kept the key. Only she was allowed to mix the leaves. It could cost between 16/- (16 shillings) and £2/10/- (two pounds ten shillings), in a world where a farm labourer would be earning

less than 10/- (ten shillings) a week. The leaves were so expensive that a black market quickly grew around it. Servants in the big houses would retrieve the tea leaves that had been used, dry them and then sell them on to poorer people. In the 1800s they tried to make tea wine, this was not successful, but tea as a drink maintained its popularity. There were problems with carrying the tea by sea from India, because it was affected by the dampness of the ships. The problem was solved when they constructed chests of wood and lined them with lead. Nowadays tea chests, or packing cases, are still lined with foil to serve the same purpose, but we can put anything in the chests - not just tea.

Also from Holland during the wars with France at the beginning of the 1700s, gin was introduced. It was called Holland Spirit and was so cheap that it became the chosen drink of the lower classes. Hogarth drew some very telling cartoons showing the evils of gin, where people would sell everything they had to drink gin, and would feed it to their babies to keep them quiet. In London it was said that you could get drunk for a 1d (one penny) or dead drunk for 2d (twopence). In fact you could get so dead drunk that you would never wake again.

One big innovation in England was the coaching inn. Travel during the Middle Ages and Elizabethan and Stuart times had been by horse. Men could travel easily on horses, but it was not considered suitable for women to travel long distances by horse, and the only other way of travelling was in a coach or a wagon. There was no suspension, and with wooden wheels on a potholed unmade road, it could not be said to be comfortable. It could also take a long time, because the weather could make the road impassable and once they had completed the journey one way, they may be marooned until they could travel back again. Therefore people only travelled when really necessary. As roads became better, women were willing and eager to travel as much as their men, and they began to travel further. Some of these journeys would be longer than one day, and even if it was shorter, the horses could not be expected to travel vast distances. They would have to be changed every 15 or so miles, so posts were established along the main road where horses could be

changed, and the

travellers own horses could be stabled until they came back and changed them again. These post houses became the centre of a community, and very often they had been opened by a local farmer who had diversified into the travel trade. He would brew his own beer, and his wife would cook her own specialities. In fact the owner of the post house had one asset that could make or break his venture - his wife. If his wife was really good at her trade she would be able to build a reputation and the venture would develop into one of the essential stopping places on that route. She had to provide food all year round for the travellers as well as for her family and household. Her husband would be the brewer, but she would devise the wine making and could make a variety of stirrup cups,

possets and caudles. She also had to make cheese; keep butter fresh for winter; store, preserve, salt, dry and smoke all sorts of food; cure meat, bacon and ham; glaze jelly and candy fruits; pickle and bottle all sorts of food. Invalid diets were needed for elderly or delicate travellers and remedies for any accidents that took place on the road. The weather could mean that the coach could be stranded for several days, and the passengers had to be fed and looked after. She would also have customers who would call in from the local area. The grooms and ostlers in the stables would require her to provide various ingredients to treat the horses, which were after all very valuable assets for the establishment. They could have had strain injuries or been involved in accidents. Along with all this work, she had to look after her family, who would then help with the business. There were servants to care for; inside servants such as chamber maids, bar maids, and kitchen maids and outside servants such as grooms, ostlers and stable lads. The posting house had to keep all rooms ready for use and all fires ready to be lit in the rooms, with beds aired for use. A lot of food had to be easily stored and able to be kept hot. Most recipes for ham, pressed beef, potted cheeses and biscuits come from this great period of coaching and posting inns. Many landladies tried to vary their food so that travellers would remember them, especially if they were regular travellers along that route, and then they would want to return. She would prepare her own sauces, preserves and condiments to give her food that extra memorable touch. Many diary entries show that travellers were aware of good and bad places to stop, those to eat at and those where they could sleep overnight. They also made notes of those places they would not be stopping at again!

This self sufficient life came to a gradual end with the enclosure of the land around the

villages and the general drift of people into the towns. Here they did not have any land to grow their own food, and they were dependent upon earning wages in order to buy all their food. This was not an overnight occurrence, but a gentle trickle that increased to a flood, and was at its height between the middle of the 18th century and the middle of the 19th century. With the slump in agricultural output and the corresponding decrease in wages, it was the greener grass of the towns, where everyone was reputed to be earning fortunes that attracted the poor country people. They thought they would be able to go into the towns for a few years, and then return to their villages with enough money to buy a good farm and set them and their descendants up in the life of luxury. That never hap-

pened because once they had left the land, there was no way that they could afford to return. Having given up the cycle of growing and producing, they needed capital to buy the first year's crop, and then have an income to last for the next year, while their crop was growing and they could harvest and sell it. Therefore they were trapped in the urban environment and they became more and more dependent upon the buying of food. They had to work longer hours to earn enough money to buy food, and therefore

did not have the time or energy to create their own menus. Readymade food was quicker.

During the Napoleonic Wars ways of preserving meat in tins was discovered, and later in the century they found ways of keeping food cool in refrigerators. The new wealth was in buying and selling food, and the new rich became the shopkeepers. The progression of that pattern has been the demise of these small shopkeepers in the towns, with the rise of the large supermarkets promoting the sale of meals that are completely ready to be eaten. They need no imagination and no effort. Will we ever go back to the rich tapestry of growing, picking and cooking our own produce, or will "The Good Life" be only a television programme?

I HAVE DRAWN ON THREE WONDERFUL BOOKS FOR THIS ARTICLE: 'FOOD IN ENGLAND' BY DOROTHY HARTLEY, 'THE YEAR 1000' BY ROBERT LACEY, AND 'THE SEVEN AGES OF BRITAIN' BY JUSTIN POLLARD. ALL OF WHICH ARE GOOD, READABLE AND VERY ENJOYABLE.

THEN

& NOW

POST OFFICE IN 1900 (FULL CIRCLE TO CO-OP)

NORTH STREET IN 1900

THEN

& NOW

WEST STREET IN 1905

SOUTH STREET IN 1890

THEN

WEST SIDE OF SQUARE WITH PAVILION CINEMA IN 1940

& NOW

THE SNOW AT DOLPHIN QUAY IN 1963

THEN

& NOW

LUMLEY MILL IN 1910

THE GODDARD BROTHERS' BLACKSMITHS IN WESTBOURNE

THEN

& NOW

VIEW FROM PROMENADE TOWARD FOSTER BOAT YARD

WESTBOURNE LOOKING TOWARDS THE CHURCH

THEN

THE HARD AT EMSWORTH

& NOW

SOUTH STREET DURING THE 1950'S

LOCAL ARTIST

MARIAN FORSTER

FIRST COME FIRST PERCHED!

THE THREE GRACES!

LITTLE TERNS

ROSEATE TERNS TUGGING

MARIAN FORSTER, ONE OF THE LOCAL EMSWORTH ARTISTS, BRINGS A QUIRKY SENSE OF HUMOUR AND AN EYE FOR THE UNUSUAL TO HER COLOURFUL INTERPRETATIONS OF EMSWORTH, ITS PEOPLE AND WILDLIFE. SHE ALSO SELLS PRINTS AND GREETINGS CARDS, AND HAS DESIGNED AND ILLUSTRATED THE WILDLIFE INFORMATION BOARDS FOR PETER POND, THE SLIPPER POND AND BROOK MEADOW IN EMSWORTH. MARIAN HAS ALSO DONE THE SAME FOR THE WILDLIFE POND AT ITCHENOR; THE OLD BRIDGE MEADOW AT BOSHAM; AND A BANK OF ILLUSTRATIONS FOR THE CHICHESTER HARBOUR CONSERVANCY.

DURING THE 1980S, MARIAN WAS A VOLUNTEER ARCHAEOLOGICAL ILLUSTRATOR FOR THE MARY ROSE TRUST BASED IN PORTSMOUTH. SHE ILLUSTRATED ARTEFACTS BROUGHT UP FROM THE WRECK OF HENRY VIII'S SHIP. LATER, MARIAN SPECIALISED IN DRAWING THE JERKINS, RESEARCHING THEIR CONSTRUCTION AND MAKING LEATHER REPLICAS FOR THE MARY ROSE MUSEUM. SHE HAS RECENTLY DONE MORE RESEARCH ON THIS SUBJECT, WHICH IS INCLUDED IN THE 2004 THREE-VOLUME PUBLICATION ON THE MARY ROSE.

MARIAN FORSTER
32 KINGS ROAD
EMSWORTH
PO10 7HN
T. 01243 372720

e. sales@scratchingaliving.co.uk
www.scratchingaliving.co.uk

HIS FIRST SQUARK!

MARIAN IS ALSO A LEADING MEMBER OF THE SOCIETY OF FELINE ARTISTS, AND REGULARLY EXHIBITS HER WITTY STYLISED SIAMESE CAT PAINTINGS AT THEIR EXHIBITIONS NATIONWIDE.

AUTUMN

SEPTEMBER

OCTOBER

NOVEMBER

The Café

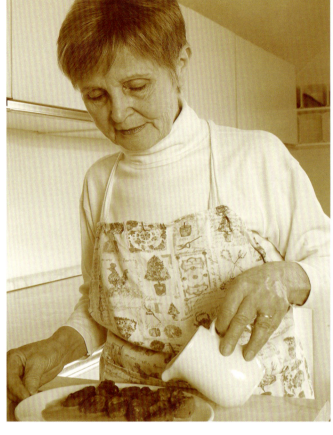

The Café
44 High Street
Emsworth
PO10 7AW
T. 01243 370549

John & Margaret Roberts

Margaret Roberts is a self-taught cook, who uses her wide knowledge of all cooking styles to produce traditional homemade dishes.

The Café is open every day, serving traditional English food, homemade specialities and vegetarian choices as well as a typical roast lunch on Sundays. The all-day breakfast is very popular with locals. The seating area in the rear garden and the pavement table offer outdoor eating in the summer months. Originally it was a clothing and haberdashery shop called 'Millers', and before it became a café, it was a greengrocer and fishmonger. Margaret and John Roberts have owned and managed the establishment for the past seven years.

MAGGIE'S PORK AND CIDER CASSEROLE

Serves 4

10g Butter
2 Tablespoons Sunflower Oil
900g Pork Shoulder (cut into
    2.5cm cubes)
12 Shallots (peeled)
570ml Cider (medium/sweet)
150ml Cider Vinegar
4 Fresh Sprigs Thyme
2 Bay Leaves
1½ Tablespoons Crème Fraîche

Pre-heat oven to 170C/325F/Gas 3

1. Gently heat a 2.5litre casserole dish on the hob, add half of the butter and half of the oil.

2. In the meantime, dry the cubes of pork on kitchen towel paper.

3. Brown the pork in the hot oil and butter, and reserve on a plate.

4. Add the remaining butter and oil to the casserole, increase the heat, add the shallots and fry until a caramel colour.

5. Add the cider and cider vinegar and stir well, scraping the sides and base of the dish with a wooden spoon.

6. Return the browned pork to the mixture, add the thyme and bay leaves and season well.

7. Bring this to a simmer, then transfer the casserole dish (without lid) to the pre-heated oven for approximately 1¼ hours until the liquid is reduced and the meat tender.

8. Remove the pork and shallots, and transfer to a warmed serving dish. Discard the herbs.

9. Place the casserole dish on direct heat and bring the liquid to the boil.

10. Simmer until reduces slightly and whisk in the crème fraîche.

11. Season to taste, and pour the sauce over the pork and shallots.

12. Serve with vegetables of your choice.

With the apple a classy unoaked Chardonnay works well here, if it's red you need, how about young Cotes du Rhone or Rioja. Failing that, why not a local traditional cider!

EMSWORTH COUNTRY MARKET

MEMBERS OF EMSWORTH COUNTRY MARKET

JUNE PRINCE & JANIS THOMSON

FOR FUTHER INFORMATION
OR IF YOU WISH TO JOIN:

SUE GRANVILLE-GEORGE
T. 01243 373421

EMSWORTH COUNTRY MARKET, FORMERLY EMSWORTH WI MARKET, IS ONE OF ABOUT 400 SIMILAR CO-OPERATIVE MARKETS IN ENGLAND AND WALES. THEY MEET EVERY THURSDAY MORNING IN THE BAPTIST CHURCH HALL, NORTH STREET TO SELL THEIR PRODUCE, FROM JAMS AND CHUTNEYS TO CAKES, BISCUITS AND VEGETABLES. NONE OF WHICH CONTAIN ANY KIND OF PRESERVATIVES. THERE IS ALWAYS A QUEUE OF CUSTOMERS OUTSIDE THE DOOR WAITING FOR THE OPENING.

AFTERNOON TEA

APPLE, ORANGE AND DATE SLICES (BY JUNE PRINCE)

Makes 12 slices

225g (8oz) Dates
2 Eating Apples
1½ Oranges
170g (6oz) Butter
85g (3oz) Caster Sugar
255g (9oz) Plain Flour

Pre-heat oven to 160C/325F/Gas 3

1. Grease a 7 x 11-inch swiss-roll tin.
2. Chop the dates and the peeled, cored apples.
3. Place these into a saucepan with the grated rind and juice of the oranges.
4. Simmer gently until soft, and put to one side to cool.
5. In a mixing bowl, cream together the butter and sugar.
6. Mix in the flour until a consistency of coarse breadcrumbs.
7. Divide this mixture into two, and press one half into the tin.
8. Top with the fruit mixture.
9. Sprinkle the remaining half of the pastry mix on top of the fruit, and slightly press down to flatten.
10. Bake in the pre-heated oven for 20-25 minutes.
11. Divide the cooked slice into finger shapes whilst still hot.
12. Remove from the tin when cool.

PINEAPPLE AND SULTANA CAKE (BY JANIS THOMSON)

Makes 2 x 7-inch Cakes

225g (8oz) Margarine
200g (7oz) Sugar
4 Eggs (beaten)
400g (14oz) Self-Raising Flour
450g (1lb) Sultanas
225g (8oz) Cherries (chopped)
1x425g Tin Pineapple (crushed)

Pre-heat oven to 170C/350F/Gas 4

1. Prepare and line 2 x 7-inch cake tins.
2. Cream together the margarine and sugar.
3. Gradually add the beaten eggs.
4. Stir in the flour, sultanas, chopped cherries and crushed pineapple.
5. Bake in the pre-heated oven for 60-70 minutes.
6. Allow to cool in tin before turning out.

EMSWORTH RASCALS (BY JUNE PRINCE)

Makes approximately 12-14

110g (4oz) Plain Flour
225g (8oz) Wholemeal Flour
4 Teaspoons Baking Powder
1 Teaspoon Mixed Spice
1 Teaspoon Nutmeg
170g (6oz) Butter
30g (1oz) Currants
30g (1oz) Sultanas
30g (1oz) Raisins
45g (1½oz) Glacé Cherries (quartered)
45g (1½oz) Walnuts (chopped)
85g (3oz) Light Brown Sugar
1 large Egg (beaten)
100-125ml (4-5fl oz) Milk
Walnuts & Cherries to decorate

Pre-heat oven to 220C/425F/Gas 7

1. Sieve the flour, baking powder, mixed spice and nutmeg into a bowl.
2. Rub in the butter.
3. Add the fruit, nuts and sugar.
4. Mix in the beaten egg and milk until the mixture is a stiff consistency.
5. Spoon the mixture into 12 or 14 heaps on a greased baking tray, and top with the spare walnuts and cherries.
6. Bake in the pre-heated oven for 15-20 minutes.
7. Sprinkle with caster sugar whilst hot.

LIME AND COCONUT CAKE
(BY JANIS THOMSON)

140g (5oz) Margarine
140g (5oz) Caster Sugar
2 Eggs
55g (2oz) Dessicated Coconut
2 Limes
140g (5oz) Self-Raising Flour

BUTTER CREAM
55g (2oz) Butter (softened)
110g (4oz) Icing Sugar (sifted)
2 Tablespoons Milk

LIME GLACÉ ICING
225g (8oz) Icing Sugar (sifted)
2 Tablespoons Lime Juice

Pre-heat oven to 180C/350F/Gas 4

1. Cream together the margarine and sugar.
2. Gradually add the beaten eggs.
3. Mix in the coconut and juice and zest of 1 lime.
4. Fold in the flour.
5. Divide the mixture between 2 prepared 7-inch cake tins.
6. Bake in the pre-heated oven for 20-25 minutes.
7. Meanwhile beat the butter cream ingredients until soft.
8. Mix together the lime glacé ingredients.
9. Once cold, sandwich together the two halves of the cake with the butter cream in the middle.
10. Top with the lime glacé icing.

CRUNCHY CEREAL SQUARES
(BY BARBARA HITCHCOCK)

225g (8oz) Butter or Margarine
340g (12oz) Cereal (Muesli) or Oats
225g (8oz) Sugar
110g (4oz) Self-Raising Flour

Pre-heat oven to 200C/400F/Gas 6

1. Melt the butter (or margarine).
2. Mix in all of the remaining ingredients.
3. Pour into a baking tin approximately 38 x 25cms (15 x 10-inch), and press down so that the mixture reaches the edges of the tin.
4. Bake in the pre-heated oven for 20 minutes until golden brown on top.
5. Cut into squares as soon as it is removed from the oven, and leave to cool in the baking tin before lifting out.
6. Will keep in an airtight container for 1 week.

ORANGE SYRUP CARROT CAKE
(BY MOLLY DEAN)

200g (7oz) Wholemeal Flour
3 Level Teaspoons Mixed Spice
1 Level Teaspoon Bicarbonate of Soda
55g (2oz) Dessicated Coconut
55g (2oz) Walnuts (chopped)
110g (4oz) Sultanas
170g (6oz) Soft Brown Sugar
2 Eggs (size 1)
125ml (¼pt) Sunflower Oil
Grated Rind 1 Orange
200g (7oz) Grated Carrots

ORANGE SYRUP GLAZE
1 Tablespoon Lemon Juice
Juice of 1 Small Orange
85g (3oz) Soft Brown Sugar

Pre-heat oven to 150C/300F/Gas 2

1. Put the flour, mixed spice, bicarbonate of soda, nuts and sultanas into a bowl.
2. In a separate bowl, combine the sugar, eggs and oil and beat together until smooth.
3. Stir in the dry ingredients from the first bowl.
4. Stir in the orange rind and carrots, and mix.
5. Put the mixture into a lined 2lb loaf tin.
6. Bake in pre-heated oven for 1½ to 2 hours.
7. Once baked, whisk together the fruit juices and sugar to make the glaze.
8. Stab the warm cake with a skewer, and flood with the syrup.
9. When cool the cake will have absorbed all of the liquid.

ALL-IN-ONE CHOCOLATE CAKE (BY MOLLY DEAN)

110g (4oz) Butter or margarine
140g (5oz) Caster Sugar
2 Eggs (small)
170g (6oz) Self-Raising Flour
30g (1oz) Cocoa Powder
½ cup Water
1 Tablespoon Vanilla Essence

Pre-heat oven to
180-190C/350-375F/Gas 4-5

1. Mix together all of the ingredients and using a food mixer, beat together on a low speed until all of the ingredients are combined.
2. Increase the speed to medium for 2 or 3 minutes until the mixture is smooth and changed in colour.
3. Spread into a lined 2lb loaf tin.
4. Bake in the pre-heated oven for approximately 1¼ hours.

SMOKED MACKEREL AND APPLE PATÉ (BY ANN BARNETT)

Serves 4 as a starter or
12 on biscuits as canapés

1 Small Dessert Apple (peeled & cored)
2 Teaspoons Lemon Juice
150g (5½ oz) Smoked Mackerel (skinned & flaked)
75g (2¼oz) Soft Cheese (cream, curd or low-fat)
30g (1oz) Butter (melted)
1 Teaspoon Creamed Horseradish
Freshly Ground Black Pepper

TO GARNISH
Lemon (sliced)
Fresh Parsley

1. Grate the apple and mix with the lemon juice in a bowl.
2. Add the mackerel, cheese, butter and horse-radish.
3. Mix well, and season to taste.
4. Spoon the paté into a large dish or individual ramekins.
5. Garnish with the lemon and parsley.
6. Chill in the fridge.
7. Serve with fingers of toast, small crackers or oatcakes; alternatively, spread onto small savoury scones.

Mackerel Paté

Ann recommends using Cox's apples if possible.

Use a food processor to mix all of the ingredients to achieve a smoother paste.

The paté mixture may be pressed into a small loaf tin lined with cling film – chill well before turning out and cut into slices to serve as a starter with a little salad garnish.

JAMS (BY SUE GRANVILLE-GEORGE)

APRICOT, ORANGE AND ALMOND JAM

450g (1lb) Dried Apricots
3 Oranges
2½ Teaspoons Ground Cinnamon
1.225kg (2½lb) Sugar
2 Lemons
55g (2oz) Flaked Almonds

1. Chop the apricots and put into a bowl with the zest from the oranges, plus the juice from the oranges made up to 1.5 litres (3 pints) with water.
2. Layer with the ground cinnamon and leave overnight.
3. The next day, put the mixture into a preserving pan and simmer on the hob until soft.
4. Add the sugar with the juice of the lemons and the almonds.
5. Bring to the boil and continue to boil, whilst stirring, until setting point is reached.
6. Pot the jam.

BLACKCURRANT JAM

1.8kg (4lb) Blackcurrants
1.5lt (3pts) Water
2.7kg (6lb) Sugar

1. Simmer the blackcurrants in the water for ¾ hour until soft and the contents of the pan are reduced.
2. Add the sugar and bring the mixture to the boil.
3. Boil hard until setting point is reached.
4. Pot the jam.

MULBERRY JAM

1.350kg (3lb) Mulberries
450g (1lb) Apples
1.575kg (3½lb) Sugar

1. In separate pans, cook the mulberries and apples until soft.
2. Combine into one pan, and add the sugar.
3. Bring to the boil and boil hard until setting point is reached.
4. Pot the jam.

STRAWBERRY AND GOOSEBERRY JAM

1.350kg (3lb) Strawberries
1.350kg (3lb) Gooseberries
2.7kg (6lb) Sugar

1. Simmer the gooseberries in a little water until soft.
2. Add the strawberries and sugar.
3. Bring to the boil and boil hard until setting point is reached.
4. Pot the jam.

With afternoon tea, how about loose leaf Darjeeling - careful with the milk, or how about a small glass of nutty Amontillado Sherry.

EMSWORTH PRIMARY SCHOOL

EMSWORTH PRIMARY SCHOOL
VICTORIA ROAD
EMSWORTH
PO10 7LX
T. 01243 375750

www.emsworth.hants.sch.uk

HEAD: ROSEMARY LAW

EMSWORTH PRIMARY SCHOOL,
UNTIL A FEW YEARS AGO BASED IN A VICTORIAN BUILD-
ING IN WASHINGTON ROAD, IS SITUATED ON VICTORIA
ROAD WITH EXTENSIVE GROUNDS RUNNING PARALLEL WITH
THE RAILWAY LINE. THE SCHOOL IS COMMITTED TO HIGH
STANDARDS AND EXCITING PLANS ARE BEING DEVELOPED
TO IMPROVE THE WHOLE SCHOOL LEARNING ENVIRONMENT.
THE CHILDREN, AGED 4-11, COME FROM A WIDE CATCH-
MENT AREA BOTH IN AND AROUND EMSWORTH. THEY ARE
ENCOURAGED TO BE INDEPENDENT LEARNERS WHO THINK
CREATIVELY AND REFLECTIVELY WITHIN A FRIENDLY,
CARING SCHOOL. PARTNERSHIP WITH ALL MEMBERS OF THE
SCHOOL AND THE LOCAL COMMUNITY IS HIGHLY VALUED IN
ORDER TO HELP PROVIDE MOTIVATING, CHALLENGING AND
ENJOYABLE LEARNING OPPORTUNITIES.

KAREN AND RAMON FARTHING OF 36 ON THE QUAY
(RESTAURANT WITH ROOMS) VISITED THE PUPILS OF YEAR 4 AND 5 (AGED 8
AND 9 YEARS) TO SET THEM A COMPETITION TO DEVELOP A RECIPE FOR THIS
BOOK. THEY WERE GIVEN A LIST OF INGREDIENTS TO USE, AND TOLD TO DRAW
OR PAINT THE FINISHED DISH AS WELL AS DESCRIBE THE METHOD OF PREPA-
RATION. FROM THIS, 16 OF THE CHILDREN WERE CHOSEN TO VISIT THE RES-
TAURANT TO HELP WITH, AND SEE THE OVERALL WINNING RECIPE PREPARED
BEFORE DEVOURING IT.

KAREN & RAMON FARTHING OF 36 ON THE QUAY WITH CHILDREN FROM YEAR 4 & 5 WITH THEIR TEACHERS, MARY SKINNER & EMMA SMITH

BETHANY GARLAND'S DRAWING OF HER 'SPONGE TURTLE SURPRISE'. HER INSPIRATION FOR HER CHOICE CAME FROM THE TURTLES ON THE SHOWER CURTAIN AT HOME.

THE FOLLOWING LIST OF INGREDIENTS WAS GIVEN TO THE CHILDREN TO WORK WITH: CASTER SUGAR, EGGS, BAKING POWDER, BUTTER, FLOUR AND MILK. OPTIONAL EXTRAS THEY COULD USE WERE: DOUBLE CREAM, GOLDEN SYRUP, SULTANAS, COCOA POWDER, RASPBERRIES, VANILLA FLAVOURING AND PEACHES.

KAREN AND RAMON HAD A DIFFICULT TIME CHOOSING 16 WINNING RECIPES, FROM THE TOTAL OF 50, BECAUSE THE STANDARD OF EACH WAS EXCELLENT. HOWEVER, THEY EVENTUALLY MANAGED THIS DIFFICULT TASK AND CHOSE RECIPES PRODUCED BY: MATTHEW STURGESS, REBECCA SAYERS, KIRSTY GLADDIS, LEWIS GARLAND, LEILA FARTHING, HOLLIE MARSHALL, GEORGE PICKERING, LAUREN KAUNHOVEN, FINN BRODIE, KATIE PHILLIPS, BETHANY GARLAND, MADISON REILLY, ROSIE LATAWSKI, ROBYN GRAY, MADELEINE HUGHES AND INDIA SWAIN. AND FROM THESE, THE OVERALL WINNER CHOSEN FOR ORIGINALITY AND PRESENTATION WAS BETHANY WITH HER TURTLE CAKE.

THE RECIPE WAS INTERPRETED AND DEVELOPED TO PRODUCE A LARGE CHOCOLATE FLAVOURED PARTY VERSION OF THE TURTLE CAKE. TO MAKE IT IN THIS SIZE YOU WILL NEED TO INCREASE THE QUANTITIES USED IN BETHANY'S RECIPE, TO 300G OF FLOUR AND SUGAR AND INCREASE OTHER INGREDIENTS ACCORDINGLY. FOR A CHOCOLATE VERSION SUBSTITUTE COCOA POWDER FOR 55G OF THE FLOUR. WHEN SHAPING THE CAKE FOR THE BODY OF THE TURTLE, RETAIN THE CUT CORNERS TO USE AS FLIPPERS AND THE HEAD.

Bethany Garland's drawing was selected from the entries of the sixteen finalists, all of whom attended the session at 36 On the Quay.

BETHANY'S RECIPE FOR SPONGE TURTLE SURPRISE

SPONGE CAKE
2 Eggs (size 3)
75g Caster Sugar
75g Self-Raising Flour

EXTRA'S
4 Peaches
50ml Double Cream
50g Raspberries

EQUIPMENT
18cm (7inch) Cake Tin
1 Whisk
1 Bowl
1 Knife
1 Plate

To make crème chantilly, whip together double cream and a little sugar.

After consulting our young chefs cold lemonade works best, with a straw please.

Pre-heat oven to 180C/350F/Gas 4

1. Grease the cake tin.

2. Break the eggs into a bowl and whisk gently. Pour in the sugar and whisk until thick and creamy.

3. Gently fold in the flour. Pour the mixture into the greased cake tin and bake in the pre-heated oven for 30 minutes. When cool, place the cake on a plate.

4. Slice 1 peach in half. Then cut 4 segments of peach to look like the flippers of a turtle.

5. Place the half of the peach on one side of the cake, in the middle of the side. This is the head. Place the 2 segments of peach on one side of the cake. Do the same to the other 2 segments. These are the flippers.

6. Pour the double cream over the cake. Lastly, place 2 raspberries on the head for the eyes, and place the remaining raspberries around the plate forming a circle around the turtle.

7. Eat and enjoy!

BETHANY GARLAND CUTS THE CAKE WITH RAMON ➤

GEORGE GALE & CO LTD

GEORGE GALE & CO LTD
THE HAMPSHIRE BREWERY
HORNDEAN
HANTS
PO8 0DA
T. 023 9257 1212

www.gales.co.uk

DEREK BEAVES, HEAD OF MARKETING

JONATHAN DALEY HAS BEEN THE CATERING DEVELOPMENT MANAGER AT THE BREWERY FOR THE PAST FOUR YEARS. PREVIOUSLY, HE WAS A HEAD CHEF FOR THE COMPANY. HE IS RESPONSIBLE FOR DEVELOPING THE MENUS, AND HELPING TO SOURCE THE INGREDIENTS SERVED AT THE MANAGED PUBLIC HOUSES.

GEORGE GALE & CO LTD IS EMSWORTH'S LOCAL BREWERY, OWNING FOUR OF THE PUBLIC HOUSES IN THE VILLAGE. DURING 2004 IT WON THE TITLE OF PUB COMPANY OF THE YEAR IN THE PUBLICAN AWARDS. THIS LEADING FAMILY BREWER WAS FOUNDED IN 1847, AND PRODUCES A RANGE OF TRADITIONAL CASK ALES, INCLUDING THE RENOWNED HSB, USING ONLY THE FINEST ENGLISH AROMA HOPS AND MARIS OTTER BARLEY MALT. THE BREWERY HAS A PORTFOLIO OF MORE THAN 100 PUBS IN HAMPSHIRE, BERKSHIRE, SURREY AND SUSSEX OF WHICH APPROXIMATELY 40 ARE MANAGED. THE BREWING WATER FOR ALL GALES BEER IS STILL EXTRACTED FROM THE BREWERY WELL WHICH EXTENDS SOME 300 FEET DOWN INTO THE CHALK.

SEARED BLACK BREAM WITH ASPARAGUS AND WATERCRESS WITH A GALES 'PRIZE OLD ALE' DRESSING

Serves 2 as a starter

2 Small Bunches Hampshire Watercress
225g Asparagus
2 x 100g Black Bream Fillets
2 Tablespoons Extra Virgin Olive Oil
Sea Salt & Freshly Ground Black Pepper

PRIZE OLD ALE DRESSING

5 Tablespoons Olive Oil
½ Onion (finely chopped)
1 Clove Garlic (chopped)
½ Bottle Prize Old Ale
3 Tablespoons White Wine Vinegar
2 Teaspoons Hampshire Honey
2 Tablespoons Whole Grain Mustard
Salt & Pepper

1. Rinse and dry the watercress.

2. Trim and steam the asparagus until tender, and refresh in iced water to stop the cooking process.

3. Brush the fillet of bream with olive oil and season with salt and ground pepper.

4. Cook the bream fillets under a hot grill for 2 minutes each side.

5. Just as the bream has finished cooking, brush the asparagus with oil, season and warm under a grill.

6. To serve, place watercress into the centre of the plate and arrange the asparagus on top, and drizzle with a little dressing.

7. Drizzle the dressing around the plate, place the bream on top of the watercress and asparagus, and glaze the bream with any remaining cooking juices.

PRIZE OLD ALE DRESSING

1. Heat 3 tablespoons of olive oil over a medium heat, in a saucepan.

2. Add the onions and garlic and sauté until soft.

3. Add the Prize Old Ale, vinegar and honey and reduce for 4 or 5 minutes.

4. Set aside to cool.

5. Place the cooled mixture in a blender with the mustard and seasoning. Whilst the motor is running, add the remaining oil.

Snap the asparagus during preparation, rather than cutting – the spear will snap at the point where it becomes tender. It can then simply be trimmed.

Good quality white Bordeaux, maybe Graves or a Semillon/Sauvignon Blanc blend from Western Australia.

FILLET OF BEEF WITH ROSEMARY ROAST POTATOES, BRAISED FENNEL AND GARLIC PARSNIP MASH

Serves 2

5 or 6 Small Potatoes (peeled)
2 Tablespoons Olive Oil
Sprigs Fresh Rosemary
10 Cloves Garlic
250g Parsnip (peeled & diced)
Salt & Pepper
100ml Beef Stock
100ml Red Wine
1 Tablespoon Balsamic Vinegar
2 x 150g Beef Fillet
150g Baby Carrots
150g Fine Beans
50g Unsalted Butter (cold)

Pre-heat oven to 200C/400F/Gas 6

1. Par boil the potatoes for approximately 5 minutes. Drain and toss in a little olive oil and the rosemary and roast in the pre-heated oven for approximately 40 minutes.

2. Add the garlic cloves to the potatoes and roast for a further 10-15 minutes.

3. Meanwhile, cook the parsnips in boiling water until tender. Drain and mash with some salt and pepper. Squeeze some of the roasted garlic into the mash and thoroughly mix.

4. Place the beef stock in a pan with the red wine and vinegar and simmer to reduce.

5. Seal the beef fillets in a hot pan with a little oil for 2-3 minutes each side. Season and place in the oven.

6. Cook the carrots and beans in a steamer.

7. The parsnip mash may be covered and kept warm with the remaining garlic cloves.

8. When the beef is done to your liking, remove from the oven. Cover and leave to rest for 5 minutes.

9. The sauce should be reduced to ¼ of the original volume.

10. Add any cooking juices from the beef to the sauce, and reduce the heat.

11. Slice the beef and place in the centre of the plate on top of the parsnip mash.

12. Arrange the vegetables, potatoes and roasted garlic around the meat.

13. Whisk the cold butter into the sauce – it will thicken slightly.

14. Pour over the sauce, and garnish with fresh rosemary.

Just the opportunity to get your best Claret out from under the stairs or any good quality Cabernet Sauvignon from California or Australia

HOLLYBANK HOUSE

Hollybank House
Hollybank Lane
Emsworth
PO10 7UN
T. 01243 375502

e. anna@hollybankhouse.com
www.hollybankhouse.com

VIV & ANNA WILLIAMS

HOLLYBANK HOUSE IS A GEORGIAN FAMILY HOME ON THE OUTSKIRTS OF EMSWORTH. ANNA AND VIV WILLIAMS ARE THE CURRENT OWNERS, AND OVER THE LAST FEW YEARS HAVE MADE THE HOUSE AND EXTENSIVE GROUNDS AVAILABLE FOR WEDDINGS AND PRIVATE FUNCTIONS. SINCE SUMMER 2003, THEY HAVE ALSO INTRODUCED BED AND BREAKFAST WITH THREE ROOMS AND OF COURSE, MUCH OF THE PRODUCE AVAILABLE AT BREAKFAST IS MADE FROM THAT GROWN IN THE GARDENS AND VICTORIAN GREENHOUSES. THE HOUSE HAS A RICH HISTORY AND HAS HAD SEVERAL OWNERS SINCE IT WAS FIRST BUILT IN THE EARLY 1820'S BY THE WIDOW OF RICHARD BARWELL OF STANSTED PARK. ORIGINALLY THE MAIN PART OF THE HOUSE HAD A THATCHED ROOF, BUT THIS WAS REPLACED BY CLAY TILES AFTER A FIRE IN THE EARLY 1900'S. SIR ROBERT MILLER MUNDY, KCMG, HER SON BY A SECOND MARRIAGE, RAISED HIS LARGE VICTORIAN FAMILY OF 13 CHILDREN AT HOLLYBANK. CONCHITA ROIG, BORN AT HOLLYBANK IN 1915, VISITED THE HOUSE A FEW YEARS AGO AND SHARED SOME OF HER MEMORIES. SHE SAID, "IN MY TIME WE HAD 3 GARDENERS AND IN THE HOUSE THERE WAS MRS BROWN, THE COOK, A KITCHEN MAID, THE BUTLER, JULIET, MAMA'S LADY'S MAID, A PARLOUR MAID AND MY NANNY". RATHER DIFFERENT FROM TODAY! DURING THE SECOND WORLD WAR, THE HOUSE WAS USED AS A CONVALESCENT HOME, AND SOME LOCAL RESIDENTS REMEMBER STAYING THERE. BRIGADIER TERRY CLARKE LIVED AT HOLLYBANK WHILE MP FOR PORTSMOUTH NORTH. THEN IN 1967, BASIL WILLIAMS BOUGHT HOLLYBANK AND RAN HIS BUS COMPANY, HANTS AND SUSSEX, FROM OFFICES AT THE HOUSE. THE COMPANY WAS FOUNDED IN 1937 WITH A BUS RUNNING FROM EMSWORTH TO THORNEY ISLAND, AND RAPIDLY EXPANDED TO BECOME ONE OF THE LARGEST PRIVATE BUS OPERATORS IN THE COUNTRY. THE MAROON COLOURED BUSES WERE A FAMILIAR SIGHT AROUND EMSWORTH UNTIL HE FINALLY RETIRED IN HIS EARLY 80'S AND SOLD THE COMPANY.

HOLLYBANK HOUSE THEN & NOW

ANNA'S BREAKFAST CONSERVES

WHICH SHE MAKES USING PRODUCE FROM HER GARDEN

COMPOTE OF SUMMER BERRIES

225g Blackcurrants & Redcurrants
225g Blackberries
225g Raspberries
225g Strawberries
175g Sugar
350ml Water

1. Gently heat the currants and blackberries with the sugar and water, and simmer until soft.

2. Add the strawberries and raspberries.

3. Remove from the heat and allow to cool.

On the assumption these are for breakfast it has to be a glass of Bucks Fizz. Please not Champagne though - such a waste.

APRICOT JAM

2kg Fresh Apricots
450ml Water
2kg Sugar
Juice 2 Lemons
Knob Butter

1. Wash, halve and stone the apricots.

2. Remove a few kernels and blanch in boiling water.

3. Simmer the apricots and kernels in the water until the fruit is tender and reduced by half.

4. Add the sugar and stir well until dissolved.

5. Add the lemon juice, turn up the heat and boil rapidly to setting point (approximately 10 minutes).

6. Remove from the heat, add a small knob of butter to disperse any scum that may have formed. Allow to settle for 10-15 minutes before pouring into warm, clean, dry jars.

7. Seal immediately with wax discs and cover with cling film and lids while still warm.

BLACKCURRANT JAM

1.8kg Blackcurrants
1.2lt Water
2.25kg Sugar
Knob Butter

1. Top and tail the blackcurrants and simmer gently in the water until the mixture is reduced by almost half, stirring frequently to avoid burning.

2. Add the sugar and stir until completely dissolved.

3. Boil rapidly to setting point (approximately 10 minutes).

4. Remove from the heat, add a small knob of butter to disperse any scum that may have formed. Allow to settle for 10-15 minutes.

5. Pour into warm, clean, dry jars and seal immediately with wax discs.

6. Cover the jars with cling film and lids while still warm.

BASIL WILLIAMS AND HIS BUS COMPANY

RENE WILLIAMS

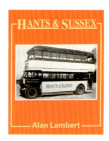

'HANTS & SUSSEX' BY ALAN LAMBERT, FORMERLY ASSISTANT AND TRAFFIC MANAGER. A FEW COPIES OF THE BOOKLET ARE STILL AVAILABLE FOR SALE AT £3.95 PER COPY, FROM:

ALAN LAMBERT
7 NURSERY CLOSE
EMSWORTH
PO10 7SP
T. 01243 431606

BASIL WILLIAMS

It was in 1933 that a Hawker aircraft crashed at Thorney Island and the Air Ministry, investigating the crash, decided to build an airfield there. Basil Williams, then too young to drive a bus, decided to apply for a licence to run a bus service to the new RAF base, which after much debate was finally granted. In 1937 he formed Hants & Sussex Motor Services Ltd which expanded quickly during the war, to such an extent that he was one of the few civilians to have a pass to all areas constructing Mulberry Harbour and to know the date of D-Day well before the event. By the end of the war, helped by his wife Rene, the fleet had grown to 140 vehicles and Basil Williams had become one of the largest independent operators in the country.

Running such a fleet in peacetime, with tremendous competition and other companies pirating the licensed routes, was very difficult and in 1954 a receiver was appointed and the company ceased trading. Basil and Rene, however, continued to run the Thorney to Emsworth route with a new company trading as 'Southern Motorways' together with many rural routes around Midhurst, Petworth, Petersfield and Chichester. In 1959 he also acquired another old established bus company, Gilder & Blue Motor Services Ltd based at Bishops Waltham, which he ran in conjunction with his son, Viv. The company still exists in a somewhat different form today. In 1966 he bought Hollybank House, from where he ran the Emsworth bus company until 1996 when the old name of 'Hants & Sussex' was again the operating name.

At the age of 82, while still running the bus service around Emsworth, he finally decided to retire and the operation was initially sold to Southampton City Bus before Emsworth & District took over the routes giving the excellent service enjoyed today.

Basil Williams died on 27 June 1999, but his memory and reputation live on both locally and also in the world of passenger transport.

IN THE 1960'S, WHEN THESE COACHES WERE PHOTOGRAPHED, THE MAIN A27 ROAD WENT THROUGH THE CENTRE OF EMSWORTH.

THE KINGS ARMS

THE KINGS ARMS
19 HAVANT ROAD
EMSWORTH
PO10 7JD
T. 01243 374941

BREWERY: GEORGE GALE & CO LTD

PENNY & ADRIAN WHITE

PENNY WHITE HAS A GREAT INTEREST IN RESEARCHING HISTORICAL RECIPES FROM THE DIM AND DISTANT PAST. THESE REGULARLY FEATURE AS PART OF THE VARIED AND EXTENSIVE SPECIAL DISHES ON OFFER FOR LUNCH AND DINNER AT THE PUB, AS WELL AS SPECIAL EVENINGS CELEBRATING EVENTS SUCH AS TRAFALGAR. SHE IS A SELF-TAUGHT COOK WHO HAS GAINED HER KNOWLEDGE WHILST RUNNING THE KITCHENS OF THE PUBS WITH HER HUSBAND, ADRIAN. THE FOOD THAT PENNY SERVES IS A MIXTURE OF TRADITIONAL OLD-FASHIONED DAILY SPECIALS WITH A WIDE RANGING CHOICE OF VEGETARIAN DISHES AS WELL AS A SELECTION OF ORGANIC MEALS AND FRESH FISH. THE HOMEMADE PUDDINGS ARE OFTEN TOO TEMPTING TO RESIST. PENNY'S KEEN INTEREST IN FOOD IS SUCH THAT SHE SOURCES MUCH OF THE FRESH PRODUCE USED FROM LOCAL SUPPLIERS.

THE KINGS ARMS WAS ORIGINALLY A STOPOVER FOR COACHES PULLED BY HORSES TRANSPORTING PEOPLE AND GOODS. THE PUBLIC HOUSE WAS FIRST RECORDED IN 1820, AND HAS BEEN RUN BY PENNY AND ADRIAN WHITE SINCE 1990 WHEN THEY MOVED FROM WICKHAM TO EMSWORTH. FOR MORE THAN 34 YEARS OF THEIR WORKING LIFE, THEY HAVE TOGETHER RUN VARIOUS PUBS AND EVEN GREW UP IN THIS ENVIRONMENT WITH BOTH HAVING PARENTS WHO WERE PUBLICANS. THIS TRADITIONAL PUB WITH ITS WONDERFULLY KEPT LARGE REAR GARDEN, ALSO HAS A SEPARATE SMALL DINING AREA. MORE THAN HALF OF THE BAR AREA IS SET ASIDE AS A NON-SMOKING AREA.

ORGANIC STUFFED MUSHROOMS   *Serves 6*

480g Organic Portabellini Mushrooms
1 Organic Medium Onion (finely diced)
30ml Organic Olive Oil
120g Organic Wholewheat Breadcrumbs
240g Organic Roquefort Cheese
1 Organic Egg (beaten)
60g Organic Grated Cheddar

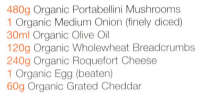

Pre-heat oven to 190C/375F/Gas 5

1. Remove the stalks from the mushrooms and blanche the mushrooms in boiling water for 1 minute.

2. Turn them upside down on kitchen paper to drain.

3. Soften the diced onion in hot oil, and add the bread-crumbs, crumbled Roquefort cheese and beaten egg.

4. Put the mixture into the drained mushrooms, divide into ovenproof dishes and sprinkle with cheddar cheese.

5. Bake in the top of the pre-heated oven for 15 minutes until browned.

Fleshy red such as St.Emilion or Reserva Rioja.

Chilled Pineapple and Curry Soup

A recipe from the 18th century when the pineapple was a symbol of wealth

Serves 6

1 Large Onion
2 Courgettes
2 Tablespoons Olive Oil
1 Dessertspoon Curry Powder
360g Fresh Pineapple (chopped)
500ml Chicken Stock
250ml Pineapple Juice
1 Dessertspoon Mango Chutney
Juice & Rind 1 lemon
250ml Double Cream
30g Toasted Almonds

1. Finely chop the onion and slice the courgettes.

2. Heat the oil in a pan and soften the onion. Add the curry powder and cook for a few minutes.

3. Add the chopped pineapple, and cover with the stock and pineapple juice.

4. Bring to the boil and add the courgettes.

5. Simmer for 5 minutes.

6. Stir in the mango chutney.

7. Remove from the heat and blend the soup – but do not make the mixture too smooth.

8. Chill the soup.

9. Add the lemon juice and rind.

10. Slightly whip the cream and stir into the bowls of soup just before serving, and sprinkle with the toasted almonds.

Simple, dry white but no oak - Alsace Pinot Blanc or Sauvignon de Touraine.

CRAB PIE

RECIPE FROM ROBERT MAY, DATED 1660

Serves 6

Shortcrust Pastry
480g Crab Meat
240g Salmon (cooked)
1 Medium Onion (diced)
60g Currants
2 Tablespoons Grapes (or Gooseberries)
15g Breadcrumbs
4 Tablespoons Tarragon
4 Tablespoons Dill
4 Tablespoons Chervil
¼ Teaspoon Nutmeg
30g Butter
125ml White Wine

Pre-heat oven to 190C/375F/Gas 5

1. Line a 20cm (8 inch) pie dish with half of the shortcrust pastry.

2. Arrange layers of the crab, salmon, onion, currants, grapes, breadcrumbs and herbs.

3. Season the layers with salt, pepper and nutmeg.

4. Dot with butter and pour the wine over the top.

5. Cover with a pastry lid and bake in the pre-heated oven for 15-20 minutes until golden brown.

6. Serve hot or cold.

ROSE EVILL, HAS WORKED WITH PENNY & ADRIAN FOR 27 YEARS, AND HER COOKING SKILLS, ESPECIALLY PASTRY, ARE SECOND TO NONE.

There may well be some richness here, so dry white with some structure would work: good quality Macon or modern style white Rioja.

STUFFED FILLET STEAKS
BASED ON A VICTORIAN RECIPE BOOKLET
Serves 6

6 Fillet Steaks (well trimmed)
120g Button Mushrooms
30g Butter
15g Flour
Salt & Pepper
1 Tablespoon Dry Sherry
2 Tablespoons Double Cream
1 Teaspoon Mustard

COATING
1 Egg (beaten)
4 Tablespoons Fresh White Breadcrumbs
2 Tablespoons Freshly Grated Parmesan
Oil

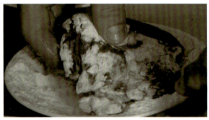

RORY GOBLE, CATERING STUDENT AT SOUTH DOWNS COLLEGE

1. Use a sharp, pointed knife to make a small slit in the side of each steak, and move around inside to make a cavity.

2. Chop the mushrooms fairly small.

3. Melt the butter in a pan and fry the mushrooms, then remove.

4. Add the flour, salt and pepper, sherry and the cream, a little at a time.

5. Stir in the mustard and mushrooms, then allow the mixture to cool.

6. Fill the cavity of the steaks with the mushroom mixture, using a small spoon.

7. Dip each steak into the beaten egg and then the breadcrumb and parmesan mixture.

8. Heat some oil in a heavy bottomed frying pan and fry the coated fillets until golden brown on each side.

Use thin fillet steaks so that it does not take too long to crisp the breadcrumb coating, and therefore does not over cook the meat.

Almost any full bodied, well structured red, try top quality Chianti or Ribera del Duero from Spain.

DAUBE OF BEEF

BASED ON A 17TH CENTURY RECIPE BY ANNE BLENCOWE

Serves 6

1kg Rump Steak
120g Bacon
2 Carrots
2 Onions
½ Stick Celery
2 Cloves Garlic (crushed)
500ml Port (or Beer)
½ Teaspoon Thyme
½ Teaspoon Marjoram
6 Cloves
60g Butter
30g Flour
250ml Beef Stock
1 Teaspoon Grated Orange Rind
Salt & Black Pepper

Pre-heat oven to 190C/375F/Gas 5

1. Trim the meat and cut into 3cm (1 inch) cubes.

2. Dice the bacon into very small pieces.

3. Dice the vegetables into 1.5cm (½ inch) chunks.

4. Put the meat and vegetables with the garlic into a dish and cover with the port, or beer.

5. Sprinkle with the freshly chopped herbs.

6. Leave the meat to marinate for at least 5 hours, or overnight.

7. Drain the meat and vegetables, retaining the marinade to use later.

8. Melt the butter in a pan and fry the bacon, and then the meat cubes to seal them.

9. Remove the meat from the pan.

10. Sprinkle the pan with the flour, stir well and add the marinade liquid and the beef stock.

11. Put the meat, bacon, vegetables, orange rind and seasoning into an earthenware casserole dish and cover with the marinade.

12. Cover and cook in the pre-heated oven for 4 hours.

Sturdy red, opened well in advance such as Cote Rotie or St.Joseph from the Rhone or one of the new breed of Shiraz from South Africa.

DARK RED FRUIT SALAD
AN 18TH CENTURY RECIPE FOR A REFRESHING PUDDING

Serves approximately 8

250ml Jasmine Tea
240g Dark Cherries (pitted)
240g Raspberries
240g Black Grapes (seedless)
240g Strawberries
240g Sweet Dark Plums
120g Caster Sugar

1. Make the jasmine tea fairly strong, and allow to cool.

2. Halve and stone the cherries and plums.

3. Wash and check other fruit.

4. Hull the strawberries, and cut in half if large.

5. Put all of the fruit into a bowl, sprinkle with the sugar and pour over the tea.

Only prepare this an hour or so before eating.

SMALL ALMOND PUDDINGS
1807 RECIPE BY MRS RUNDLE

Makes 8 - 10

240g Ground Almonds
30g Whole Almonds (chopped)
120g Butter
4 Eggs
60g Sugar
2 Tablespoons Double Cream
1 Tablespoon Brandy

Pre-heat oven to 180C/350F/Gas 4

1. Mix all of the almonds together.

2. Melt the butter in a tablespoon of water, and add to the almonds.

3. Reserve 2 egg whites.

4. Beat 2 eggs and the 2 egg yolks, and stir together with the sugar, cream and brandy into the almond mixture..

5. Whisk the egg whites until stiff and fold into the mixture.

6. Butter small individual soufflé dishes or ramekins and half fill with the mixture.

7. Stand the dishes in a tray of water and bake in the pre-heated oven for 15 minutes.

8. Turn out and serve with the fruit salad or any other sweet sauce.

Muscat de Rivesaltes or similar from the South of France or maybe a glass of Amaretto.

The Lord Raglan

The Lord Raglan
35 Queen Street
Emsworth
PO10 7BJ
T. 01243 372587

e. les@thelordraglan.com
www.thelordraglan.com

Brewery: George Gale & Co ltd

Les & Trish Young

Trish Young cooks a wide-range of traditional good pub food, including her now renowned steak, stout and mushroom pies and a daily choice of fresh homemade soups. On her travels abroad she collects regional cookery books, as is evidenced in the daily specials on offer. Trish is a self-taught chef who found she had a flair for the job, having gained her experience whilst running their first pub, the King's Head near Chichester. She manages to relax with her husband, Les by listening to live music and taking long walks on the South Downs. During May 2004, she completed the Moonwalk in London with a team of bar staff, raising money for Breast Cancer Research.

The Lord Raglan with its south facing rear garden overlooking the Slipper Millpond and the River Ems, is Emsworth's only waterside public house. This traditional flint-built pub has been under the tenancy of Les and Trish Young since December 1993. Retaining many of its original features, including an oak-beamed bar area and inglenook fireplace with real log fires during the colder months, the pub has become a popular venue for locals and visitors alike. The separate restaurant area provides a quieter ambience for lunch and dinner. Live music is a regular feature, with bands playing every Sunday night as well as every second Wednesday night.

3-COURSE MENU

SMOKED HADDOCK MELTS

APRICOT AND GINGER STUFFED PORK

BOOZY CHOCOLATE ICE CREAM

OVERLOOKING THE SLIPPER MILL POND, THE LORD RAGLAN HAS EMSWORTH'S ONLY WATERSIDE BEER GARDEN. REGULAR VISITORS INCLUDE A FAMILY OF DUCKS WHO CONSIDER TRISH AND LES THEIR ADOPTED PARENTS.

SMOKED HADDOCK MELTS

Serves 1

1 Slice French Bread
55g (2oz) Poached Smoked
    Haddock (flaked)
Double Cream
30g (1oz) Cheddar Cheese (grated)
Salad Leaves
Baby Plum Tomatoes
Lemon (to garnish)

Pre-heat oven to 200C/400F/Gas 6

1. Butter the slice of French bread on both sides, and pop into the pre-heated oven until golden brown and crisp. Allow to cool.

2. Mix the flaked smoked haddock with a small amount of the double cream to moisten.

3. Spread the smoked haddock mixture onto the bread and top with the grated cheddar cheese.

4. Put under a hot grill to melt the cheese.

5. Serve on a bed of mixed salad leaves, and garnish with the tomatoes and lemon.

Chablis would work well but not Premier or Grand Cru, if not head south for a good Macon.

APRICOT AND GINGER STUFFED PORK

Serves 4-6

Red with some spice to match the ginger, good quality South African Pinotage or Southern Italian red.

1.450/1.8kg (3-4lbs) Joint Belly Pork (boned)
2 Tablespoons Apricot Jam
110g (4oz) Dried Apricots
1 Teaspoon Ground Ginger

Pre-heat oven to 200C/400F/Gas 6

1. Score the skin of the pork joint.

2. Spread the apricot jam over the inside of the pork joint.

3. Cover the surface evenly with the dried apricots.

4. Sprinkle the ground ginger over the apricots.

5. Tightly roll the pork, and secure by tying with string.

6. Rub salt into the skin of the pork to help crisp the crackling.

7. Wrap the pork in foil and roast in the pre-heated oven for approximately 25 minutes per 450g (1lb) plus 25 minutes.

8. Unwrap the pork for the last half hour and return to the oven until the crackling is golden and crisp.

9. Serve with potatoes and vegetables of your choice.

BOOZY CHOCOLATE ICE CREAM

Serves 1

Sprinkling Raisins
25ml Rum
3 Scoops Chocolate Ice Cream
Sprinkling Chocolate Chips
Whipped Cream (to taste)
Chocolate Sauce
Wafers

1. Soak the raisins in the rum overnight.

2. Put the ice cream into a serving bowl and pour over the rum and raisin mixture.

3. Sprinkle with the chocolate chips.

4. Top with the whipped cream and chocolate sauce.

5. Decorate with the wafer and serve.

Trainee chef, Les says:

You could use grated chocolate instead of chocolate chips.

Use dark Belgian chocolate and ice cream if preferred.

Australian Liqueur Muscat is a must here or maybe a small glass of Baileys – try pouring a little of either on the ice cream!

NICOLINO'S ITALIAN RESTAURANT

NICOLINO'S ITALIAN RESTAURANT
34 NORTH STREET
EMSWORTH
PO10 7DG
T. 01243 379809

NICOLINO DIODOVICI WITH
GIORGIO BOUSSIA, RESTAURANT MANAGER

NICOLINO DIODOVICI HAS WORKED IN THE KITCHEN SINCE THE EARLY AGE OF 15 YEARS WHILST LIVING IN ITALY, INITIALLY PRODUCING AND SELLING HOMEMADE ICE CREAM. HE THEN WORKED IN MILAN AT TRATTORIA MAMMA ITALIA, BEFORE MOVING TO THE QUIET RESORT OF LAKE MAGGIORE IN STRESA WHERE HE CONTINUED TO GAIN EXPERIENCE AS A COMMIS CHEF. DURING 1984 NICOLINO ARRIVED IN THE UK WHERE HE WORKED AT GIULIANO ITALIAN RESTAURANT IN CHICHESTER AND THE WHITE HORSE INN AT CHILGROVE. FOLLOWING THIS, NICOLINO BEGAN HIS OWN BUSINESS IN PORTSMOUTH BEFORE MOVING TO EMSWORTH TO OPEN HIS CURRENT RESTAURANT.

NICOLINO'S ITALIAN RESTAURANT HAS SERVED TRADITIONAL RUSTIC ITALIAN CUISINE SINCE IT OPENED IN FEBRUARY 1993. THE TRATTORIA-STYLE INTERIOR ALONG WITH THE FRIENDLY ITALIAN APPROACH TO SERVICE AND FOOD AS AN IMPORTANT PART OF LIFE, HAS PROVED A VERY POPULAR COMBINATION FOR THE MANY CUSTOMERS WHO EAT THERE. NICOLINO PRODUCES A NUMBER OF DAILY SPECIAL DISHES FOR HIS RESTAURANT, MANY OF WHICH ARE TYPICAL OF THE REGION FROM WHICH HE COMES.

5-COURSE CELEBRATION MENU

CAPONATINA DI MELANZANE IN AGRODOLCE CON SCAMPI E CAPESANTE IN PADELLA

ZUPPA DI FAGIOLI E COZZE

PAPPARDELLE CON SUGO D'ANITRA

FILETTO DI CERVO CON FUNGHI RIPIENI E CIPOLLINE GLASSATE

PASTICCIO DI MELE CON GELATO ALL AMARETTO

CAPONATINA DI MELANZANE IN AGRODOLCE CON SCAMPI E CAPESANTE IN PADELLA
(CAPONATINA OF SWEET AND SOUR AUBERGINES WITH SCAMPI AND KING SCALLOPS)

Serves 4

50ml Extra Virgin Olive Oil
300g Aubergines (finely diced)
1 Medium Red Onion (chopped)
80g Celery (chopped)
4 Plum Tomatoes (seeded & diced)
50g Black Olives (stoned & halved)
20g Capers (rinsed)
20g Pine Kernels
30g Sugar
4 Soupspoons White Wine Vinegar
4 Slices Parma Ham
200g Fresh King Scallops (shelled)
30g Butter
200g Scampi (shelled)
100ml Shellfish Stock
50ml White Wine
Lemon Juice

1. Heat the olive oil in a saucepan, and add the aubergines, onion and celery and cook until soft.

2. Add the tomatoes, olives, capers and pine kernels and simmer for 3-4 minutes. Then put to one side.

3. In another saucepan, heat the sugar until becomes caramel, and then add the wine vinegar and simmer until reduced.

4. Add the sugar and vinegar to the cooked vegetables and mix thoroughly.

5. Divide the mixture (caponatina) into an 8cm wide mould.

6. Wrap the scallops in the parma ham and secure with cocktail sticks.

7. Heat the butter and a drop of olive oil in a non-stick frying pan, seal and cook the scallops and scampi in this.

8. Put the caponatina on serving plates, and arrange the cooked shellfish around. Keep warm.

9. Add the shellfish stock and white wine to the frying pan used to cook the shellfish, and simmer until reduced by half. Season with salt and pepper, and add a few drops of lemon juice.

10. Pour the sauce over the plated shellfish, and garnish the dish with quartered lemon to serve.

Langoustine is another term for scampi in this dish.

Dry white - good quality Verdicchio or Vernaccia di San Gimignano.

ZUPPA DI FAGIOLI E COZZE
(BORLOTTI BEAN AND MUSSEL SOUP)

Serves 4

200g Dry Borlotti Beans
1 Bay Leaf
50ml Extra Virgin Olive Oil
2 Garlic Cloves (chopped)
20g Parsley (chopped)
1 Medium Red Onion (chopped)
2 Celery Stalks (chopped)
1 Medium Carrot (chopped)
1 Soupspoon Tomato Purée
500ml Vegetable Stock
500g Fresh Mussels in Shells (prepared)
1 Glass White Wine

1. Soak the beans in water overnight.

2. Bring the beans and water to the boil in a saucepan, add the bay leaf and simmer until cooked. Add seasoning to taste.

3. Put the pan to one side, and liquidise half of the cooked beans.

4. Into another saucepan, add the olive oil, garlic, parsley and chopped vegetables and cook until soft.

5. Add the tomato purée, vegetable stock, liquidised beans and whole beans, and simmer for 20 minutes.

6. Using another saucepan, cook the cleaned mussels with the white wine and a drop of olive oil (covered) until the shells have opened.

7. Remove the mussels from the shells, but retain a few in shells for garnish. Retain the sauce.

8. Add the cooked mussels with the cooking liquor into the saucepan of beans, and stir.

9. Serve the soup with toasted Italian bread.

You may wish to garnish the soup with grated parmesan cheese.

Robust Italian white Orvieto Classico or Gavi di Gavi.

PAPPARDELLE CON SUGO D'ANITRA
(PAPARDELLE PASTA WITH DUCK SAUCE)

Serves 4

4 Tablespoons Olive Oil
1 Medium Onion
2 Celery Stalks
2 Medium Carrots
200ml White Wine
1 Bay Leaf
200g Passata (tomato sauce)
25g Dried Porcini Mushrooms
1 Large Tablespoon Sage (chopped)
1 Large Tablespoon Rosemary (chopped)
1 Whole Duck (liver removed)
400g Pappardelle Pasta
Parmesan Cheese

1. Chop the vegetables.

2. Soak the dried mushrooms in 100ml water. Strain through a sieve and retain the liquid. Chop the mushrooms.

3. Pour the olive oil into a saucepan and add the chopped vegetables, wine, bay leaf, passata, soaked mushrooms with the strained liquid, sage and rosemary.

4. Bring the mixture to the boil, and simmer.

5. Meanwhile, cut the duck in half and remove the fat and bones.

6. Roughly chop the duck meat, add to the cooking sauce mixture and simmer for 1 hour.

7. Season to taste.

8. Bring a large saucepan of salted water to the boil, add the pasta and reduce the heat. Cook until al dente.

9. Divide the cooked pasta into 4 pasta bowls, and pour the duck sauce over. Serve with parmesan cheese.

Try a Primitivo from Puglia or Barbera d'Asti.

FILETTO DI CERVO CON FUNGHI RIPIENI E CIPOLLINE GLASSATE
(VENISON FILLET WITH STUFFED MUSHROOMS, BABY ONIONS IN A RED WINE AND THYME SAUCE)

Serves 4

FOR THE VENISON
700g Venison Fillet
    (boned, trimmed & cut into 4)
1 Teaspoon Crushed Black Peppercorns
100g Smoked Streaky Bacon
50g Butter
2 Tablespoons Olive Oil
12 Baby Onions
150ml Red Wine
150ml Port Wine
1 Bay leaf
150ml Game or Beef Stock
50g Redcurrant Jelly
1 Teaspoon Fresh Thyme Leaves

FOR THE STUFFED MUSHROOMS
50g Butter
4 Tablespoons Olive Oil
4 Portabella Mushrooms
2 Garlic Cloves
50g Button Mushrooms (sliced)
20g Dry Cep Mushrooms
    (soaked in 50ml warm water)
4 Plum Tomatoes
50ml Sweet Sherry or Marsala Wine
2 Slices White Bread (for breadcrumbs)
2 Tablespoons Freshly Grated Parmesan
    Cheese
1 Egg
Salt & Pepper

Pre-heat oven to 180C/350F/Gas 4

1. Spread the crushed peppercorns on the venison and wrap each piece with 2 slices of the smoked bacon and secure with a cocktail stick.
2. Heat a non-stick frying pan with half of the butter and the olive oil.
3. Seal the venison on all sides.
4. Remove the sealed venison to a roasting tray and finish the cooking in the pre-heated oven. 10 minutes for rare; 15 minutes for medium rare.
5. Remove the excess fat from the frying pan, and add the baby onions and cook until coloured.
6. Then add the wines, bay leaf, stock, and redcurrant jelly and simmer until the sauce has reduced by half.
7. To finish the sauce, add the thyme leaves and the rest of the butter.

FOR THE MUSHROOM FILLING
1. In a frying pan, add the butter and olive oil and cook the sliced button mushrooms with the garlic.
2. Add the soaked mushrooms and the filtered water from these, the tomatoes and sherry and cook until the liquid has almost evaporated.
3. Allow to cool and add the breadcrumbs, parmesan cheese, egg and seasoning and mix thoroughly.
4. Fill the large mushrooms with the mixture, and using a large spoon carefully transfer these to a roasting tray and cook in the pre-heated oven for 15-20 minutes until the mushrooms are cooked.
5. Arrange the cooked mushrooms onto serving plates with the venison on top, and pour the sauce and shallots around.

If you can afford it this cries out for top quality Barolo, if not try a Nebbiolo d'Alba.

PASTICCIO DI MELE CON GELATO ALL AMARETTO
(APPLE FLAN WITH SAMBUCA LIQUEUR, AND AMARETTO ICE CREAM)

Serves 6

PASTRY

200g Butter (unsalted)
400g Flour
100g Sugar
Grated Rind ½ Lemon
1 Egg
4 Tablespoons Milk

FILLING

4 Eggs
200g Sugar
50g Plain Flour
300g Single Cream
Grated Rind 1 Lemon
75g Sultanas – Soaked with
50ml Sambuca Liqueur
8 Granny Smith Apples (peeled, cored & sliced)
5 Amaretto Biscuits (crumbled)
50g Pine Kernels

AMARETTO ICE CREAM

5 Egg Yolks
150g Sugar
50ml Amaretto Liqueur
300ml Milk
300ml Whipping Cream
50g Amaretto Biscuits (crushed)

Pre-heat oven to 180C/350F/Gas 4

PASTRY

1. Mix the butter with the flour and sugar.
2. Add the lemon rind, and then add the egg and milk and bind together until firm.
3. Wrap the pastry in cling film and allow to rest in a fridge for 30 minutes.
4. Line a 20-26cm (8-10 inch) greased flan case with the rolled pastry.
5. Allow to rest in a fridge while making the filling.

FILLING

1. Using a mixing bowl, mix together the egg and sugar.
2. Slowly add the flour whilst mixing.
3. Add the cream, lemon rind and strained Sambuca (from the soaked sultanas).
4. Remove the flan case from the fridge, and arrange the sliced apples in the pastry. Add the sultanas and amaretto biscuits on top.
5. Pour the egg mixture over, and add the pine kernels.
6. Cook in the pre-heated oven for 30 to 40 minutes.
7. Allow to cool, and serve with the amaretto ice cream.

AMARETTO ICE CREAM

1. Mix together the egg yolks, sugar and Amaretto liqueur in a bowl.
2. Boil the milk and cream.
3. Add the hot milk and cream to the eggs and sugar.
4. Return to the saucepan and add the amaretto biscuits.
5. Simmer gently on a low heat until it has thickened. Do not allow it to boil.
6. Remove from the heat and allow to cool.
7. Churn and freeze in an ice cream machine, and store in a freezer until required.

You can make individual pastry cases if preferred.

Vin Santo, Amaretto or maybe a Grappa purely to revive yourself!

LE PETIT PAIN

LE PETIT PAIN
14 NORTH STREET
EMSWORTH
PO10 7DG
T. 01243 373375

PAT FRISBY WITH HER MOTHER, FLORRIE KIRK

LE PETIT PAIN BAKERY AND SANDWICH BAR SELLS A SELECTION OF FILLED ROLLS, BREADS AND PASTRIES, INCLUDING BAGUETTES AND CROISSANTS MADE FROM REAL FRENCH DOUGH FOR THAT AUTHENTIC TASTE AND TEXTURE. ORIGINALLY THIS BOULANGERIE WAS SITUATED IN THE LOWER PART OF SPENCERS RESTAURANT IN NORTH STREET. PAT FRISBY TOOK OVER THE ESTABLISHMENT FROM DENIS AND LESLEY SPENCER MORE THAN EIGHT YEARS AGO WHEN IT MOVED FURTHER ALONG NORTH STREET TO ITS CURRENT POSITION.

FLORRIE'S BREAD PUDDING

Makes 8-10 slices

340g (12oz) Bread – Crust Removed
(cut into fingers or cubes)
225g (8oz) Sultanas
225g (8oz) Raisins
110g (4oz) Cherries
225g (8oz) Brown Sugar
55g–110g (2-4oz) Mixed Spice
110g (4oz) Suet
250ml (½ pt) Milk
2 Eggs
Caster Sugar or Demerara for Dusting

Pre-heat oven to 180C/350F/Gas 4

1. Place the bread in a bowl with enough water to soak the bread, and leave for 30 minutes.

2. Squeeze out the excess water from the bread.

3. In a separate bowl, mix together all of the dry ingredients.

4. Add the dry ingredients to the bread, together with the beaten milk and eggs, and mix.

5. Grease a 1-litre (2-pint) baking tin or ovenproof dish.

6. Pour the bread mixture into the dish, ensuring it is smoothed out to the edges.

7. Bake in the pre-heated oven for between 1 hour and 1½ hours until spongy in the middle to touch.

8. Dust with sugar to serve.

Use a quantity of mixed spice according to taste and desired colour.

Can be eaten hot or cold.

Hungarian Tokay Azsu or botrytised Semillon from Australia.

ST AUBIN-SUR-MER

MEMBERS OF THE ST AUBIN-EMSWORTH TWINNING ASSOCIATION

ST AUBIN-SUR-MER
CÔTE DE NACRE
NORMANDY
FRANCE

FOR FURTHER INFORMATION:
www.emsworthtwinning.org.uk
OR FROM EMSWORTH LIBRARY

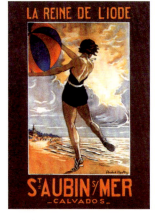

BERYL JOBLING & SARAH TURNER

ST AUBIN-SUR-MER, AN ATTRACTIVE SMALL SEASIDE TOWN ON THE CÔTE DE NACRE IN THE CALVADOS 'DÉPARTEMENT' OF NORMANDY, IS THE TWINNED TOWN OF EMSWORTH. THE COMMUNITIES HAVE A GREAT DEAL IN COMMON HAVING BOTH DEVELOPED FROM OLD FISHING VILLAGES PARTICULARLY RENOWNED FOR THEIR SEAFOOD. ST AUBIN IS LOCATED ON JUNO BEACH, ONE OF THE D-DAY LANDING BEACHES BETWEEN BAYEUX AND OUISTREHAM AND PLAYED A PROMINENT ROLE IN THE JUNE 2004 60TH ANNIVERSARY CELEBRATIONS. THE TWINNING RELATIONSHIP BETWEEN THE TWO COMMUNITIES WAS ESTABLISHED IN 1986 AND HAS FLOURISHED SINCE. THE ASSOCIATION AIMS TO PROMOTE FRIENDSHIP AND LINKS BETWEEN INDIVIDUALS, FAMILIES, SCHOOLS, GROUPS AND CLUBS. ONE OBJECTIVE IS TO ENCOURAGE AND SUPPORT YOUNG PEOPLE AS MEMBERS OF THE ASSOCIATION TO MAKE FRIENDS WITH YOUNG ST AUBINAIS.

KIR NORMAND

1/5th Crème de Cassis (or Mure or Myrtille) **4/5th** Dry (Brut) Normandy Cider Twist of Lemon (optional)	Pour the cassis (or other fruit liqueur) into a glass. Top up with chilled cider and, if you wish, a twist of lemon.

NORMANDY HAS ITS OWN PARTICULAR CHARM. THE COUNTRYSIDE IS CHARACTERISED BY THATCHED AND BEAMED COTTAGES, PASTURES AND APPLE ORCHARDS, AND IS PARTICULARLY RENOWNED FOR THE QUALITY OF ITS CIDER, CALVADOS AND LOCAL CHEESES: CAMEMBERT, PONT L'EVEQUE, PAVÉ D'AUGE AND LIVAROT. THE FOLLOWING RECIPES INCORPORATE THIS LOCAL PRODUCE AND HAVE BEEN ENJOYED BY MEMBERS OF THE ST AUBIN-EMSWORTH TWINNING ASSOCIATION DURING THEIR VISITS TO ST AUBIN.

PEOPLE OF THIS REGION PROUDLY PROCLAIM THEIR CIDER TO BE VASTLY SUPERIOR TO THAT OF NEIGHBOURING BRITTANY, AND CIDER FROM LE VALLÉE D'AUGE IS PARTICULARLY CELEBRATED.

KIR NORMAND MIXES BRUT (DRY) NORMANDY CIDER WITH LIQUEURS MADE FROM EVERY IMAGINABLE FRUIT – CASSIS (BLACKCURRANT), MURE (BLACKBERRY) OR MYRTILLE (BILBERRY). IN NORMANDY A TRADITIONAL LOCAL VERSION OF CRÈME DE CASSIS IS MADE BY STEEPING THE FRUIT IN CALVADOS.

FAISAN AUX POMMES
(NORMANDY PHEASANT)

Serves 4

1 Pheasant
6 Dessert Apples
150g Fromage Frais
½ Teaspoon Freshly Ground Black Pepper
Salt
75g Butter (melted)
3 Tablespoons Calvados

A simple dish incorporating Calvados (an apple brandy after which the Département is named). According to the Michelin guide 'Calvados is to the apple what brandy is to the grape'. As the spirit distilled from cider, Calvados needs up to 15 years to mature to perfection. It develops its unique bouquet from the oak barrels in which it is stored and the nuts which are added.

Pre-heat oven to 200C/400F/Gas 6

1. Prepare and clean the pheasant.

2. Peel and core the apples. Dice 2 and cut the remaining 4 in half.

3. Combine the diced apple with the fromage frais and season with a pinch of salt and the pepper.

4. Stuff the cavity of the pheasant with the mixture and secure the opening (either sew or use wooden skewers).

5. Place the pheasant in a greased ovenproof dish and brush with melted butter.

6. Cook in the pre-heated oven for 30 minutes.

7. Remove from the oven.

8. Toss the halved apples in melted butter and place around the pheasant.

9. Return the dish to the oven and cook for a further 30-40 minutes.

10. At the point of serving, gently heat the Calvados and spoon over the pheasant and (carefully) flame at the table.

11. Garnish with watercress and serve with braised chicory.

Good quality Pinot Noir with a little bottle age would work well here.

NEWS IN BRIEF

Moped and car in arson attacks

■ **SOUTHSEA:** Arsonists set fire to a moped and car in two separate attacks in Southsea late at night.

A moped in Fawcett Road was torched about midnight on Wednesday and destroyed by the fire.

Two and a half hours later yobs set alight a car parked in Maxstoke Close.

Both fires are believed to have been started deliberately and are being investigated by police.

Church meeting

■ **FAREHAM:** Racial awareness in our communities will top the agenda at a gathering tomorrow.

An ecumenical day conference entitled Our Christian Response To The Stranger is being held in Fareham United Reformed Church in Osborn Road South from 10am to 4pm.

For more information, telephone (023) 8022 0533.

AA ROADWATCH

■ M27 between junctions eight and three: Roadworks overnight both ways for communication upgrade work, various lane closures.

■ Farnham Road, Liss: Closed for roadworks, both ways.

■ Liberty Road, Sobert

Blyth spirit inspires crews

THE Global Challenge pits 12 identical 72ft yachts against one another for a race around the world from east to west.

Each yacht has 17 crew made up of men and women from all walks of life and nationalities plus a skipper – the only professional sailor on board. They all have one aim: to win the Princess Royal trophy on their return.

Conditions during the race will range from unpredictable currents to gale-force winds.

The route follows that taken by Sir Chay Blyth when, in 1971, he became the first person to sail around the world non-stop and single-handedly from east to west. He left from Hamble aboard the yacht British Steel.

There have been three races that all set off from Southampton, but this will be the first time that Portsmouth has been the embarkation point.

Event organiser Challenge Business estimates the event could be worth £7m to the city. Project manager Anne-Marie Wood said: 'When Southampton last held it, the figure was around £7m, and the same in Boston, one of the ports on the route.'

Gosport businessman Alex Alley, 33, from Titchfield, who will be sailing aboard Team Seven, can't wait for it to start. 'I always wanted to sail around the world,' he said.

People can find out how each yacht is doing by logging on the internet at www.global-challenge2004.com

jeremy.dunning@thenews.co.uk

GLOBAL CHALLENGE

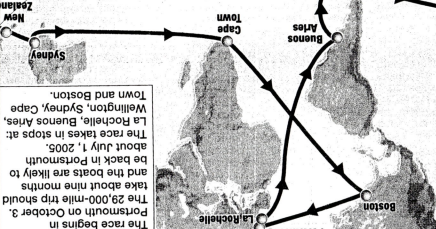

The race begins in Portsmouth on October 3. The 29,000-mile trip should take about nine months and the boats are likely to be back in Portsmouth about July 1, 2005.

The race takes in stops at: La Rochelle, Buenos Aires, Wellington, Sydney, Cape Town and Boston.

MEANS TO US

Catherine Jones, 30, formerly of Alverstoke, now in Kent, said: 'It will be a life-changing experience.' She is aboard Kunachi.

...anfield, ...Davies, 59, ...this as a ...hrow of the ...nge dice ...e retiring. ...a crewman ...oard the ...The Firm.

...tionally.' ...e media nationally and ...us a showcase on TV ...e in the city but it ...ill not only bring lots ...e in Portsmouth. ...osen to start and finish ...y that Global Challenge ...dence in the future of ...on, said: 'It's a real vote ...ouncillor Gerald Vernon- ...tsmouth's Lib Dem lead- ...t,' she said. ...for us. It's not just a one- ...those cities, which is su- ...h will be up there along- ...the stopovers, and Ports- ...'There will be spin-offs ...the city would be cashing ...egeneration department,

...Alley, of Titchfield, seen here at the helm of Fandango, is raring to go in the Global Challenge

CONTEST: Portsmouth is poised to rake in millions of pounds thanks to epic adventure

It's steady as she goes for oceans' 12 racers

GLOBAL CHALLENGE
2004/05

by Jeremy Dunning
The News

THE countdown to the Global Challenge round-the-world yacht race that is set to boost Portsmouth's economy by £7m has begun.

City chiefs are gearing up for a cash bonanza when the 12 competing yachts set sail from Portsmouth for the first time in the event's history.

They leave on October 3 and will return more than nine months and 29,000 miles

TROU NORMAND
(CALVADOS SORBET)

Serves 4

4 Granny Smith Apples
Juice 1 Lemon
300g Sugar
300ml Water
80ml Calvados

The Norman custom of drinking 'un trou Normand', a small glass of Calvados, as a digestive between courses or at the end of the meal, may also be transformed into a Calvados sorbet.

If an ice cream maker is not available, the syrup may be poured into a shallow bowl and placed in the freezer, ensuring that it is taken out and beaten regularly during the freezing process to prevent the formation of ice crystals. Sorbets take at least 5 hours to freeze.

1. The day before, wash and finely grate the unpeeled, cored apples. Place these into a bowl, sprinkle with the lemon juice and place in a freezer overnight.

2. The next day, make a hot syrup by boiling the sugar with the water for 5 minutes.

3. Remove the apples from the freezer. Pour over the hot syrup and mix thoroughly, crushing up the apples. This is best done in a heavy based saucepan with a fork or potato masher.

4. Place the mixture into an ice cream maker to produce the sorbet, and store in the freezer.

5. Remove from the freezer to the fridge 45 minutes before serving.

6. Serve in individual glasses, and drizzle a little Calvados over the sorbet.

La Tarte Aux Pommes Normande
(Normandy Apple Tart)

Serves 4-6

FILLING
5-6 Crisp Dessert Apples
55g (2oz) Butter (unsalted)
3 Tablespoons Caster Sugar

PÂTE SABLÉE
85g (3oz) Butter (unsalted)
170g (6oz) Plain Flour
1 Dessertspoon Caster Sugar
2-4 Tablespoons Iced Water

Just cries out for good
quality Sauternes or Barsac, the best you can afford.

Pre-heat oven to 200C/400F/Gas 6

FILLING
1. Peel, core and thinly slice the apples.

2. Melt the butter in a large frying pan, and add the apples and sugar.

3. Cook very gently until the fruit is transparent but the slices remain intact.

4. Put to one side.

PÂTE SABLÉE
1. Make shortbread-style pastry by rubbing the butter into the flour and sugar.

2. Add as little water as possible to keep the pastry light and buttery.

3. Do not roll the pastry.

4. Take a 20cm (8inch) flan ring, greased with butter, and mould the pastry mix by hand into the base and sides.

5. Drain the cooked apples, but retain the cooking juices.

6. Top the pastry with circles of the cooked apples.

7. Put the flan ring onto a baking sheet and bake in the pre-heated oven for 30-35 minutes.

8. Remove from the oven and sprinkle the top of the tart with the reserved cooking juices and a sprinkling of sugar.

9. Return to the oven for a further 2 minutes.

10. Best served hot.

PHOTO: BRIAN FELLOWS

WINTER

TWO SNOW PHOTOGRAPHS BY MARIAN FORSTER

DECEMBER

JANUARY

FEBRUARY

THE CROWN HOTEL

ANDREW COUSINS IS HEAD CHEF AT THE CROWN, SERVING HOME-MADE TRADITIONAL PUB FOOD AS WELL AS MORE ADVENTUROUS MULTINATIONAL DISHES, LOCAL AND EXOTIC FISH AND OF COURSE, HIS SPECIALITY, HOMEMADE PIES. ANDREW HAS PREVIOUSLY WORKED AT THE GEORGE HOTEL, AMESBURY, THE DICK WHITTINGTON IN GLOUCESTER, THE BUCKINGHAM ARMS IN SHOREHAM AND THE RODMILL IN EASTBOURNE.

THE CROWN HOTEL DATES BACK TO THE 16TH CENTURY AND THE DAYS WHEN IT WAS A COACHING INN. REFURBISHED IN MAY 2004, WITH WOODEN FLOORS AND DÉCOR THROUGHOUT, THIS HOTEL IS OPEN ALL DAY AND SERVES A MULTINATIONAL MENU WITH LOCAL FISH AS WELL AS A SELECTION OF MORE THAN 12 DIFFERENT HOMEMADE PIES AT LUNCH AND DINNER. A SEPARATE RESTAURANT AREA, AS WELL AS A REAR ENCLOSED COURTYARD, IS AVAILABLE FOR THOSE WHO PREFER TO BE AWAY FROM THE BAR. THERE ARE 9 EN-SUITE BEDROOMS PLUS A PRIVATE FUNCTION ROOM AVAILABLE FOR HIRE. MAGGIE COUSINS AND SEAN FLANAGAN HAVE MANAGED THE CROWN SINCE 2002, WITH THEIR SON ANDREW IN CHARGE OF THE KITCHEN.

THE CROWN HOTEL
8 HIGH STREET
EMSWORTH
PO10 7AW
T. 01243 372806
F. 01243 370082

SEAN FLANAGAN & MAGGIE COUSINS

SAUCES AND DIPS FOR TAPAS
SATAY SAUCE

Serves 4-6

Party style sparkling wine such as Cava or probably an ice cold Mexican beer.

1 Large Onion (quartered)
6 Small Dried Red Chillies
2 Cloves Garlic
1 Tablespoon Pine Nuts
1 Tablespoon Lemon Rind (finely grated)
2 Tablespoons Walnut Oil
400ml Coconut Milk
180g Crunchy Peanut Butter
1 Teaspoon Sugar
Salt

1. Put the onion, chillies, garlic, pine nuts and lemon rind in a food processor or blender and mix until puréed.

2. Heat the oil in a heavy saucepan and add the blended mixture.

3. Cook over a low heat for 3-4 minutes, stirring continuously.

4. Add the coconut milk to the pan and bring to the boil whilst stirring.

5. Lower the heat and add the peanut butter, sugar and salt and simmer for approximately 3 minutes.

6. Allow to cool for 1 hour before serving.

CACHUMBER (TOMATO, ONION AND CORIANDER RELISH) *Serves 4-6*

225g (8oz)Tomatoes
1 Medium Onion (peeled)
1 Green Chilli (de-seeded)
30ml (2 Tablespoons) Fresh Coriander
    Leaves (chopped)
15ml (1 Tablespoon) Lemon Juice
Salt & Pepper

1. Finely chop the tomatoes, onion and chilli and put into a salad bowl.

2. Add the coriander and lemon juice, with salt and freshly ground pepper to taste.

3. Toss the ingredients together.

4. Cover tightly and chill for about 1 hour before serving.

The 2 different relishes can be stored for up to 1-2 days in a fridge.

PIAZ KA IACCHA (ONION RELISH) *Serves 4*

1 Medium Onion (peeled)
Juice 1 Lemon
2.5ml (½ Teaspoon) Paprika
Salt & Pepper

1. Cut the onion crossways into very thin rings, and put into a bowl.

2. Add the remaining ingredients, with salt and freshly ground pepper to taste.

3. Toss the ingredients together and leave to marinate for approximately 1 hour.

4. Chill for 1 hour before serving.

TZATZIKI (CUCUMBER AND YOGHURT DIP) *Serves 4*

1 Small Cucumber
300ml (1/2pt) Authentic Greek Yoghurt
1 Clove Garlic (crushed)
1 Tablespoon Fresh Mint (chopped)
Salt
Can use dill instead of mint if preferred.)

1. Coarsely grate the cucumber, and put into a sieve to squeeze out as much of the water as possible.

2. Place the cucumber into a bowl.

3. Add the yoghurt, garlic and chopped mint (reserve a small amount for the garnish).

4. Sprinkle a little salt to the mixture.

5. Mix well together and chill in a fridge for approximately 2 hours before serving.

6. To serve, stir the cucumber and yoghurt dip, transfer to a serving bowl and sprinkle top with mint.

CHILLI SAUCE
Serves 4-6

10 Cloves Garlic
4-6 Large Onions (finely chopped)
125ml Olive Oil
200g Fresh Red Chilli Peppers
    (de-seeded & chopped)
375g Tomato Ketchup

1. Peel and finely chop the cloves of garlic.

2. In a heavy saucepan, gently fry the onions in a little olive oil until soft.

3. Add the garlic and cook for a further 2 minutes.

4. Add the chilli and simmer for approximately 5 minutes.

5. Put the mixture into a food processor, add the tomato ketchup and mix.

6. Return the mixture to the saucepan and simmer for 15 minutes.

7. Allow to cool for 1 hour before serving.

EMSWORTH DELICATESSEN

EVELYN & TONY PEARCE

EMSWORTH DELICATESSEN
WEST STREET
EMSWORTH
PO10 7DU
T. 01243 389181

EVELYN PEARCE HAS WORKED IN THE FOOD INDUSTRY SINCE LEAVING SCHOOL. ALONGSIDE HER HUSBAND TONY, SHE OWNED AND MANAGED FOR A PERIOD OF NINE YEARS HOTELS WITH RESTAURANTS AND FUNCTION SPACE. EVELYN ENJOYS THE HANDS-ON WORK AS WELL AS THE RETAIL BUSINESS AND SINCE OPENING THE SHOP IN EMSWORTH HAS BEEN ABLE TO COMBINE THESE INTERESTS.

EMSWORTH DELICATESSEN HAS TRADED IN THE VILLAGE SINCE 1999. IN ADDITION TO SELLING A VARIETY OF FRESH AND PACKAGED DELI ITEMS, EVELYN AND HER HUSBAND TONY PEARCE ALSO SUPPLY WINES, FRESHLY BAKED BREADS, A LARGE SELECTION OF FILLED ROLLS AND BAGUETTES AND RECENTLY INTRODUCED TEAS AND COFFEES WITH SEATING AREA JUST INSIDE THE DOORWAY. AS WELL AS MANAGING THE SHOP, EVELYN OFFERS A FULL BUFFET SERVICE FOR SPECIAL FUNCTIONS AND PRIVATE PARTIES.

EASY PARTY BUFFET

Serves 12

RED LENTIL AND SUN DRIED TOMATO PATÉ

500g Patchwork Paté
1 Cucumber
Cherry Tomatoes

1. Defrost the paté for a minimum of 4 hours.
2. Slice the cucumber and halve the tomatoes.
3. Place the paté onto a serving dish and garnish with the cucumber and tomatoes.

ROSETTES OF PROSCIUTTO AND SALAMI

12 Slices Prosciutto Ham
12 Slices Napoli Salami
12 Slices Milano Salami
24 Artichokes in Oil
36 Sun Blush Tomatoes
36 Green Olives

1. Roll the slices of ham and salami and arrange onto a serving platter.
2. Place the artichokes, tomatoes and olives around the meats.

RED THAI CHICKEN CURRY

4 Tablespoons Oil
6 Chicken Breast Fillets (diced)
2 Tubs (475g) Thai Red Curry Sauce

1. In a saucepan, heat the oil and fry the diced chicken.
2. Stir in the curry sauce.
3. Simmer for 1 hour, stirring regularly.

COCONUT RICE

4 Tablespoons Oil
500g Basmati Rice
½ Block Coconut Cream

1. Heat the oil in a saucepan.
2. Add the rice and stir to coat with the oil.
3. Pour in 625ml of boiling water, and bring the mixture to the boil.
4. Cover with a lid and simmer for 15 minutes until all of the liquid has been absorbed.
5. Stir in the coconut cream.

POACHED SALMON

1kg Salmon Fillet
Cucumber Slices
Lemon Slices
Dill Mustard

Pre-heat oven to 200C/400F/Gas 6

1. Place the salmon into a large flat pan.
2. Add 250ml of water and cover.
3. Poach in the pre-heated oven for 20 minutes.
4. Leave the salmon in the pan until cold.
5. Serve on a platter garnished with cucumber and lemon slices, with dill mustard sauce.

Crowd pleasing and food friendly dry white such as New Zealand or South African Sauvignon Blanc.

EASY PARTY BUFFET

Serves 12

LAMB PASTA AU GRATIN

750g Minced Lamb
2 Packs (300g) Roasted Vegetable
  Pasta Sauce
500g Pasta Bows
2 Eggs
250ml Milk
400g Greek Yoghurt
100g Grated Parmesan

Pre-heat oven to 180C/350F/Gas 4

1. Dry fry the minced lamb in a saucepan until brown.
2. Add the pasta sauce and simmer for 45 minutes.
3. Cook the pasta in a saucepan of boiling water for 8 minutes, and drain.
4. Mix together the eggs, milk and yoghurt with half of the parmesan cheese.
5. Put the meat sauce into an ovenproof dish 30cm x 25cm x 6cm.
6. Top with the pasta and then the egg mixture.
7. Sprinkle with the remaining parmesan and bake in the pre-heated oven for 45 minutes until browned.

NEW POTATOES WITH BLUSH WINE DRESSING

1kg Baby New Potatoes
¼ Bottle Blush Wine Dressing

1. Boil the potatoes for 25 minutes.
2. Strain and place into a serving bowl.
3. Pour over the Blush Wine Dressing.
4. Can be served hot or cold.

STRAWBERRY & KIWI PAVLOVA

2 Kiwi Fruits
250g Strawberries
500ml Double Cream
1 Large Meringue Base

1. Peel and slice the kiwi fruit, and wash and halve the strawberries.
2. Whip the cream until stiff, and spread over the meringue base.
3. Arrange the kiwi and strawberries on top of the cream.

RASPBERRY BISCUIT CREAM

2 Bags (200g) Soft Amaretti Biscuits
5 Tablespoons Grand Marnier
  or liqueur of choice
2 Punnets (125g) Raspberries
6 Egg Yolks
90g Caster Sugar
250g Mascarpone Cheese
Double Cream (whipped)
Chocolate Flake

1. Break the biscuits into the base of a serving dish and pour over the Grand Marnier.
2. Wash the raspberries (reserve 10 for garnish), and crush onto the biscuits.
3. Whisk the egg yolks and sugar over a pan of hot (not boiling) water until thick and pale.
4. Stir in the mascarpone.
5. Pour the mixture over the raspberries and biscuits.
6. Pipe the top with cream whirls and place a raspberry onto each one.
7. Sprinkle on the crumbled chocolate flake, and chill.

All ingredients other than the fresh meat and vegetables can be purchased in the deli.

WEST STREET THEN AND NOW

EMSWORTH WOMEN'S INSTITUTE (NORTH)

MEMBERS OF THE
NORTH EMSWORTH WI

IF YOU ARE INTERESTED IN
JOINING OR FOR MORE
INFORMATION CONTACT
01243 373365

ANN BARNETT IS AN ACTIVE MEMBER OF THE WI. SHE TRAINED IN GLOUCESTER AS A DOMESTIC SCIENCE TEACHER, AND IN THE EARLY 70'S SHE TAUGHT CITY AND GUILDS COOKERY CLASSES, AS WELL AS A VARIETY OF NON-VOCATIONAL COOKERY CLASSES IN NOTTINGHAM. FOR SOME 20 YEARS ANN RAN 'EATING WELL ON A PENSION' CLASSES WHERE THOSE ATTENDING EACH PREPARED THEIR OWN LUNCH, FOLLOWING A STAGE-BY-STAGE INSTRUCTION AND DEMONSTRATION. AT THE END OF EACH SESSION, THE CLASS SAT DOWN TO EAT TOGETHER. FOLLOWING RETIREMENT IN 1997 ANN AND HER HUSBAND MOVED TO EMSWORTH TO BE NEARER THEIR GRANDCHILDREN. SHE JOINED THE WI AND IS ALSO A PRODUCER FOR THE EMSWORTH COUNTRY MARKET FOR WHICH SHE TEACHES THE FOUNDATION CERTIFICATE IN FOOD HYGIENE FOR THE MARKETS IN HAMPSHIRE AND WEST SUSSEX.

EMSWORTH WOMEN'S INSTITUTE (NORTH) WAS FORMED IN 1966 AND NOW MEET DURING THE EVENING OF THE FIRST TUESDAY OF EVERY MONTH AT WESTBOURNE PARISH CHURCH HALL. THE WI IS NOT ONLY ABOUT BAKING CAKES AND MAKING JAM. EACH MEETING WILL GENERALLY HAVE A SPEAKER ATTEND COVERING A DIVERSE RANGE OF SUBJECT MATTER. WITH REGULAR COFFEE MORNINGS, CHEESE AND WINE PARTIES AND LUNCHES, MEMBERS TAKE A GREAT INTEREST IN THE LOCAL COMMUNITY. DURING 1984 A GROUP OF WOMEN WHO FOUND THEIR LIFESTYLE MADE IT DIFFICULT TO ATTEND EVENING MEETINGS, FORMED A SECOND WI GROUP IN EMSWORTH WHICH MEETS DURING THE MORNINGS AT THE COMMUNITY CENTRE.

BACON AND LENTIL HOTPOT
(AN 'EATING WELL ON A PENSION' FAVOURITE)

Serves 4

225g (8oz) Streaky Bacon
2 Medium Carrots
1 Medium Onion
1 Large Potato
2-3 Sticks Celery
1 Tablespoon Cooking Oil
110g (4oz) Red Lentils
500ml (1pt) Water, Chicken or Vegetable
Stock
Seasoning

Pre-heat oven to 190C/375F/Gas 5

1. Remove the rind from the bacon and cut into 2cm (1inch) pieces.

2. Peel the vegetables and cut into 1cm (½ inch) chunks.

3. In a medium saucepan, heat the oil and fry the bacon.

4. Add the vegetables, a few at a time, and fry for a further 5-10 minutes.

5. Stir in the lentils and the water or stock and mix well.

6. Bring to the boil.

7. Pour the mixture into a casserole dish, cover and cook in the pre-heated oven for approximately 1 hour, stirring occasionally. Add more liquid if necessary.

8. Season with salt and pepper to taste.

9. Serve with green vegetables or a crisp green salad with some wholemeal bread.

Can be frozen in individual meal-sized portions.

Other vegetables of choice can be substituted.

For economy, the cooking may be completed in the saucepan but you will need to keep covered and stir frequently.

Lentils are a pulse vegetable – a good source of protein and fibre, and low in fat.

Robust, inexpensive red from the South of France such as Fitou or Corbieres.

LEMON AND ALMOND ROULADE (A PARTY SWEET)

Serves 6-8

3 Large Eggs (separated)
110g (4oz) Caster Sugar
Grated rind & juice **1** Lemon
55g (2oz) Ground Almonds
15g (½oz) Semolina or Ground Rice

FILLING
2 Tablespoons Lemon Curd
125ml (¼pt) Double Cream
(lightly whipped)
Caster Sugar (to sprinkle)
Whipped Cream for Piping
Mandarin Orange Segments or
Crystallised Orange/Lemon Slices
(to decorate)
Sprig of Fresh Mint

Pre-heat oven to 170C/325F/Gas 3
Line and grease a Swiss roll tin 20.5 x 30.5cm (8 x 12inches)

1. Whisk the egg yolks with the sugar until pale in colour and very thick (the whisk should leave a ribbon trail when lifted).

2. Carefully – using a metal spoon – stir in the lemon rind and juice with the ground almonds and semolina.

3. Whisk the egg whites until soft peaks (not rocky), and fold into the mixture in 2 batches using the metal spoon.

4. Slide the mixture into the tin and spread evenly.

5. Bake in the pre-heated oven for 20-25 minutes until golden brown.

6. Leave to cool in the tin, covered by a clean damp tea towel.

7. When cool, turn out onto a sheet of greaseproof paper sprinkled with a little caster sugar and peel off the lining paper.

8. Trim the edges of the sponge if they are crisp.

9. Fold the lemon curd into the whipped cream, and spread over the sponge.

10. Roll up using the greaseproof paper to help.

11. Stand the roll – along the join – on an oblong dish or plate.

12. Pipe with cream and decorate with the orange segments.

13. Eat within 24 hours.

Be very careful to grate only the lemon zest and not the white pith which is bitter.

Try using crème fraîche or thick yoghurt instead of cream.

Non-stick Bakewell paper/ baking parchment is good for lining the tin (wet the tin before lining to hold the paper in place) and for rolling.

Lighter style Bordeaux sweet wine from a lesser area, St Croix du Mont would fit the bill.

NANNIE'S GINGER AND HONEY COOKIES
(A GOOD RECIPE TO MAKE WITH CHILDREN OR GRANDCHILDREN)

Makes approximately 30

120g (4½oz) Caster Sugar
120g (4½oz) Soft Margarine
1 Good Tablespoon Runny Honey
1 Egg Yolk
180g (6½oz) Self-Raising Flour
1 Level Teaspoon Ground Ginger

FOR ROLLING
1 Tablespoon Caster Sugar
½ Level Teaspoon Ground Ginger

Pre-heat oven to 180C/350F/Gas 4
Grease 2 large baking trays

1. Beat the sugar and margarine together in a bowl until creamy using an electric hand mixer or a wooden spoon.

2. Beat in the honey.

3. Beat in the egg yolk.

4. Sieve together the flour and ginger, and add little by little while mixing with a wooden spoon to form a soft dough.

5. Take a teaspoonful of the mixture at a time, and lightly roll in your hands into a ball. Roll the ball in the sugar and ginger mixture.

6. Place on the prepared baking trays – remembering to space them out as they will spread during baking. Flatten slightly.

7. Bake in the pre-heated oven for 12-15 minutes until golden brown.

8. Remove from the oven and leave on the tray for 5 minutes – the biscuits will flatten and firm up.

9. Lift onto a cooling rack using a palette knife.

Use a spoon dipped in hot water to measure the honey – this stops the honey sticking to the spoon.

The biscuits are soft when cooked – they firm up as they cool.

MOLLIE (7YRS), BECCY (11YRS), & BEN (9YRS) LIPPETT BAKING NANNIE'S COOKIES

FAT OLIVES

FAT OLIVES
30 SOUTH STREET
EMSWORTH
PO10 7EH
T. 01243 377914

e. info@fatolives.co.uk
www.fatolives.co.uk

LAWRENCE & JULIA MURPHY

LAWRENCE MURPHY MET HIS WIFE JULIA WHILE BOTH WERE EMPLOYED AS TRAINEE HOTEL MANAGERS, A CAREER THEY PURSUED IN VARIOUS HOTELS BEFORE TAKING THE DECISION TO CHANGE CAREER PATHS AND OPEN THEIR OWN RESTAURANT IN EMSWORTH. LAWRENCE HAS WORKED IN THE FOOD INDUSTRY FOR A NUMBER OF YEARS; HE BEGAN WORKING IN A KITCHEN AT THE AGE OF 16 YEARS. HE IS A SELF-TAUGHT CHEF WHO IS GAINING AN EXCELLENT REPUTATION FOR SERVING MODERN ENGLISH FOOD WITH A MEDITERRANEAN INFLUENCE. JULIA HAS TAKEN ON RESPONSIBILITY FOR LOOKING AFTER THE FRONT OF HOUSE. THEY ARE AN ACTIVE COUPLE, WHO SPEND WHAT LITTLE LEISURE TIME THEY HAVE PURSUING THEIR INTEREST IN SPORTS — MOUNTAIN BIKING, DIVING AND HORSE RIDING.

FAT OLIVES RESTAURANT IS SITUATED IN WHAT WAS ORIGINALLY A FISHERMAN'S COTTAGE WHICH DATES BACK TO 1670. APPARENTLY THERE USED TO BE AN UNDERGROUND TUNNEL LINKING EACH PROPERTY WHICH RAN THE WHOLE LENGTH OF SOUTH STREET UP TO WHERE THE OLD PHARMACY IS IN THE HIGH STREET, WHICH WAS EXTENSIVELY USED BY SMUGGLERS. JULIA AND LAWRENCE MURPHY HAVE OWNED THE RESTAURANT SINCE JANUARY 2000, HAVING DEVELOPED THEIR OWN SIMPLE STYLE OF DÉCOR USING WOODEN FLOORS AND TABLES TO GIVE A MODERN FEEL TO THE PLACE. TO THE REAR OF THE BUILDING IS A LOVELY ENCLOSED COURTYARD AREA FOR AL-FRESCO EATING DURING THE SUMMER MONTHS. AS THE NAME SUGGESTS, THEY SERVE LARGE OLIVES AS AN APPETISER, AND SINCE 2003 HAVE BOTTLED THESE TO SELL TO CUSTOMERS.

3-COURSE MENU

RED MULLET, SAFFRON BROTH,
BLACK OLIVE TAPENADE

WILD BOAR, BLACK PUDDING MOUSSELINE,
GRAIN MUSTARD SAUCE

RED WINE AND CRANBERRY JELLY, POACHED
PEARS, CARDAMOM ICE CREAM

RED MULLET, SAFFRON BROTH, BLACK OLIVE TAPENADE

Serves 4

1 Onion
1 Leek
1 Carrot
1 Baby Fennel
1 Stick Celery
2 Tomatoes (blanched, peeled, de-seeded & chopped)
Olive Oil
Pinch Saffron
150ml White Wine
5 Peppercorns
1 Star Anise
1lt Fish Stock
2 Medium Red Mullet (filleted & pin-boned)
Chervil
Black Olive Tapenade

1. Prepare the vegetables and cut into small interesting shapes.

2. Gently sauté the chopped onion in olive oil until soft, but without colouring.

3. Add the rest of the vegetables – except the tomatoes – and the saffron and cover with the white wine.

4. Add the peppercorns and star anise and simmer until reduced by half.

5. Add the fish stock and simmer for a further 5 minutes.

6. Add seasoning to taste and the tomatoes.

7. Score the skin of the red mullet fillets and sauté in a frying pan of hot oil, skin side down, until cooked halfway through. Turn the fish over and cook the other side.

8. Pour the broth into bowls and lay sprigs of chervil on top of the broth.

9. Arrange the red mullet on top of the broth and top with the tapenade to serve.

You can buy good quality fresh fish stock and olive tapenade if you do not have time to prepare your own.

Dry, tasty white such as a good quality southern Rhone white or for something a little different try a Spanish Albarino.

FISH STOCK

Makes approximately 1lt

450g Fish Bones (use flat fish or monkfish)
3 Tablespoons Olive Oil
900g Mixed Vegetables (chopped)
      Leeks
      Celery
      Onion
      Fennel
150ml White Wine
1 Bay Leaf
1 Teaspoon Peppercorns
Parsley Stalks

1. Wash the fish bones thoroughly in cold water.

2. Heat the olive oil in a large saucepan, and gently cook the chopped vegetables until soft.

3. Add the white wine, fish bones and sufficient water to cover the bones.

4. Bring to the boil and skim the surface.

5. Reduce the heat, add the remaining ingredients and simmer for 20 minutes.

6. Strain through a fine sieve and allow to cool.

7. Store in a fridge (it will last for 3 days).

BLACK OLIVE TAPENADE

100g Black Olives (pitted)
2 Anchovy Fillets (use marinated not salted)
1 Clove Garlic
125ml Olive Oil
1 Teaspoon Lemon Juice

1. Put all of the ingredients into a small blender and pulse until smooth.

2. Refrigerate until required (it will keep for up to 5 days).

Wild Boar with Black Pudding Mousseline and Grain Mustard Sauce

Serves 4

Pre-heat oven to 220C/425F/Gas 7

Mousseline

Mousseline
1 Chicken Breast
1 Egg White
300ml Double Cream
Seasoning
100g Black Pudding

2 Wild Boar Fillets
12 Pieces Caul Fat

Sauce
1 Onion
1 Leek
150ml White Wine
250ml Chicken Stock
250ml Double Cream
2 Tablespoons Mustard (grain or Dijon)

Olive Oil
250g Spinach
Butter

Mousseline
1. Blend the chicken breast in a blender or liquidiser.
2. Add the egg white and blend until mixed into the chicken.
3. Slowly add the double cream whilst pulsating the mixture.
4. Add seasoning and the black pudding and pulse to mix.
5. Refrigerate for 10 minutes.

Wild Boar
1. Trim and cut the wild boar fillets into 12 noisettes.
2. Top each noisette with the black pudding mousseline.
3. Wrap each in caul fat.
4. Refrigerate for 3 hours to set.

Sauce
1. Sweat the onion and leak in a pan with a little olive oil.
2. Add the white wine and simmer until reduced.
3. Add the chicken stock and double cream and reduce until a consistency to cover the back of a spoon.
4. Pass the mixture through a sieve into a clean saucepan.
5. Add the grain mustard, and heat when ready to serve.

Noisettes
1. Heat a frying pan with a little olive oil and fry the noisettes, sealing the caul fat.
2. Transfer to an oven tray and bake in the pre-heated oven for 8-10 minutes.

To Serve
1. Sauté the spinach in butter, and arrange on a plate.
2. Put the boar on top.
3. Pour the mustard sauce around the meat.

Wild Boar is a darker meat than pork, but you can substitute pork fillets.

Corn fed chicken gives the best flavour.

Black pudding mixes easier if first cut into cubes.

Caul fat comes from the pig and has a texture rather like a string bag. You can buy from your butcher.

If you sweat down spinach in butter rather than water it gives a better flavour and texture.

Good quality, full bodied, robust red - Shiraz from the Barossa Valley or a fine Chateauneuf du Pape.

RED WINE AND CRANBERRY JELLY WITH POACHED PEARS

RED WINE & CRANBERRY JELLY

250ml Red Wine
250ml Cranberry Juice
110g Caster Sugar
4 Gelatine Leaves

POACHED PEARS

4 Baby Pears
½ Cinnamon Stick
110g Sugar
250ml Red Wine
1 Bay Leaf
3 Peppercorns

CARDAMOM ICE CREAM

15 Cardamom Pods
250ml Double Cream
250ml Milk
6 Egg Yolks
170g Caster Sugar

RED WINE & CRANBERRY JELLY

1. Put the red wine, cranberry juice and sugar into a saucepan.
2. Heat and simmer until reduced to 250ml of liquid.
3. Add the gelatine.
4. Pour the mixture into moulds.
5. Allow to cool, then place into a fridge to set. This should take 1-2 hours.

POACHED PEARS

1. Peel the pears but keep the stalk intact.
2. Put all of the other ingredients into a saucepan and bring to the boil, then simmer for 10 minutes.
3. Add the pears, cover and simmer for a further 20 minutes or until the pears are knife tender.
4. Leave to cool in the liquid.
5. Take some of the liquid to reduce down to form a syrup to decorate the plate.

CARDAMOM ICE CREAM

1. Split the cardamom pods to extract the seeds.
2. Crush the seeds in a pestle and mortar to form a fine dust.
3. Put the cream, milk and crushed cardamom seeds into a saucepan and slowly bring to the boil.
4. Meanwhile, whisk the egg yolks and sugar until white.
5. Pour the hot milk slowly onto the egg and sugar mixture whilst whisking.
6. Return the mixture to a clean saucepan and gently bring to 80°C whilst stirring continuously. Do not allow to boil or you will split the custard.
7. Allow to cool and then churn in an ice cream machine.

TO SERVE

1. Cut the poached pears in half and remove the pips.
2. De-mould the jelly and place onto a plate next to the lower half of the pear.
3. Decorate the plate with the syrup.
4. Place a ball of ice cream onto the pear, and then put the top of the pear onto the ice cream.

If you leave the pears in the poaching liquid overnight they absorb more colour.

Not easy, but try a chilled Banyuls from the South of France.

AND CARDAMOM ICE CREAM

GLENWOOD SCHOOL

GLENWOOD SCHOOL
WASHINGTON ROAD
EMSWORTH
PO10 7NN
T. 01243 373120
F. 01243 373103

www.glenwood.hants.sch.uk

HEAD: PHILIP JOHNSON
FOOD STUDIES TEACHER: LESLEY WATTON

GLENWOOD SCHOOL IS A SECONDARY SCHOOL FOR PUPILS AGED 11 TO 16 YEARS WITH MODERATE LEARNING DIFFICULTIES. IT HAS BEEN BASED IN EMSWORTH SINCE NOVEMBER 1998, IN A CONVERTED AND EXTENDED VICTORIAN SCHOOL BUILDING WHICH WAS UNTIL THEN THE EMSWORTH PRIMARY SCHOOL BUILDING. PUPILS ATTENDING THE SCHOOL COME FROM ALL OVER SOUTH EAST HAMPSHIRE BUT MOST OF THEM COME FROM THE BOROUGH OF HAVANT. THE FULL NATIONAL CURRICULUM IS TAUGHT, WITH A STRONG EMPHASIS ON PERSONAL AND SOCIAL DEVELOPMENT. ALL OF THE PUPILS UNDERTAKE A COURSE IN FOOD STUDIES WHICH AIMS TO TEACH THEM THE SKILLS, ATTITUDES AND SAFE WORKING PRACTICES TO ENSURE THEY WILL BE ABLE TO MAKE JUDGEMENTS ABOUT WHAT CONSTITUTES A HEALTHY LIFESTYLE.

YEAR 10 PUPILS WITH DENIS SPENCER, SPENCERS RESTAURANT & BRASSERIE

PASTRY PARCELS

200g Puff Pastry
200g Shortcrust Pastry
200g Filo Pastry

FILLINGS

CHEESE & PICKLE
150g Grated Cheese
1 Tablespoon Sweet Pickle

CHEESE & HAM
150g Grated Cheese
100g Ham (roughly chopped)

CURRIED CHICKEN
2 Chicken Breasts (sliced & cooked)
1 Teaspoon Curry Powder

APPLE & SULTANAS
1 Tin (400g) Apples
50g Sultanas

THE YEAR 10 PUPILS DEVELOPED THESE RECIPE IDEAS IN CLASS. THEY WANTED TO PRODUCE FOOD WHICH APPEALED TO TEENAGERS AS WELL AS ADULTS, EITHER AS A SNACK OR CANAPÉS FOR A PARTY. THE FILLINGS USED HERE ARE THEIR CHOICE, BUT THE LIST IS ENDLESS AND ONLY LIMITED BY YOUR IMAGINATION. DENIS SPENCER, OF SPENCERS RESTAURANT & BRASSERIE, SPENT A MORNING WITH THE PUPILS HELPING THEM TO DEVELOP THEIR IDEAS AND COOK (AND EAT!) THEIR PASTRY PARCELS.

Pre-heat oven to 220C/425F/Gas 7

1. Roll out the shortcrust and puff pastry. Cut into small squares before rolling to avoid waste, roll into a round using your hands and flatten with the palm of your hand.

2. Do not allow shortcrust pastry to become too warm or it will stick to the board when rolling out. Puff pastry is best left to rest in a fridge for 30 minutes after rolling.

3. Carefully separate the leaves of filo pastry and lightly brush with clarified butter - this makes it easier to work with.

4. When making the filo pastry parcels, build up the squares at angles to fold into parcels with the filling inside.

5. Alternatively, you can blind bake the filo as baskets using cake tins, and fill once cooked. Use sweet or savoury fillings, for example cooked pear with chocolate sauce; ice cream with fruit drizzled with coulis. For savoury fillings, they can be heated in the oven to serve warm.

6. Roll out and cut the pastry shapes (triangles, circles or squares) and use a small amount of filling of choice (do not use too much or it will leak out during cooking).

7. Brush the edges of the pastry with beaten egg or milk to seal and fold into shape as required. You can brush the top to glaze if required.

8. Remember to pre-cook raw meat before using in the parcels.

9. Place parcels onto a greased baking sheet and cook in the pre-heated oven for 10-15 minutes until golden brown.

These pastry parcels are quick, easy and fun to make. The combination of different sweet or savoury fillings chosen by the pupils means there is something to appeal to everyone. Choose from filo, puff or shortcrust pastry, and experiment with different shapes and sizes.

Other favourite fillings tried and tested in the class include: apple & blackberry; cherry; ham and couscous; cheese & onion; Cornish pasty.

While the kids are making these it's probably a good excuse to open a bottle of whatever you really enjoy and …enjoy!

PANTRY WEIGH

PANTRY WEIGH
7 HIGH STREET
EMSWORTH
PO10 7AQ
T. 01243 372719

ADRIAN & ROS OAKLEY

ROS OAKLEY HELPS HER HUSBAND, ADRIAN TO RUN THE SHOP IN BETWEEN LOOKING AFTER THEIR CHILDREN. SHE LEARNT TO COOK IN HER MOTHER'S KITCHEN AND IS KEEN THAT HER OWN CHILDREN LEAVE HOME WITH THE ABILITY TO COOK WITH CONFIDENCE AND IMAGINATION. AFTER LEAVING A CAREER IN QUANTITY SURVEYING IN LONDON TO TRAVEL EXTENSIVELY, SHE MET ADRIAN, WHERE THEY DISCOVERED THAT THEY SHARED AN ENJOYMENT OF NEW FOODS AND FLAVOURS. THIS HAS INFLUENCED THE CHOICE OF PRODUCE STOCKED IN THE SHOP.

PANTRY WEIGH OPENED IN 1993, OWNED AND MANAGED BY ADRIAN AND ROS OAKLEY. THIS WHOLEFOODS AND GROCERY STORE BEGAN AS A 'SCOOP' SHOP, SELLING LOOSE FOODS TO ENABLE CUSTOMERS TO CHOOSE THE AMOUNTS REQUIRED. ALTHOUGH STILL A PART OF THE STORE, THEY NOW SELL A WIDE VARIETY OF OTHER PACKAGED STORE CUPBOARD ITEMS AS WELL AS A RANGE OF MORE LUXURIOUS FOOD PRODUCTS INCLUDING SEASONAL INGREDIENTS AND GIFT FAYRE. THE BUILDING WAS FIRST A FINE TOWN HOUSE, AND HAS ALSO BEEN A HABERDASHERY AND IRONMONGERS.

SWEET TREATS TO MAKE AND GIVE
CHOCOLATE TRUFFLES

Makes 18

125g Plain Chocolate
(70% cocoa)
50g Unsalted Butter (softened)
1 Tablespoon Brandy (or rum)
3 Egg Yolks (medium)
50g Ground Almonds
75g Icing Sugar (sifted)

COATING (CHOICE OF)
Chocolate Vermicelli
Icing Sugar
Desiccated Coconut
Cocoa Powder
Chopped Nuts

1. Break the chocolate into small pieces and place into a heatproof bowl over a pan of hot water, ensuring that none of the water gets into the bowl.

2. Add the butter, and stir until melted.

3. Remove the bowl from the heat and allow to cool for approximately 10 minutes.

4. Beat in the brandy and egg yolks.

5. Gradually stir in the ground almonds and then the icing sugar. Beat until thoroughly mixed.

6. Cover and place into a fridge for approximately 1 hour until set.

7. Form the mixture into small balls, and roll in a coating of choice.

8. Package in petit four cases.

Perfect at the end of a meal with a glass of Tawny Port or rich Madeira.

Most of the ingredients can be purchased at the shop.

SWEET TREATS TO MAKE AND GIVE
STUFFED DATES

Makes approximately 60

2 x 250g Boxes Dates
15 Whole Almonds
(decoration)

MARZIPAN FILLING
50g Ground Almonds
25g Icing Sugar
40g Caster Sugar
1 Egg Yolk (large)
2-4 Drops Almond Essence
1 Teaspoon Lemon Juice

APRICOT & WALNUT FILLING
90g Soft Dried Apricots (finely chopped)
30g Walnuts (finely chopped)
1 Teaspoon Clear Honey
½ Teaspoon Dried Rosemary

1. Slit each of the dates without halving, and remove the stones.

2. To make the marzipan filling, mix the ground almonds and sugars in a bowl. Beat in the egg yolk, almond essence and lemon juice and mix until a smooth, firm paste.

3. Slip a small roll of the filling into each date, and top with half an almond.

4. To make the apricot and walnut filling, combine all of the ingredients and mix well. Mould into small rolls and fill the cavities of the dates.

Perfect at the end of a meal with a glass of Tawny Port or rich Madeira.

All of the ingredients can be purchased at the shop.

SWEET TREATS TO MAKE AND GIVE
TRADITIONAL MINCEMEAT

Makes 2.8kg (6lb 4oz)

450g Currants
450g Sultanas
450g Raisins
225g Mixed Peel
50g Chopped Almonds
50g Chopped Brazil Nuts
450g Dark Soft Brown Sugar
170g Vegetable or Beef Suet
1 Teaspoon Ground Nutmeg
1 Teaspoon Ground Cinnamon
250ml Brandy
Juice & Grated Zest 1 Orange
Juice & Grated Zest 1 Lemon

OPTIONAL
200g Cooking Apples
   (peeled & grated)

Most of the
ingredients can
be purchased at
the shop.

Make at least 2 weeks before required

1. Thoroughly mix together all of the
    ingredients in a large bowl.

2. Spoon the mixture into clean glass
    jars and seal with waxed paper
    discs and cellophane tops or
    screw top jars.

3. Store in a cool dark place until
    ready to use.

THE SHIP INN

JANE MURRAY WAS A CREW MEMBER ON THE WINNING YACHT, BP EXPLORER WITH SKIPPER DAVID MELVILLE IN THE 1800-MILE NON-STOP ROUND BRITAIN AND IRELAND CHALLENGE 2004. EIGHT GLOBAL CHALLENGE YACHTS TOOK PART IN THIS RACE.

JANE IS ALSO A RESERVE FOR THE 2004 GLOBAL CHALLENGE, WHICH LEAVES FROM GUNWHARF, PORTSMOUTH DURING OCTOBER.

THE SHIP INN
24 HIGH STREET
EMSWORTH
PO10 7AW
T. 01243 377151
F. 01243 389163

BREWERY: GEORGE GALE & CO LTD

JANE MURRAY

THE SHIP INN PUBLIC HOUSE SITUATED IN THE SQUARE HAS TRADED SINCE THE 1700S. JANE MURRAY HAS BEEN THE LANDLADY SINCE 1996, AND FOR THE LAST FOUR YEARS HAS BEEN THE WINNER OF THE GALES BREWERY CELLAR-CRAFT COMPETITION. THE PUB IS OPEN ALL DAY, CATERING FOR DIFFERENT CLIENTELE DURING THE DAYTIME WHEN FOOD IS SERVED — ATTRACTING PEOPLE OF ALL AGES. WHILST AT NIGHT IT CATERS FOR THE YOUNGER DRINKERS WHO ENJOY A LIVELY ATMOSPHERE. THE REAR, ENCLOSED COURTYARD IS AN IDEAL PLACE TO SIT DURING THE BETTER WEATHER.

LINDA COLE (NÉE POWER) IS THE CHEF, SERVING TRADITIONAL GOOD PUB FOOD AND DAILY SPECIALS. SHE TRAINED AT HIGHBURY COLLEGE DOING A TWO-YEAR HOTEL AND CATERING MANAGEMENT COURSE. FOLLOWING THIS SHE WORKED AT THORNHAM MARINA FOR FOUR YEARS, BEFORE TAKING OVER AT THE SHIP IN 1998.

SAUSAGES IN CIDER

Serves 2

6 Sausages
Vegetable Oil
Olive Oil
1 Large Onion (diced)
225g (8oz) Carrots (peeled & sliced)
2 Celery Sticks (washed & chopped)
220ml Cider
375ml (¾ pt) Vegetable Stock
Vegetable Gravy Granules (optional)

1. Brown the sausages in a frying pan with a little vegetable oil.

2. Meanwhile, heat some olive oil in a reasonable size saucepan.

3. Fry the chopped onion in the olive oil until transparent, then add the sliced carrots and fry for a couple of minutes.

4. Add the chopped celery, and continue to fry for a further minute.

5. Add the browned sausages to the mixture.

6. Pour in the cider and vegetable stock, and bring to the boil.

7. Simmer on a very low heat, stirring occasionally, for approximately 45 minutes or until the vegetables are cooked. You may need to add more stock. Alternatively, transfer the ingredients to a casserole dish and cook in a pre-heated (180C/350F/Gas 4) oven for 1 hour.

8. Thicken the casserole with gravy granules as required.

9. Season to taste.

Linda recommends pork & chive sausages from MR Starr.

Sturdy red, new wave Spanish red from La Mancha or how about the long forgotten Cahors from South west France.

MR STARR

MR STARR
1 HIGH STREET
EMSWORTH
PO10 7AB
T. 01243 372058

MICHAEL & LINDA STARR
WITH THEIR SONS, PAUL & NEIL,
& PETER ROCK & ROGER WILSON

LINDA STARR, KNOWN IN THE VILLAGE AS LOU, NOT ONLY HELPS RUN THEIR FAMILY BUSINESS BUT ALSO TEACHES CLASSES IN QUILTING AND PATCHWORK AND IS AN ACTIVE MEMBER OF THE BOURNE QUILTERS, BASED IN EMSWORTH. SHE ENJOYS COOKING, AND THE RECIPES FOR THE PIES SOLD AT THE SHOP ARE IN FACT HER OWN.

MR STARR IS A FAMILY OWNED BUTCHER AND FISMONGER, ESTABLISHED IN EMSWORTH IN 1989. MICHAEL AND LINDA STARR'S SONS, PAUL AND NEIL WORK ALONGSIDE THEM IN THE SHOP. PAUL RUNS THE FISHMONGERY AND SELLS LOCALLY CAUGHT FISH AND SHELLFISH WHEN AVAILABLE. NEIL COOKS THE HOMEMADE PIES AND STEAK PUDDINGS IN ADDITION TO MAKING THEIR OWN RANGE OF SAUSAGES, BURGERS AND FAGGOTS. THE BUILDING DATES FROM THE 1800S, AND HAS LONG BEEN OPERATED AS A BUTCHER'S SHOP, ORIGINALLY ALSO ACTING AS A SLAUGHTER HOUSE FOR THE MEAT SOLD AS IS EVIDENCED BY THE ORIGINAL TETHERING RINGS AT THE REAR OF THE BUILDING.

BOURNE QUILTERS, EMSWORTH

MEMBERS OF BOURNE QUILTERS AT THE 2004 QUILT SHOW, WITH THEIR RAFFLE QUILT

FOUNDED IN 1997 AFTER FOUR QUILTING FRIENDS DECIDED TO HIRE THE LOCAL COMMUNITY CENTRE TO SEE IF THERE WERE ANY OTHER LIKE MINDED LADIES WHO WOULD BE INTERESTED IN FORMING A QUILTING GROUP. THE INITIAL FOUR HAVE NOW GROWN TO 70 PAID-UP MEMBERS AND A HEALTHY WAITING LIST. BOURNE QUILTERS HOLDS MONTHLY EVENING MEETINGS WHEN MEMBERS CAN LISTEN TO SPEAKERS ON VARIOUS ASPECTS OF QUILT MAKING AS WELL AS WORK ON SMALL PROJECTS OR MEET WITH OTHER VISITING GROUPS. IN 2002, BOURNE QUILTERS HELD ITS VERY FIRST QUILT SHOW AND RAISED £3,300 FOR THE ROWANS HOSPICE. FOR FURTHER DETAILS TELEPHONE SHEILA LILLINGTON 023 9247 5958

CHICKEN AND CHEESE WITH MUSTARD SAUCE *Serves 4*

   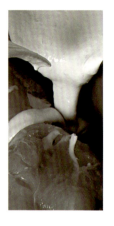  

4 Boneless Chicken Breasts
100g Cream Cheese
200ml Double Cream
1 Tablespoon French Mustard
25g Butter
Salt & pepper
Freshly Ground Pink Peppercorns

Pre-heat oven to 200C/400F/Gas 6

1. Make a deep slit into the side of each chicken breast to form a pocket.

2. Put a piece of cream cheese into each pocket and place chicken into an ovenproof dish.

3. Mix the cream and half of the mustard together and pour around the base of the chicken.

4. Melt the butter, add seasoning and the remaining mustard and mix, then brush onto the exposed chicken.

5. Bake in the pre-heated oven for 40 minutes until golden and the chicken is cooked.

6. Once cooked, top the chicken with the pink peppercorns and serve with either jacket or new potatoes, fresh vegetables or salad and baby mushrooms.

The cream cheese can be replaced by blue cheese if preferred.

Red or white work here, well made new world Chardonnay with some oak, as for red, try a Chilean Carmenere.

THE SUSSEX BREWERY

THE SUSSEX BREWERY
36 MAIN ROAD
EMSWORTH
PO10 8AU
T. 01243 371533
F. 01243 379684

BREWERY: YOUNG'S

MALCOLM & PAM ROBERTS

BOB LANGLEY, PAM'S BROTHER, HAS, FOR MORE THAN TEN YEARS, BEEN THE CHEF AT THE SUSSEX BREWERY, SERVING UP A VARIETY OF DAILY SPECIALS AS WELL AS SERVING TRADITIONAL PUB FOOD, FRESH LOCAL FISH AND, OF COURSE, THE EXTENSIVE SAUSAGE MENU, FOR WHICH HE AND THE PUB ARE NOW KNOWN. HE GAINED HIS EXPERIENCE IN THE KITCHEN WORKING FOR VARIOUS PUBS AND RESTAU-RANTS IN LONDON BEFORE MOVING SOUTH FOR THE QUIETER LIFE OF EMSWORTH.

THE SUSSEX BREWERY, ALTHOUGH NOW A PUBLIC HOUSE, WAS ORIGINALLY A LOCAL BREWERY ATTACHED TO A SMALL BUILDING WHICH ALSO SOLD THE BEER BREWED. WITH ITS FLOORS OF MUD AND SAWDUST AND CHICKENS RUNNING THROUGH, IT WAS VERY MUCH AN ALE HOUSE IN THOSE DAYS. TODAY, THE TRADITION OF USING SAWDUST ON THE BAR FLOOR REMAINS, ALTHOUGH THE PUB HAS CHANGED GREATLY AND NOW HAS TWO SEPARATE RESTAURANT AREAS TO THE REAR, BOTH OF WHICH ARE NON-SMOKING, IN ADDITION TO AN OUTSIDE COURTYARD AREA WITH TABLES AND CHAIRS. PAM AND MALCOLM ROBERTS HAVE RUN THIS TRADITIONAL OLD-FASHIONED PUB SINCE 1985. THE FOOD SERVED INCLUDES THE RENOWNED OFFERING OF MORE THAN 50 VARIETIES OF SAUSAGE AS WELL AS BOB'S HOMEMADE PIES AND LOCAL FISH DISHES.

PHEASANT CASSEROLE WITH DUMPLINGS

Serves 8

8 Pheasant Breasts
1lt English Stout
55g (2oz) Plain Flour
110g (4oz) Suet
Seasoning

Seasonal Root Vegetables
  (roughly diced)
4 Leeks
1 Swede (large)
1 Turnip (large)
2 Parsnips
1 Onion
450g (1lb) Potatoes
450g (1lb) Carrots

Pre-heat oven to 220C/425F/Gas 7

1. Marinate the pheasant breasts in the English stout for 24-28 hours.

2. Make the dumplings by sifting the flour and mixing with the suet, 5 tablespoons water, and seasoning.

3. Shape the dough into 4cm (1½ inch) balls and put into a fridge.

4. Put all of the diced vegetables into a pan of boiling water. Return to the boil, and rapid boil for 2 minutes, then drain.

5. Place the pheasant breasts, stout, par-boiled vegetables and the dumplings into a large casserole dish and cook in the pre-heated oven for 20-30 minutes.

6. Serve with roasted new potatoes and minted garden peas.

Top quality red, with some bottle age if you can, from Burgundy or the Rhone, particularly Chateauneuf du Pape.

HH TREAGUST & SONS

HH TREAGUST & SONS
17 HIGH STREET
EMSWORTH
PO10 7AQ
T. 01243 372484

RICHARD & SUE TREAGUST

SUE TREAGUST COMES FROM A LONG-ESTABLISHED LOCAL EMSWORTH FAMILY. SHE WORKS IN THE SHOP ALONGSIDE HER HUSBAND, RICHARD, OCCASIONALLY HELPED BY THEIR SON BEN. SUE HAS A GREAT INTEREST IN FOOD AND COOKING, AND ALSO BAKES ALL OF THE TREAGUST OWN PIES AND PORK PIES. DURING THE WINTER MONTHS HER HOMEMADE FAGGOTS ARE A TRADITIONAL FAVOURITE, AND IN THE SUMMER HER HAND-PRESSED, 100% BEEF BURGERS ARE VERY POPULAR.

HH TREAGUST & SONS HIGH CLASS FAMILY BUTCHERS HAS BEEN IN THE FAMILY FOR FOUR GENERATIONS SINCE THE MID-1920S WHEN THE PROPERTY WAS PURCHASED BY RICHARD'S GREAT GRANDFATHER, HARRY TREAGUST FOR THE SUM OF £500. A HAWKER BY TRADE, HARRY ORIGINALLY SOLD MEAT FROM HIS PIGS RAISED AND SLAUGHTERED ON LAND AROUND PRINSTED, DOOR TO DOOR. THE RECIPE FOR THE POPULAR TREAGUST'S OLD ENGLISH PORK SAUSAGES HAS BEEN HANDED DOWN FROM GENERATION TO GENERATION, GAINING MANY AWARDS AND MERITS. SINCE MARCH 2000, RICHARD TREAGUST HAS OWNED THE BUSINESS AND CONTINUES IN MICHAEL'S, HIS FATHER'S, FOOTSTEPS BEING LICENSED TO SELL ABERDEEN ANGUS SCOTCH BEEF. IN ADDITION, A RANGE OF HOMEMADE PIES AND ORGANIC PRODUCTS ARE AVAILABLE.

SAVOURY SAUSAGE SLICE

Serves 4

85g Sage & Onion Mix
450g Treagust Sausage Meat
25g Cooked Ham (chopped)
1 Leek (finely chopped)
Olive Oil
400g Puff Pastry
English Mustard (optional)
Milk (to seal pastry)
Beaten Egg (to glaze)

Pre-heat oven to 200C/400F/Gas 6

1. Mix the sage and onion with hot water and a knob of butter.

2. Using a spoon, mix together the sausage meat, chopped ham, sage and onion, and the chopped leek until thoroughly combined.

3. Shape the meat into a rectangular loaf shape, on a floured surface.

4. Heat a small amount of olive oil in a frying pan and seal each side of the meat for 5-10 minutes.

5. Roll out the puff pastry to required size, and spread the inside with a thin layer of English mustard.

6. Roll the meat loaf onto the pastry and seal the edges with a little milk (or water).

7. Score the top with a criss-cross pattern and brush with beaten egg.

8. Put onto a baking tray and cook on the middle shelf of the pre-heated oven for 30 minutes or until golden brown.

9. Turn down the temperature to 180C/350F/Gas 4, cover the pastry with tin foil to prevent burning, and cook for a further 20-30 minutes.

A versatile meat loaf which can be eaten hot with vegetables or cold with salad.
Equally good for picnics or packed lunch boxes.

Light to medium bodied red, maybe from the Loire and try slightly chilled.

SUET-CRUST BACON, CHEESE AND LEEK ROLY-POLY   *Serves 3*

100g Plain Flour
100g Self-Raising Flour
100g Shredded Suet
Large Pinch Salt & Pepper
5 Rashers Green Back Bacon
1 Leek (finely chopped)
Small (250g) Can Sweetcorn
55g Grated Cheese

Pre-heat oven to 200C/400F/Gas 6

1. Mix together the flours, suet and salt and pepper, then add enough cold water (approximately 3 tablespoons) to form a dough.

2. Once the dough is thoroughly mixed, flour your hands and turn out onto a floured work surface.

3. Roll the dough into a rectangular shape approximately 30 x 22cm (111/2 x 81/4 inch).

4. Remove rind from the bacon, and place bacon onto the rolled dough. Remember to leave 1-2cm space around the edges for sealing.

5. Sprinkle with the chopped leeks (retain a small amount for later), sweetcorn and 2/3rds of the cheese onto the bacon.

6. Brush edges with cold water and then begin to roll the dough over from one edge to the other to form the roly-poly.

7. Ensure that all edges are sealed.

8. Place in a dish or on a baking tray and cover with foil.

9. Bake in the pre-heated oven for 40 minutes.

10. Remove the foil and sprinkle some leeks and the remaining grated cheese on top of the roly-poly.

11. Return to the oven and cook for a further 15 minutes until golden brown.

An old-fashioned winter warmer and can be served with colourful vegetables.

Can use original or vegetarian suet

Cabernet/ Shiraz blend from Australia or good quality Cotes de Rhone.

STRAWBERRY SHORTBREAD

Serves 8

125g Plain Flour
100g Cornflour
50g Caster Sugar
175g Butter
250ml Double Cream
2-3 Teaspoons Icing Sugar
Punnet Strawberries

Pre-heat oven to 180C/350F/Gas 4

1. Sift together the flour, cornflour and caster sugar.

2. Rub in the butter until well blended into a dough.

3. Roll out on a well-floured surface into 2 round shapes approximately 18-20cm (7-8inch).

4. Prick both sides with a fork, and on one round only pinch the edges for decoration and run a knife gently over the top to divide into 8 petticoat tail shapes.

5. Bake in the pre-heated oven for 12-15 minutes or until lightly browned and firm to touch.

6. Allow to cool on a rack before cutting out the petticoat tails.

7. Whisk the double cream and add 2 teaspoons of icing sugar.

8. Spread generously over the complete shortbread base.

9. Top with halved strawberries.

10. Arrange the petticoat tails on top and pipe with extra cream.

11. Finish with more strawberries and a dusting of icing sugar.

If you can find it, Clairette de Die from the Rhone, if not Moscato d'Asti.

SPRING

MARCH

Photos by Brian Fellows

APRIL

MAY

BC's Catering Capers

Mountbatten House, dating from 1768, Official residence of Deputy Commander-in-Chief, Fleet

BC's Catering Capers
6 Farm View
Emsworth
PO10 7TN
T. 01243 378827
M. 07733 264795

e. abc333@ntlworld.com

Andrew Bellchambers has been a chef in the Royal Marines since he joined in 1979. Initially based with 42 Commando and then Commando Logistics, before moving to Portsmouth where he cooks for the Second Sea Lord and Commandant General Royal marines. His role often involves preparing meals for visiting members of the royal family, dignitaries and mps. During 1997 Andrew won the Royal Navy Chef of the Year award. He has also worked in many restaurants, including for Rick Stein, gaining experience as a chef. Outside his work in the navy, Andrew runs his own catering business for people who love to entertain, but do not have the time to source and prepare the food.

BC's Catering Capers is operated by Sgt Andrew Bellchambers, a fully qualified chef in the Royal Marines, as a part-time catering business where, in his spare time, he specialises in cooking at your home for you and your guests. Whatever the occasion may be, whether lunch, dinner or a party, Andrew can provide the food to remove the hassle from your busy schedule.

3-Course Menu

Open Ravioli of Minted Asparagus with Mascarpone Potatoes and a Mint Leaf Oil Dressing

Cajun Spiced Salmon Darne with Roasted Tri-colour Peppers and Artichokes on a Bed of Rocket Salad and Couscous, served with a Sea-scented Sauce

Light Mango Mousse on a Cointreau Soaked Sponge

OPEN RAVIOLI OF MINTED ASPARAGUS WITH MASCARPONE POTATOES AND A MINT LEAF OIL DRESSING

Serves 4

3 Large Baking Potatoes
500g (16oz) Mascarpone
2 Teaspoons Italian Herbs & Spices
Salt & Pepper
6 Tablespoons Olive Oil
1 Bunch Mint Leaves
50g (2oz) Butter (melted)
8 Sheets Fresh Lasagne Pasta
24 Fine Asparagus Tips

1. Peel and cut the potatoes into 5mm squares, and boil in enough water to cover, for 5 minutes.

2. Strain and put to one side.

3. Mix the mascarpone, herbs and spices and add seasoning to taste. Add this mixture to the potatoes and heat gently.

4. For the mint leaf dressing, take the oil, chopped mint, salt and pepper and warm through with the melted butter.

5. Cut the pasta into 5 x 5cm (2 x 2inch) sheets, and cook in boiling salted water until aldente.

6. Quickly blanche the asparagus in the same water as the pasta.

7. Place the potato and mascarpone mix onto the middle of a plate, followed by 1 sheet of the pasta.

8. Place 6 asparagus tips onto the pasta and add some of the mint leaf dressing.

9. Top with another sheet of the pasta and a drizzle of the dressing and add a mint leaf to garnish.

Northern Italian white would go well, maybe a good quality Pinot Grigio or Sauvignon Blanc from Collio.

CAJUN SPICED SALMON DARNE WITH ROASTED TRI-COLOUR PEPPERS AND ARTICHOKES ON A BED OF ROCKET SALAD AND COUSCOUS, SERVED WITH A SEA-SCENTED SAUCE

Serves 4

4 Salmon Darne (medium size)
200g Couscous
1 Small Glass White Wine
570ml (1pt) Fish Stock
½ Chicken Stock Cube
2 Teaspoons Swiss Vegetable Seasoning
2 Teaspoons Pink Peppercorns (crushed)
570ml Double Cream
50g Butter
½ Large Onion (finely chopped)
3 Sweet Peppers (1 of each colour)
   Quartered, Roasted and Peeled
2 Jars Chargrilled Artichokes in Olive Oil
200g Wild Rocket

CAJUN MIX
½ Teaspoon Chopped Garlic
½ Teaspoon Paprika
½ Teaspoon Chilli
½ Teaspoon Thyme
½ Teaspoon Black Pepper
½ Teaspoon Salt
½ Teaspoon Oregano

Pre-heat oven to 190C/375F/Gas 5

1. Mix together all of the ingredients for the Cajun marinade and cover the salmon with the mixture and marinate for at least 1 hour.

2. Cook the couscous according to the instructions on the packet, cover and leave to one side to absorb the water.

3. For the sauce, bring to the boil and reduce by half the white wine and fish stock with the chicken stock cube, vegetable seasoning and the pink peppercorns.

4. When the liquid has reduced, turn down to the lowest heat and add the double cream.

5. Heat half the butter in a heavy-based pan and fry the onion until clear. Add to the couscous.

6. Put the remaining butter into an oven dish along with the salmon darne skin side up, and place under a hot grill until crisp. Finish cooking the salmon in the pre-heated oven for 5 minutes.

7. Meanwhile, re-heat the roasted peppers and the artichokes in the same pan with the onion. Set aside and keep hot.

8. Place a small handful of rocket leaves onto the centre of a plate, followed by 2 or 3 spoonsful of couscous.

9. Next add the roasted peppers and artichokes and top with the salmon darne. Drizzle with the sauce.

.

Salmon can work with lighter reds and with the spices try an Oregon Pinot Noir or even a lighter style Californian Zinfandel.

LIGHT MANGO MOUSSE ON A COINTREAU SOAKED SPONGE *Serves 4*

175g Mangos (sliced)
1 Tablespoon Caster Sugar
7g Powdered Gelatine
150ml Double Cream (lightly whipped)
2 Egg Whites
Victoria Sponge
8 Tablespoons Cointreau

1. Simmer the mango slices in a heavy saucepan with half of the sugar and 150ml of water until the sugar is dissolved and the mango is soft.

2. Liquidize the mango slices to a soft purée, and leave to cool.

3. Put 3 tablespoons of water into a small saucepan, sprinkle on the gelatine and leave for 5 minutes.

4. Dissolve the gelatine over a low heat, without boiling, until the liquid is clear.

5. Stir in the mango purée and allow to cool.

6. Fold in the lightly whipped cream.

7. Whisk the egg whites with the remaining sugar until stiff.

8. Using a metal spoon, fold the egg whites into the mango mixture.

9. Cut the Victoria sponge into 4 thin circles to fit your ring-moulds.

10. Put a slice into the bottom of each mould, add 2 tablespoons of cointreau per disk, and spoon the mango mixture over.

11. Leave to set in the fridge for at least 2 or 3 hours.

12. Carefully remove the mousse and sponge from the ring and position in the centre of a plate and garnish with mango and raspberry coulis and a tuile biscuit.

Line the moulds with either cling film or baking parchment for ease of removal of contents.

Heat a flat metal spatula and rub it across the top and sides of the mousse for a smooth, glazed effect.

Coteaux du Layon from the Loire or light, sweet Muscat.

*MULBERRY TREE
BROUGHT BACK FROM
HIS TRAVELS BY DARWIN*

*MANY HERBS ARE
AVAILABLE FRESH
IN THE GARDEN OF
MOUNTBATTEN HOUSE*

THE BLUE BELL INN

THE BLUE BELL INN
29 SOUTH STREET
EMSWORTH
PO10 7EG
T. 01243 373394

A FREE HOUSE

THOMAS M BABB WITH HIS SON, THOMAS GILES &
THEIR DOGS, BRACKEN. MAX, & POMPEY

THOMAS GILES BABB HAS COMPLETED AN NVQ3 IN CATERING AT SOUTH DOWNS COLLEGE. THE SON OF THE LANDLORD, HE GAINED HIS INTEREST IN FOOD WHILST WORKING IN HIS FATHER'S PUB AS A KITCHEN ASSISTANT. HIS COLLEGE WORK EXPERIENCE PLACEMENTS HAVE INCLUDED WORKING LOCALLY AT FAT OLIVES AS WELL AS ESTABLISHMENTS WITH ROYAL CONNECTIONS. THOMAS -REGULARLY HELPS OUT IN THE KITCHENS AT THE BLUE BELL, AND ALSO RUNS THE PUB WHEN HIS FATHER TAKES DAYS OFF.

THE BLUE BELL INN, FOR MANY YEARS A FAVOURITE HAUNT OF LOCAL FISHERMEN SITUATED, AS THIS PUBLIC HOUSE IS, WITHIN YARDS OF THE PICTURESQUE HARBOUR IN EMSWORTH. THOMAS BABB HAS BEEN THE OWNER AND LANDLORD SINCE 1994. OPEN ALL-DAY IT IS A POPULAR VENUE FOR VISITORS AS WELL AS RESIDENTS, WITH THE OUTSIDE SEATING PROVIDING A VIEW OF THE WATERFRONT. NATURALLY, WITH ITS HISTORY, THE PUB SERVES LOCALLY CAUGHT FISH AND SHELLFISH, AS WELL AS A HOST OF OTHER DAILY SPECIALS AND TRADITIONAL FOOD.

3-COURSE MENU

BEER BATTERED SEA BASS FILLETS ON MUSHY PEAS WITH A TOMATO VINAIGRETTE

NEW SEASON LAMB IN CRUSHED PEPPERCORNS WITH GARLIC MASHED POTATO AND PORT JUS

BRAEBURN APPLE AND CINNAMON CRUMBLE TART WITH CINNAMON CREAM

PHOTOGRAPHS FROM 1950's, COURTESY OF JENNY HENDERSON WHOSE PARENTS RAN THE PUB

BEER BATTERED SEA BASS FILLETS ON MUSHY PEAS WITH A TOMATO VINAIGRETTE

Serves 4

TOMATO VINAIGRETTE
4 Tablespoons Tomato Purée
400ml Olive Oil
3 Tablespoons Balsamic Vinegar
4 Tomatoes (peeled, de-seeded and diced)

BEER BATTER
2 Eggs (large)
1 Tablespoon Mayonnaise
2 Tablespoons Turmeric
Self-Raising Flour
500ml Beer or Lager

MUSHY PEAS
300g Fresh Peas
50ml Double Cream
Seasoning

4 Fillets Sea Bass
Vegetable Oil

1. Make the vinaigrette by putting the tomato purée into a bowl and adding, whilst whisking, the olive oil and balsamic vinegar. Season to taste and mix in the finely diced tomatoes.

2. Make the beer batter using a food mixer to whisk the eggs and mayonnaise with the turmeric to form a light and fluffy mixture. Mix in the flour to form a paste, and add the beer. Continue to mix until a coating consistency is achieved.

3. To make the mushy peas, warm the fresh peas in a pan, add the cream and simmer until the liquid is reduced. Season to taste and whisk to form a mushy consistency.

4. Coat the sea bass fillets with the batter, and deep fry in a pan of vegetable oil at 180C for 5-7 minutes.

5. Use an individual ring-mould to shape the mushy peas, and place in the centre of a plate.

6. Position the sea bass fillets on top of the peas, and drizzle around with the vinaigrette.

To prepare the fresh tomatoes (concasser), first cut a cross over the stalk and remove the 'eye'. Then boil a pan of water, and drop-in the tomatoes for 10 seconds. Peel and de-seed, and cut into finely diced pieces.

Australian Riesling or why not a half of a tasty summer ale.

NEW SEASON LAMB IN CRUSHED PEPPERCORNS WITH GARLIC MASHED POTATO AND PORT JUS

Serves 4

GARLIC MASHED POTATO
500g Potatoes
50ml Double Cream
3 Cloves Garlic (crushed)
50g Butter

PORT JUS
75ml Ruby Port
200ml Lamb or Beef Stock
25g Butter

225g Lamb Canon
100g Cracked Black Pepper
Vegetable Oil

Pre-heat oven to 190C/375F/Gas 5

GARLIC MASHED POTATO

1.   Peel the potatoes and cook in boiling salted water.

2.   Meanwhile, warm the cream and butter.

3.   Drain the potatoes and dry mash over heat.

4.   Mix in the cream, garlic, butter and seasoning to taste.

PORT JUS

1.   Simmer the port in a saucepan until reduced by half.

2.   Add the stock and simmer until reduced by half.

3.   Keep warm, and when ready to serve whisk in the butter.

LAMB

1.   Season the lamb and seal on all sides in a hot pan with vegetable oil.

2.   Coat the sealed lamb in the cracked black pepper.

3.   Place into an oven dish and cook in the pre-heated oven for 7-10 minutes for rare meat, or longer if preferred.

Ask your butcher to prepare the lamb canon.

Some heat from the peppercorns, so not top-notch red, but good quality Cabernet Sauvignon from Coonawarra or Stellenbosch.

BRAEBURN APPLE AND CINNAMON CRUMBLE TART WITH CINNAMON CREAM

Serves 4

PASTRY
250g Butter
500g Plain Flour
2 Eggs (whisked)

CRUMBLE
120g Butter
250g Plain Flour
100g Brown Sugar
20g Cinnamon

FILLING
2 or 3 Braeburn Apples
4 Tablespoons Brown Sugar
4 Tablespoons Cinnamon

CINNAMON CREAM
250ml Double Cream
20g Cinnamon
20g Icing Sugar

When blind baking, line the pastry case with greaseproof paper and fill base with baking beans. This will prevent the pastry from rising.

The cream can be made in advance and stored in a fridge for up to 1 day.

Austrian or German Riesling such as Spatlese or Auslese - serve ice cold, great taste sensation with the warm crumble.

Pre-heat oven to 190C/375F/Gas 5

PASTRY

1. Rub the butter into the flour until the mixture forms breadcrumb texture.

2. Add the eggs and combine into the pastry.

3. Roll out on a floured surface and line a large, or individual, tart case.

4. Chill in the fridge for 10 minutes. This will prevent the pastry from shrinking.

5. Blind bake the pastry in the pre-heated oven for 10 minutes until lightly browned.

CRUMBLE

1. Rub the butter into the sifted flour until the mixture forms breadcrumb texture.

2. Mix in the sugar and cinnamon.

FILLING

1. Wash, core and thinly slice the apples.

2. Line the pastry case with the sliced apples, and sprinkle with the sugar and cinnamon.

3. Cover the top with the crumble mix.

4. Cook in the pre-heated oven (200C/400F/ Gas 6) for 20-25 minutes until bubbling and golden brown.

CINNAMON CREAM

1. Whisk together the cream, cinnamon and sugar until stiff.

2. Place a spoonful on top of each tart just before serving.

THE BROOKFIELD HOTEL AND HERMITAGE RESTAURANT

THE BROOKFIELD HOTEL
93-95 HAVANT ROAD
EMSWORTH
PO10 7LF
T. 01243 373363
F. 01243 376342

e. bookings@brookfieldhotel.co.uk
www.brookfieldhotel.co.uk

AMANDA THOMAS, HOTEL MANAGER

RAYMOND HARRISON HAS WORKED IN THE KITCHENS AT THE BROOKFIELD HOTEL SINCE 1988, AND IN 1989 WAS APPOINTED HEAD CHEF. BEFORE THEN HE WORKED AS A CHEF DE PARTIE AT THE METROPOLE HOTEL IN BRIGHTON AND AS A JUNIOR SOUS CHEF AT THE METROPOLE CASINO IN LUTON.

THE BROOKFIELD HOTEL IS AN INDEPENDENT HOTEL OWNED BY THE GIBSON FAMILY SINCE 1973. THE RESTAURANT OVERLOOKS LANDSCAPED GARDENS WITH A WATERFALL FEATURE, AND OFFERS A WIDE CHOICE OF DISHES USING LOCALLY PRODUCED FRESH INGREDIENTS. THE HOTEL IS A POPULAR VENUE FOR RECEPTIONS, FUNCTIONS AND CONFERENCES, AND REGULARLY HOSTS THEMED EVENINGS. IT IS ALSO OPEN FOR LUNCH AND DINNER EVERY DAY, WITH AN EVER CHANGING SELECTION OF FINE WINES ON OFFER SUPPLIED THROUGH ALISTAIR GIBSON'S WHOLESALE WINE COMPANY, HERMITAGE CELLARS.

3-COURSE MENU

LOBSTER SALAD

SPRING LAMB FOR AN EARLY BARBECUE

RHUBARB CRUMBLE WITH CLOTTED CREAM

LOBSTER SALAD

Serves 4

10 Black Peppercorns
1 Celery Stalk
2 Bay Leaves
½ Onion
Red Wine Vinegar
1 x 1.3kg Fresh Lobster

DRESSING
½ Green Pepper
1 Small Red Onion (chopped)
1 Tomato (chopped)
1 Celery Stalk (peeled & chopped)
3 Pitted Green Olives
5 Tablespoons Red Wine Vinegar
5 Tablespoons Tomato Ketchup
1½ Cups Extra Virgin Olive Oil

SALAD
2 Bunches Watercress
1 Lemon
Mayonnaise

1. Using a large saucepan, bring to the boil enough water to cover the lobster, and add the peppercorns, celery, bay leaves, onion and wine vinegar.

2. Take the live lobster and place it in the boiling water. This should kill it instantly.

3. Cover with a lid, bring back to the boil and simmer for 15 minutes.

4. Remove from the heat and allow to cool in the liquid. If you do not have the time for this, then remove the lobster from the hot liquid and wrap it in cold wet towels and cool in a fridge.

5. When cold, cut the lobster lengthways into 2 pieces from the head to the tail.

6. Remove the white flesh running down the back of it.

7. You will see a grey coloured line ending in black at the tail – remove this carefully with the point of a knife and discard.

8. Slice the flesh, crack open the claws and the joints with the back of a heavy knife and remove all of the flesh. Cut into bite size pieces.

9. Wrap lobster meat in cling film and refrigerate until required.

DRESSING
1. Place all of the ingredients, other than the olive oil, into a food processor.

2. Process until very finely chopped.

3. Gradually add the olive oil until it is all emulsified, using the lowest speed.

4. Lightly season.

SALAD
1. Wash (using lightly salted water) and dry the watercress, and place into a bowl.

2. Add 4 spoonfuls of the dressing and mix through the watercress until you have a good coating.

3. Add the lobster, and mix well.

4. Divide the mixture amongst the plates, and garnish with a dollop of mayonnaise and a lemon wedge.

Do not try to cool off the cooked lobster under running water as you will wash away the delicate flavours.

Always an excuse for Champagne or top quality, no expense spared white Burgundy!

SPRING LAMB FOR AN EARLY BARBECUE

Serves 4

CHERMOULA SAUCE

2 Bunches Fresh Coriander
4 Teaspoons Ground Cumin
1-1½ Teaspoons Cayenne Pepper
4 Teaspoons Sweet Paprika
1 Roasted Red Pepper (peeled & de-seeded)
6 Cloves garlic
Juice 2 Lemons
60ml Extra Virgin Olive Oil
1 Tablespoon Coarse Sea Salt

4 Lamb Steaks (cut from chump of animal)
Jersey Royal Potatoes
Sprig Rosemary or Mint
500g Spinach Leaves
2 Bunches Watercress
1 Bunch Radishes
Crème Fraîche

1. To make the chermoula, put all of the ingredients, other than the pepper, into a food processor and blitz until almost smooth. Add the pepper and quickly pulse to give a little texture to the mixture.

2. An hour or so before eating, take the lamb steaks and rub over some of the chermoula sauce. Cover, and keep cool and leave to marinade, turning over at least once.

3. Cook the potatoes with salt and a sprig of rosemary or mint if preferred.

4. Mix together the washed and dried spinach and watercress with the washed and sliced radishes in a bowl. Add some of the chermoula and mix gently.

5. Place salad onto serving plate.

6. In the meantime, grill the lamb steaks to your liking, and place onto the salad.

7. Top with some more chermoula and a small dollop of crème fraîche, and a radish to finish.

8. Serve the potatoes separately with a little melted butter.

The chermoula will keep in an airtight container in the fridge for approximately 2 weeks.

Good value South American red here, Chilean Cabernet Sauvignon or Argentinean Malbec, anyway you haven't got much money left after the lobster!

RHUBARB CRUMBLE WITH CLOTTED CREAM

Serves 4

5 Stalks Forced Rhubarb
2 Tablespoons White Wine
75g Caster Sugar
Pinch Mixed Spice
175g Plain Flour
100g Butter (softened)
Good Pinch Ground Cardamom
50g Brown Sugar
25g Raisins (chopped)
25g Hazelnuts (toasted & chopped)
Clotted Cream

Pre-heat oven to 180C/350F/Gas 4

1. Wash and chop the rhubarb, and place into a stainless steel pot with the wine, caster sugar, and mixed spice.

2. Cook until tender, and allow to cool.

3. Put the cooked rhubarb into a large, or individual, serving dish.

4. Rub together the flour and butter with the cardamom until a fine breadcrumb consistency is obtained.

5. Add the brown sugar, chopped raisins and chopped hazelnuts.

6. Place the mixture onto the rhubarb, and bake in the pre-heated oven for 20-25 minutes.

7. Serve with clotted cream.

Has to be a sweet, exotic Riesling from almost anywhere, try a New Zealand example if you can find one.

EMSWORTH SLIPPER SAILING CLUB

EMSWORTH SLIPPER SAILING CLUB
THE QUAY MILL
THE QUAY
SOUTH STREET
EMSWORTH
PO10 7EG
T. 01243 372523

e. secretary@emsworthslippersc.org.uk
www.emsworthslippersc.org.uk

COMMODORE: JULIAN MANDIWALL

EMSWORTH SLIPPER SAILING CLUB HAS ITS ROOTS DATING BACK TO 1912 WHEN A GROUP OF LOCAL BUSINESSMEN WHO KEPT BOATS ON THE MUD ADJACENT TO EMSWORTH SHIPYARD FORMED THE EMSWORTH SAILING COMMITTEE AND ORGANISED RACES BETWEEN LOCAL BOATS. RACING CEASED AT THE OUTBREAK OF WAR IN 1914 UNTIL 1919 WHEN THE COMMITTEE RESUMED ACTIVITIES. AT THE END OF 1921 A GENERAL MEETING WAS CALLED AT THE SHIP INN, CHAIRED BY THE LANDLORD, CHARLIE WINGHAM AND A SAILING CLUB WAS FORMED, THE EMSWORTH MUD SLIPPERS SAILING CLUB. THE FIRST PRESIDENT AND COMMODORE ELECTED WAS MR EW KINNELL, OWNER OF THE BREWERY, KINNELL & HARTLEY SITUATED BEHIND THE BLUE BELL INN IN SOUTH STREET. DURING 1924 THE NAME WAS CHANGED TO EMSWORTH SLIPPER SAILING CLUB. HOWEVER, INTEREST WANED UNTIL IN 1933 THE NAME BECAME EMSWORTH SLIPPER SAILING AND MOTOR BOAT CLUB AND RACING WAS RESUMED. IN 1948 THE CLUB USED A ROOM AT THE COMMUNITY CENTRE, WHICH WAS SITUATED OVER THE THEN CO-OP BUILDING AND WAS USED BY MEMBERS UNTIL IN 1958 THEY RENTED THE BOAT STORE IN KING STREET WHICH PROVIDED NOT ONLY A BASE FOR STORAGE BUT ALSO A CLUB ROOM. THE SEARCH FOR OWNED PREMISES CONTINUED, AND IN 1963 THE CLUB SUC-CESSFULLY PURCHASED THE ANCHOR PUB (NOW BETTER KNOWN AS RESTAURANT 36 ON THE QUAY) FOR THE SUM OF £10,000. BUT TIME MOVES ON AND A BIGGER CLUB HOUSE WAS NECESSARY. SO, IN 1977 DISCUSSIONS BEGAN TO PURCHASE THE MILL AND THE MALTHOUSE – THE PRESENT HOME OF THE CLUB – AND SELL THE ANCHOR. ALL OF WHICH DID TAKE PLACE, AND WORK BEGAN TO TURN THE QUAY MILL FROM A DERELICT SHELL INTO WHAT IT IS TODAY.

(TAKEN FROM 'IN SEARCH OF A SLIPPER: TALES FROM THE BAR' BY CLIVE FROST, ESSC)

3-COURSE MENU

AVOCADO, BACON AND STILTON SALAD

BREAST OF CHICKEN WITH ROSTI POTATOES, AND A ROAST RED PEPPER AND MANGO SALSA

STRAWBERRY HEARTS

BEV & MARK WHEELER OPERATE THEIR OWN CATERING BUSINESS, PROVIDING FOOD FOR WEDDINGS, FUNCTIONS AND PARTIES. THEY MET WHILST WORKING IN THE KITCHENS AT AMBERLEY CASTLE, WHERE BEV WAS THE PASTRY CHEF IN CHARGE OF A SECTION AND MARK WAS CHEF-DE-PARTIE. THEY BOTH HAVE A PASSION FOR FOOD AND COOKING AND TOOK THE DECISION TO START THEIR OWN BUSINESS IN 1996. EVERY WEEKEND, AND FOR SPECIAL CLUB OCCASIONS, THEY CAN BE FOUND AT ESSC COOKING MEALS FOR LUNCH AND DINNER FUNCTIONS.

BEV & MARK WHEELER
T. 023 9223 2809

AVOCADO, BACON AND STILTON SALAD

Serves 4

4 Rashers Streaky Bacon or Pancetta
2 Dessertspoons Olive Oil
1 Dessertspoon Balsamic Vinegar
1 Teaspoon Dijon Mustard
2 Cloves garlic
½ Dessertspoon Caster Sugar
Salt & Pepper
2 Small Ripe Avocados
75g Stilton Cheese
4 Tomatoes
½ Packet Fresh Chives
Mixed Salad Leaves
2 Dessertspoons French Dressing
Garlic Croutons

1. Finely shred the bacon and gently fry in a pan until crisp.

2. Use a bowl to whisk together the olive oil, balsamic vinegar, mustard, crushed garlic, sugar and salt and pepper.

3. Peel and slice the avocados, crumble the stilton cheese and peel, de-seed and chop the tomatoes. Add together in a bowl (retaining some of the tomatoes for later).

4. Add the chopped chives (retain some for later), and the cooked bacon and carefully mix together. Check the seasoning.

5. Lightly oil 4 ramekins and line with cling film.

6. Divide the mixture into the ramekins and compress down.

7. Toss the salad leaves in the French dressing.

8. Turn out the ramekins onto plates and arrange the salad leaves around the outer edge.

9. Sprinkle the garlic croutons over the leaves, and place the remaining chopped tomatoes and chives on top of the avocado mix.

Lots of flavours here, dry white with some acidity would be best, Sancerre or a dry German Riesling from the Pfalz.

BREAST OF CHICKEN WITH ROSTI POTATOES AND A ROAST RED PEPPER AND MANGO SALSA

Serves 4

2 Red Peppers
750g Peeled Potatoes
Butter
1 Lime
2 Teaspoons Sugar
3 Cloves Garlic
4 Dessertspoons Olive Oil
1 Dessertspoon Ground Coriander
2 Teaspoons Tomato Puree
1 Large Mango
4 Tomatoes (de-seeded & chopped)
½ Spanish Onion (finely diced)
1 Packet Fresh Coriander
1 Red Chilli Pepper
4 Skinned Chicken Breasts

BASKETS
4 Flour Tortillas
1 Egg (beaten)

1. Place the 2 peppers onto an oven tray and cook in a hot oven until almost black. Allow to cool slightly before peeling.

2. Grate the peeled potatoes, and mix in salt and pepper.

3. Put a large buttered frying pan over medium heat. Add the potatoes and fry, adding butter to the edges as required.

4. When browned, flip over using a plate on the top of the pan, then slide the potato back into the pan on the other side. When almost cooked, turn down the heat to a low setting.

5. To make the salsa, juice the lime into a pan, add the sugar and whisk until dissolved.

6. Add the chopped garlic, olive oil, ground coriander, tomato purée and salt and pepper and whisk together.

7. Add the peeled and chopped mango, the skinned, de-seeded and chopped tomatoes, finely diced onion, chopped fresh coriander (retain 1/3rd un-chopped), and skinned de-seeded roasted chopped red pepper, finely chopped chilli pepper. Mix and check for seasoning.

8. In the meantime, fry the skinned chicken breasts in a hot frying pan on both sides until cooked through.

9. Place the pan of salsa onto the heat and bring to a gentle simmer. Turn off the heat.

10. Divide the rosti into 12 rounds using a round cutter. Place onto plates.

11. Cut each piece of chicken into 6. Present on plate and garnish with mango.

12. Spoon salsa into each tortilla basket, and garnish with coriander.

13. Serve with a green salad.

The salsa can be made well in advance to allow the flavours to infuse and stored in the fridge until required.

Add more chilli to the salsa for a hotter taste.

The rosti potatoes can be made 1 hour in advance and warmed through in an oven when required.

For roasted peppers, the blacker the better. The longer they're in the oven, the sweeter they will become. Allow to cool slightly before peeling.

BASKETS

*Pre-heat oven to
200C/400F/Gas 6*

1. Cut 1 large round
   and 12 small
   rounds out of each
   tortilla.

2. Brush with
   beaten egg.

3. Using an oiled cap
   dish, or ramekins,
   place the large
   round on the
   bottom and
   overlap the small
   rounds to form the
   sides.

4. Cook in the
   pre-heated oven
   for 10 minutes.

Young, fruity red,
Chilean Merlot or
mid range
Californian
Merlot.

STRAWBERRY HEARTS   Serves 2

TULIP PASTE
85g (3oz) Plain Flour
85g (3oz) Sugar
55g (2oz) Egg Whites
55g (2oz) Melted Butter

STRAWBERRY COULIS
110g (4oz) Sugar
110g (4oz) Puréed Strawberries

FILLING
110g (4oz) Sliced Strawberries
250ml (½pt) Whipped Cream

WILL ALSO NEED
Heart Shaped Stencil
  (cut out of a plastic lid)
Plastic Scraper or Spatula
Icing Sugar
Strawberries (to garnish)

1. Make the tulip paste by mixing the flour, sugar and egg whites in a bowl. At the last minute, add the melted butter. Leave the mixture to rest for at least 4 hours, or overnight, in a fridge.

2. When ready to make the heart shapes, place a buttered baking sheet into a freezer for 5 minutes to chill.

3. Take your heart shape stencil and scraper, and carefully add the paste over the stencil and scrape away excess to leave the shape on the cold baking tray. You will need 3 hearts per person.

4. Return tray to freezer to chill for 5 minutes – this will prevent the mixture running during the cooking process.

5. Meanwhile, pre-heat the oven to 200C/400F/Gas 6.

6. Cook the heart biscuits in the pre-heated oven for 5 minutes, turning them over every minute.

7. Allow to cool on a cooling tray.

8. Dust 1 heart per person with icing sugar, and using a hot knife or skewer score a lattice design onto the heart.

9. Make the strawberry coulis by boiling the sugar with enough water to cover, in a pan to make the syrup (104ºC). The syrup will bubble more slowly when it is ready.

10. Add the syrup to the puréed strawberries whilst hot. Chill the mixture.

11. Make the filling by adding the sliced strawberries (retain the best ones to garnish the hearts) and 1 tablespoon of the coulis to the whipped cream. Chill the mixture.

12. Decorate the plates with the remaining coulis, using a paint brush to create brush strokes and splatters.

13. Secure a heart in the centre of the plate with a blob of cream underneath.

14. Top with filling 3cm (1inch) thick. Repeat.

15. Top with the decorated heart and garnish with strawberries.

Can make the hearts the day before and store in airtight container.

If not all of the hearts are perfect when cooked, use these on the bottom layers where they will not be seen.

Always choose the garnish strawberries first, so that the most perfect are used.

Use an ice cream container lid to cut the heart stencil template (or any other shapes).

It may not be fashionable, but Asti Spumante would be great with this.

HEIDI'S SWISS PATISSERIE

HEIDI'S SWISS PATISSERIE
37 HIGH STREET
EMSWORTH
PO10 7AL
T. 01243 376814

e. heidis.patisserie@virgin.net

ERNST STRASSMANN & HEIDI ELLIOTT

VICKY FISHER ORIGINALLY TRAINED AS A MEN'S BARBER. HER HUSBAND'S JOB THEN TOOK THEM OVERSEAS FOR A FEW YEARS. WHEN THEY RETURNED, SHE WORKED AS A SUPERVISOR IN ONE STOP AND THEN COST CUTTER. THREE YEARS AGO, VICKY DECIDED TO HAVE A CHANGE IN CAREER AND BECAME A COOK AT HEIDI'S. FOR THE PAST 18 MONTHS SHE HAS BEEN HAPPILY MANAGING THE SHOP IN EMSWORTH, AND IS STILL INVOLVED WITH COOKING LIGHT SNACKS AND LUNCHES.

HEIDI'S SWISS PATISSERIE IS A FAMILY BUSINESS ESTABLISHED IN 1969, OWNED BY HEIDI ELLIOTT AND HER FATHER, ERNST STRASSMANN. THE MAIN BAKERY AT HAYLING ISLAND PRODUCES THE VARIETY OF BREADS (BRITISH AND CONTINENTAL) AND CONFECTIONARY SOLD THROUGH THE EIGHT PATISSERIES LOCATED IN THE AREA. EACH SHOP ALSO HAS A COFFEE LOUNGE SERVING HOT AND COLD SNACKS.

SMOKED MACKEREL TOAST

Heidi's recommend using Ninecorn bread for added taste and texture.

Serves 2 (as a snack)
or 4 (as a starter)

100g Smoked Mackerel Fillets
125g Natural Yoghurt
1 Tablespoon Creamed
  Horseradish Sauce
½ Teaspoon Lemon Juice
Seasoning
4 Slices of Bread
1 Spring Onion (chopped)
1 Tomato (sliced)

1. Skin the mackerel fillets and discard any small bones.

2. Mash the fillets in a bowl.

3. Add the natural yoghurt and creamed horseradish to the mashed mackerel.

4. Add the lemon juice and seasoning to the mixture, and blend ingredients together using a fork.

5. Toast the slices of bread, and spread the paté onto the hot toast.

6. Top with a sprinkling of the chopped spring onions and slices of tomato.

Manzanilla Sherry or a dry Vinho Verde from Portugal.

EASTER BISCUITS

Makes approximately 25

350g Plain Flour
Large Pinch Salt
2 Level Teaspoons Mixed Spice
150g Butter
100g Caster Sugar
75g Currants
Finely Grated Rind 1 Lemon
1 Egg (beaten)
1 Tablespoon Milk

Vin Santo from Tuscany or a rich Malmsey Madeira.

Pre-heat oven to 190C/375F/Gas 5

1. Sift the flour, salt and mixed spice into a bowl.

2. Rub in the butter, then add the sugar, currants and lemon rind.

3. Stir the mixture.

4. Mix in the beaten egg and milk to make a firm dough.

5. Roll out to approximately 5mm thickness.

6. Cut out the biscuits using a 7.5cm (3-inch) fluted cutter.

7. Transfer to lightly greased baking sheets on a tray.

8. Bake in the pre-heated oven for 10–12 minutes.

9. Allow to cool on a wire rack.

QUEEN STREET

VICTORIA ROAD

TOWER STREET

BRIDGEFOOT PATH

THE QUEEN STREET GREENHOUSE

JANIS & JERRY WITH SUE HINGSTON, JACQUI JOOSTEN & HALINKA CHASTON

THE QUEEN STREET GREENHOUSE
4-6 QUEEN STREET
EMSWORTH
PO10 7BL
T. 01243 376414

THE QUEEN STREET GREENHOUSE IS SITUATED JUST AROUND THE CORNER FROM THE SQUARE, AND AS ITS NAME SUGGESTS, AT THE TOP OF QUEEN STREET. THE DOUBLE-FRONTED SHOP IS FORMED FROM TWO LISTED GEORGIAN BUILDINGS, AND WAS PREVIOUSLY A HARDWARE STORE AND, MORE RECENTLY, A YACHT CHANDLERS. JANIS AND JEREMY OPENED THEIR BUSINESS IN JULY 2000, SELLING FRESH FLOWERS, PLANTS, VASES AND TERRACOTTA POTS. IN ADDITION, THEY PROVIDE ARRANGEMENTS FOR LOCAL BUSINESSES, WEDDING DESIGNS AND BOUQUETS FOR ALL AND SUNDRY.

JANIS & JEREMY ESCAPED FROM TEACHING IN THE 1980'S TO OPEN THEIR FIRST SHOP THE GREENHOUSE IN GREENWICH, LONDON. AFTER 12 SUCCESSFUL YEARS RUNNING THIS BUSINESS, THEY DECIDED TO LEAVE THE BUSY CITY LIFE BEHIND AND MOVED TO BOSHAM. THEY STARTED THE QUEEN STREET GREENHOUSE WHERE THEY AND THEIR STAFF CONTINUE TO OFFER AN INDIVIDUAL AND FRIENDLY SERVICE.

A SPRING ARRANGEMENT FOR THE DINING TABLE

YOU WILL NEED
Oasis Ring
Foliage & Flowers
Miniature Terracotta Pots
Small Sticks
Moss
Decorated Eggs (optional)

1. First thoroughly soak the oasis ring.

2. Cover with the foliage.

3. Insert flowers into the oasis in natural groupings
   (see fig. 3-6).

4. Fix the terracotta pots into position by pushing small sticks
   through the drainage hole and into the oasis.

5. Fill the pots with moss or foliage and flowers to hide the
   stick.

6. Continue to work around the ring, filling any gaps with
   flowers.

7. For an Easter table decoration, try adding a few decorated
   eggs to the arrangement.

TIPS FOR KEEPING YOUR FLOWERS FRESH

1. Always use a clean vase – soak in a bleach solution
   after use to remove any bacteria.

2. Use flower food, making sure that the powder is
   properly dissolved before adding flowers.

3. Cut the stems of foliage and flowers as they are
   arranged – make a clean diagonal cut. Strip away any
   leaves that will be below the water line.

4. Always place your flowers in the coolest place and
   never in direct sunlight.

5. Change the water as often as you can –
   daily if possible.

A SIMPLE IDEA FOR A TABLE DISPLAY IS TO MAKE A COLLECTION OF SMALL VASES AND TEA-LIGHTS. USE A SINGLE STEM IN EACH VASE FOR A STUNNING EFFECT.

TESSA'S

TESSA IS BASED IN HOLLYBANK LANE WHICH LEADS UP TO THE WOODS

TESSA SMITH

3-COURSE MENU

FRIED CHEESE PUFFS

STUFFED FILLETS OF FLOUNDER IN WHITE WINE

GINGERLY RHUBARB

TESSA'S
34 HOLLYBANK LANE
EMSWORTH
PO10 7UE
T. 01243 375464

TESSA'S COMPANY HAS BEEN ESTABLISHED IN EMSWORTH FOR MORE THAN 30 YEARS, PROVIDING CATERING FOR PRIVATE FUNCTIONS SUCH AS WEDDINGS, FUNERALS, AND PARTIES OF ALL KINDS. SINCE 1960, OTHER THAN FIVE YEARS' TRAINING AND PRACTICE FOR GENERAL NURSING SRN AND MIDWIFERY, TESSA SMITH HAS BEEN INVOLVED IN THE FOOD BUSINESS. HER WORK IN EMSWORTH BEGAN ON A SMALL SCALE, MAKING WEDDING AND ANNIVERSARY CAKES AND ESCALATED TO PROVIDING CATERING FOR CORPORATE COMPANIES. SHE CONTINUES TO PROVIDE A CATERING SERVICE, BUT ON A MUCH SMALLER SCALE.

FRIED CHEESE PUFFS

(A DELECTABLE HOT HORS-D'OEUVRE)

Serves 4

2 Large Egg Whites (lightly beaten)
125g Grated Swiss Cheese
Fine Breadcrumbs
Oil (for frying)

1. Make a paste of the beaten egg whites mixed with the cheese.

2. Form the paste into small balls, no bigger than marbles.

3. Roll these in the breadcrumbs.

4. Fry in deep, very hot oil for a few seconds until golden brown. Do not fry too many at one time – whilst cooking they puff up.

5. Drain off the excess oil on kitchen paper.

6. Serve whilst hot and garnish with a sprig of watercress or fried parsley, or on a bed of baby salad leaves drizzled with French dressing.

The pre-cooked cheese balls can be stored in the fridge for a few hours until required.

Tasty dry white - Australian Semillon or South African Chenin Blanc.

STUFFED FILLETS OF FLOUNDER IN WHITE WINE

Serves 4

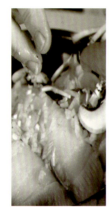

8 Small/Medium Flounder Fillets
170g Fresh Prawns (peeled)
1 Cup Dry White Wine
2 Shallots (finely chopped)
125g Mushrooms (sliced)
Butter
2 Large Egg Yolks
½ Small Cup Double Cream

Pre-heat oven to 190C/375F/Gas 5

1. Roll the fish fillets skin side up with the prawns inside.

2. Place into a shallow baking dish, and add the white wine.

3. Sprinkle the fish with salt and freshly ground black pepper, and the chopped shallots and mushrooms.

4. Dot the fish with butter and bake in the pre-heated oven for 20 minutes until the fish is cooked but still firm.

5. Drain off the liquid into a saucepan (put the fish to one side and keep warm) and simmer to reduce to approximately 1-1½ cups. Add any spare prawns.

6. Mix the egg yolks with the cream and carefully stir into the reduced fish stock. Gently simmer until thickened, but do not allow the sauce to curdle.

7. Season as required.

8. Place the fish onto a serving dish and pour over the sauce.

9. Garnish with a sprig of watercress or parsley and a twist of lemon.

If using frozen prawns, ensure that they are thoroughly de-frosted before use.

Some character needed here, a Marsanne or Viognier from the Midi.

GINGERLY RHUBARB

Serves 6-8

900g Fresh Rhubarb
1 Teaspoon Fresh Ginger (grated)
100g Caster Sugar
1 Teaspoon Grated Orange Peel
2 or 3 Leaves Gelatin
Small Carton Double Cream

Pre-heat oven to 190C/375F/Gas 5

1. Wash and cut the rhubarb into 3cm lengths and place into an ovenproof dish with the ginger, sugar and orange.

2. Cover and cook in the pre-heated oven for approximately 20-30 minutes until well cooked.

3. Drain the rhubarb into a colander and reserve the juice. Leave to cool.

4. Soak the gelatin in cold water until soft. Then squeeze out the excess water.

5. Heat a small amount of the juice reserved from the rhubarb and stir in the gelatin until dissolved.

6. Add the gelatin mixture to the rest of the juice.

7. Pour half of this mixture into the bottom of the serving glasses and leave to set in the fridge – this will take approximately 2 hours.

8. Meanwhile add the rest of the juice to ¾ of the cooked rhubarb. Spoon this over the top of the set juice in the glass, and return to the fridge.

9. Whisk the cream until thick, then blend 2 tablespoons of the cream with the remaining rhubarb.

10. Put a layer of the cream and rhubarb mix into the glasses.

11. With the remaining whipped cream, pipe a rosette on the top of each glass and garnish with a little crystalised or stem ginger and a few strands of orange peel.

Use 4 sheets gelatin to each 500ml juice.

This can also be made into a terrine. Line a loaf tin with clingwrap, pour all the juice and gelatin into the tin until set. Then add the rhubarb and juice mixture. Refrigerate until set. Turn out onto a serving plate and garnish with the rest of the rhubarb and whipped cream.

Sweet Riesling from Alsace if you can afford it, if not try the New World.

RA TIER & SON

RA TIER & SON
9 HIGH STREET
EMSWORTH
PO10 7AQ
T. 01243 372447

JULIE
&
STEPHEN
TIER

JOSIE & RAY TIER WITH THEIR DAUGHTERS,
DEBBIE KEMISH & SARAH LONG,
& SON, STEVE

RA TIER & SON IS A LONG-ESTABLISHED FAMILY RUN GREENGROCER
AND FLORIST OWNED BY THE TIER FAMILY SINCE 1966. THEY ARE AN OLD
ESTABLISHED EMSWORTH FAMILY, AND WHILST THE SHOP IS OWNED BY JOSIE AND
RAY, THEIR DAUGHTERS HAVE RUN THE BUSINESS SINCE THEIR PARENTS'
RETIREMENT. IT IS SITUATED IN A LISTED BUILDING DATING BACK TO 1789.

BOMBAY POTATOES

Serves 4 (as a side dish)

Julie prefers the taste from Co-op own brand of curry powder

3 Tablespoons Vegetable Oil
1 Teaspoon Mustard Seeds
1 Medium Onion (finely chopped)
2 Cloves Garlic (crushed)
2 Tablespoons Mild Curry Powder
450g Cooked New Potatoes (cubed)
Seasoning

1. Heat the oil and add the mustard seeds and allow to 'pop'.

2. Add the onion and garlic and fry until cooked.

3. Add the curry powder and gently fry for 2 minutes.

4. Add the cooked potatoes and seasoning to taste.

5. Continue to fry until potatoes have browned.

Some curry overtones here, so fairly neutral white such as Italian Pinot Grigio or Soave.

SPICY VEGETABLE STIR FRY

Serves 4

5-6 New Potatoes (thinly sliced)
1 Medium Red Onion (finely sliced)
Bunch Spring Onions (sliced diagonally)
1 Red Pepper (thinly sliced lengthways)
1 Red Chilli (de-seeded & finely diced)
2 Cloves Garlic (thinly sliced)
1 Pack Mangetout
1 Pack Baby Sweetcorn
  (halved lengthways)
125g Button Mushrooms (thinly sliced)
1 Small Courgette (sliced in strips,
  leaving the centre)
1 Medium Carrot
  (thinly sliced – leaving centre)
1 Small Parsnip
  (thinly sliced – leaving centre)
1 Pack Bean Sprouts
2 Tablespoons Olive Oil
1 Dessertspoon Light Soya Sauce
1 Dessertspoon Dark Soya Sauce
1 Tablespoon Worcestershire Sauce
2 Packs Singapore Curry Sauce
  (Blue Dragon)
300g Ready to Wok Noodles

1. Wash and prepare all of the vegetables before starting to cook.

2. Heat the oil in a wok or large frying pan, and add seasoning.

3. Add both soya sauces and the Worcestershire sauce and heat until hot.

4. Add the potatoes and cook for 4 minutes.

5. Add the onion, spring onions, pepper, chilli and garlic and cook for 3 minutes.

6. Add the mangetout, mushrooms and sweetcorn and cook for a further 5 minutes.

7. Add the remaining vegetables and the stir fry sauce and cook for 2 minutes.

8. Add the noodles and cook until warmed through.

Use a mandolin or potato peeler to thinly slice the vegetables.

You can use any combination of vegetables or stir fry sauce flavours.

You can add cooked prawns to the mixture at the point of cooking the noodles.

You can use diced chicken breast added with the potatoes.

If the mixture sticks to the pan, add a splash of boiling water.

Sancerre, Sauvignon de St-Bris or a zesty English Sevyal Blanc.

Then and Now

The building in early 1900's

Tier's building in 2004

SUMMER

JUNE

FRIENDS OF HOLLYBANK WOODS

ALLIED TROOPS WERE BILLETED IN THESE AND
NEARBY WOODS PRIOR TO TAKING PART IN THE
D-DAY LANDINGS OF 6TH JUNE 1944.

THIS PLAQUE COMMEMORATES THE 60TH ANNIVERSARY
OF THAT EVENT

July

AUGUST

36 ON THE QUAY (RESTAURANT WITH ROOMS)

36 ON THE QUAY
(RESTAURANT WITH ROOMS)
47 SOUTH STREET
EMSWORTH
PO10 7EG
T. 01243 375592

e. 36@onthequay.plus.com
www.36onthequay.co.uk

RAMON & KAREN FARTHING
WITH THEIR DAUGHTER, LEILA

36 ON THE QUAY (RESTAURANT WITH ROOMS) IS IN A 17TH
CENTURY LISTED BUILDING ON THE QUAY FRONT WITH STUNNING VIEWS ACROSS THE
PICTURESQUE HARBOUR. THE BUILDING HAS SEEN A NUMBER OF USES DURING ITS
TIME: IN 1820 IT WAS FIRST RECORDED AS A PUBLIC HOUSE – THE ANCHOR; DUR-
ING 1878 THE PUB PREMISES WAS ALSO USED AS THE CUSTOMS HOUSE. DURING
1926 THE PUB CLOSED, AND DURING THE 1950S THE BUILDING, ALONG WITH
OTHERS AT THE BOTTOM OF SOUTH STREET, WAS DUE TO BE DEMOLISHED. LUCKILY
FOR EMSWORTH NONE OF THIS HAPPENED, AND DURING 1963 THE
BUILDING BECAME THE HOME OF THE NOW EMSWORTH SLIPPER SAILING CLUB.
KAREN AND RAMON FARTHING TOOK OVER THE RESTAURANT IN 1996, AND HAVE,
EACH YEAR, BEEN AWARDED A MICHELIN STAR IN ADDITION TO OTHER RENOWNED
FOOD AWARDS. THIS FRIENDLY AND RELAXING, YET EFFICIENT, RESTAURANT IS RATED
IN THE TOP 10% OF UK RESTAURANTS, SERVING FOOD WHICH IS MODERN BRITISH,
WITH A EUROPEAN INFLUENCE. DURING 2003 KAREN AND RAMON OPENED 4
EN-SUITE ROOMS ON THE FIRST FLOOR OF THE RESTAURANT, AND DURING 2004 A
SELF-CONTAINED 1-BEDROOM COTTAGE ACROSS THE ROAD WAS ADDED.

RAMON FARTHING AND WITH HIS WIFE KAREN HAVE SPENT ALL OF THEIR WORKING LIVES FOLLOWING THEIR CAREERS IN THE CATERING INDUSTRY, WORKING AT MANY PRESTIGIOUS RESTAURANTS AROUND THE COUNTRY. THEY MET WHILST BOTH WERE WORKING AS CHEFS AT THE SAME ESTABLISHMENT. RAMON HAS WORKED AT ALTHORP HOUSE AS PERSONAL CHEF TO EARL AND COUNTESS SPENCER. HOWEVER, IT WAS WHILST WORKING AS HEAD CHEF AT CALCOT MANOR THAT HE BECAME ONE OF THE YOUNGEST TO RECEIVE A MICHELIN STAR. SINCE THEN HE HAS CONTINUED TO WIN THIS ACCOLADE, AT HARVEYS RESTAURANT AND OF COURSE AT HIS OWN IN EMSWORTH. KAREN BEGAN HER CAREER IN THE KITCHENS AS A COMMIS CHEF, THEN PASTRY CHEF AND CHEF DE PARTIE, BUT SHE HAS NOW TAKEN ON THE ROLE OF RUNNING THE FRONT OF HOUSE, AND THE ROOMS, AT THEIR OWN RESTAURANT.

3-COURSE MENU

CRISP VEAL SWEETBREADS IN HAZELNUT OIL WITH RED ONIONS, GIROLLE MUSHROOMS AND WILTED SPINACH LEAVES

OR

BONED QUAIL WITH PICKLED ENOKI MUSHROOMS, POACHED PRUNES WITH BALSAMIC & OLIVE OIL DRESSING

MEDALLIONS OF MONKFISH WITH ASPARAGUS, BABY FENNEL AND SAFFRON POTATOES COMPLEMENTED BY A SHALLOT, TOMATO BUTTER NAGE

PRUNE AND ARMAGNAC ICE CREAM WITH SPICE BISCUITS AND A FRAGRANT TEA AND PRUNE SYRUP

GARY PEARCE , JUNIOR SOUS CHEF

THE 36 KITCHEN BRIGADE

CRISP VEAL SWEETBREADS IN HAZELNUT OIL WITH RED ONIONS, GIROLLE MUSHROOMS AND WILTED SPINACH LEAVES   ALL-IN-ONE PAN COOKING   *Serves 4*

 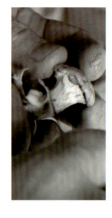    

1kg Veal Sweetbreads
White Wine Vinegar
300ml White Wine
300ml Chicken Stock with
  ½ Onion
  1 Carrot
  1 Leek
  2 Cloves Garlic
200g Girolle Mushrooms (or similar)
2 Red Onions
50ml Hazelnut Oil
25ml Olive Oil
Lemon Juice
200g Baby Spinach Leaves
125ml Double Cream
55g Butter (cubed)

1. Blanche the sweetbreads in a small amount of vinegar and white wine with salt by simmering for 3-4 minutes. Remove from the pan and refresh in iced water.
2. Put the sweetbreads into chicken stock with the fresh vegetables and braise for 30 minutes until tender.
3. Allow to cool in the stock, and rest overnight in a fridge.
4. The next day, remove all of the fat, membrane and sinew until left with the lean nugget. Cut these into 3 or 4 small chunks.
5. Prepare the girolle mushrooms by scraping down to the stalks with a small knife, and rinse quickly in cold water to remove any debris. Dry on kitchen towel.
6. Prepare the onions by peeling down the outside 2 layers until left with the tender inner part. Chop in half and square off the edges, then cut into 3 lengthways pieces and remove the inner core. Trim and cut into squares.
7. Take a medium sized pan and heat (moderate) the hazelnut oil and olive oil. Add the onions (they will seal as they hit the oil), and cover with a lid to allow them to sweat down slowly for a few minutes.
8. Add a little salt and pepper, then remove the onions and reserve.
9. Add a little more hazelnut oil to the pan over a moderate heat and then add the mushrooms to seal very quickly in the oil. Add a little more salt and pepper and a drop of lemon juice. Remove from the pan and reserve.
10. Wipe out the pan with a piece of kitchen towel and add a little olive oil and heat until hot.
11. Lightly season the sweetbreads with salt and pepper and seal on all sides in the hot oil until crisp on all of the edges – this should take approximately 10 minutes. You may need to add a little more oil. The sweetbreads will now be crisp and browned on all sides, but remain soft in the centre.

12. Remove the stalks from the baby spinach leaves, rinse in cold water and dry on kitchen towel.
13. Remove the sweetbreads from the pan and put to one side.
14. A sediment will be left in the bottom of the pan. Pour away excess fat from this, then put the pan back onto the stove and add 100ml white wine and use a spatula to scrape the sediment from the bottom and side of the pan.
15. Reduce the liquid until it is a light syrup consistency.
16. Add 250ml of chicken stock to the wine syrup in the pan and reduce by half.
17. Then add 125ml double cream while whisking and gently simmer until reduced to a thicker consistency – by about 1/3rd.
18. Pour into the pan the drained oil from the 'rested' sweet-breads, add salt and pepper.
19. Add the cubed butter and whisk into the sauce, over heat, until smooth and simmering.
20. Pass the sauce through a sieve into a clean jug and keep warm.
21. Now rinse the pan and dry, return to heat, add a small amount of hazelnut oil and add the sweetbreads to the hot oil then turn to warm through (approximately 1 minute).
22. Add the onions and the mushrooms plus the spinach leaves and toss and turn for 30 seconds until the spinach leaves wilt in the pan (the whole process should not take more than 2 minutes).
23. Arrange on a dish, bring the sauce back to a gentle simmer and pour around all the other finished ingredients. Serve immediately.

Ramon prefers Dutch sweet-breads for flavour and texture.

You can substitute calves liver or kidneys if you do not like sweetbreads, which come from around the heart, throat, or pancreas of the animal. Heart variety are the best.

For a vegetarian dish, leave out the meat and add other vegetables, such as artichokes or aubergines.

A grand quite rich dish so Alsace Grand Cru Pinot Gris or maybe a Condrieu from the Rhone.

BONED QUAIL WITH PICKLED ENOKI MUSHROOMS, POACHED PRUNES
FINISHED WITH BALSAMIC AND OLIVE OIL DRESSING

Serves 4

 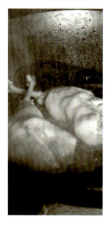   

8 Prunes d'Agen
110g Sugar
2 Teabags
200ml Water
150ml Extra Virgin Olive Oil
100ml White Wine Vinegar
2 Sprigs Thyme
Maldon Salt
Black Pepper
2 x 100g Packs Enoki Mushrooms
4 Quail (breasts & legs removed)
110g Butter
8 Small Shallots
4 Quail Eggs

DRESSING
100ml Good Balsamic Vinegar
150ml Extra Virgin Olive Oil
Juice ½ Lemon
Maldon Salt & Pepper

1. Soak the prunes overnight in a warm tea syrup, made from the sugar, teabags and water simmered for 5 minutes.
2. Warm half of the olive oil and the vinegar together in a stainless steel pan. Add the thyme, salt and pepper. Cut the bottoms from the enoki mushrooms, rinse, drain and add to the vinegar mixture and stir together for 1 minute. Remove from heat and allow to cool in the pan.
3. Use an ovenproof sauté pan to seal the quail legs in a little butter for a few minutes. Peel the shallots and place in the pan with the legs. Put the pan into a low to moderate oven until the legs are tender (this prevents over colouring the legs and shallots).
4. When the legs are tender, remove from the pan and allow to rest. Sprinkle a little sugar over the shallots and add a little more butter and gently allow to colour on the stove until tender (on a very low heat).
5. Take a clean pan and heat a little butter and oil. Place the quail breasts in the pan, skin side first, and allow to cook gently on both sides until just pink.
6. When the breasts are cooked, leave to rest with the legs. Then remove the wing bones from the breast and twist the bottom thigh bone out of the leg, leaving only the drumstick bone intact.
7. Remove the prunes from the syrup, drain and add to the shallot pan. Allow to warm through with the shallots for a few minutes. Remove and drain through a sieve.
8. Warm the enoki again in the original pan, then place in the sieve with the prunes and shallots. Place a round or oval cutter on the plates, and fill with a good mix of the ingredients.
9. Heat the quail legs and breasts in an oven for a few minutes (do not overcook). While they are warming, place a small frying pan with a little oil on the stove on a moderate heat. Use a sharp knife to crack open the quail eggs and fry as a normal egg, keeping them a little runny.
10. When breasts and legs are ready, place breasts first onto prune, shallot, mushrooms. Remove the cutter, and arrange the legs on the breasts. Take a small pastry cutter, cut carefully around the eggs and lift gently on top of the legs. Spoon dressing all around and serve.

DRESSING
1. Place the balsamic vinegar, olive oil and lemon juice in a pan with salt and pepper to taste.
2. Warm gently whilst stirring gently with a teaspoon.

The dressing is meant to have a separated appearance, so don't whisk it.

Get your butcher to remove the breasts and legs if you are not confident to do this.

Red Burgundy can be a perfect match with quail, but try also New Zealand South Island Pinot Noir. If you need to go white, try a good quality white Burgundy.

MEDALLIONS OF MONKFISH WITH ASPARAGUS, BABY FENNEL AND SAFFRON POTATOES COMPLEMENTED BY A SHALLOT, TOMATO BUTTER NAGE *Serves 4*

 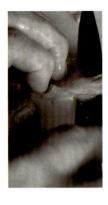    

1.5kg Monkfish Tail Loin
100ml Olive Oil
275g Butter (unsalted)
Maldon Rock Salt
12 Spears Asparagus
½ Lemon
12 Heads Baby Fennel
375ml Chicken Stock
4 Star Anise
Good Pinch Black Peppercorns
6 Shallots
55g Diced Mushrooms
   - Chestnut or Oyster
150ml Dry Vermouth
100g Fresh Chives (chopped)
2 Plum Tomatoes (skinned, de-seeded & sliced & diced)

SAFFRON POTATOES
500ml Water
250ml White Wine
10g Saffron
Pinch Thyme
12 Romano Potatoes (medium/large) or similar Red Potato

Full white or lighter red here, a Western Australian Chardonnay or how about the New Zealand Pinot Noir you had with the quail!

Pre-heat oven to 180C/350F/Gas 4

1. If a whole monkfish tail, remove the sinew and membrane (like a skin), and remove 2 fillets per tail. Wrap the fillets tightly into a cling film sausage shape parcel the day before required and leave in a fridge. This produces the best shape for the medallions, but is not necessary if you don't have time.
2. Take a non-stick frying pan and add some olive oil and a knob of butter and heat until the butter is melted.
3. Season the fish with Maldon rock salt and pepper, and gently settle the fish, with a little lemon juice, into the pan and cook on a moderate heat to seal all sides.
4. Prepare the asparagus, and cut off all of the ears from the head down the stalk. Then blanche in boiling salted water for 2-3 minutes. Plunge into iced water to stop the cooking process.
5. Remove the fish and leave to rest for 3-4 minutes.
6. Braise the baby fennel in 250ml of chicken stock with salt and pepper, star anise, peppercorns, and shallots in a roasting tray and simmer for 20 minutes to allow all of the flavours to infuse. Cover with foil and place into the pre-heated oven for 35-40 minutes.
7. Allow the fennel to cool down in the stock, then prepare by removing the outer coarse leaves and trim until neat and tidy.
8. Take a small saucepan and add a knob of butter, then add the chopped shallots and gently sweat. Add the diced mushrooms (any type) and sweat gently. Add the dry vermouth and allow this to be absorbed and glaze the shallots and mushrooms, then 125ml chicken stock and 250ml of the fennel cooking liquor. Reduce the liquid by 1/3rd.
9. Once the sauce has reduced, whisk in 250g butter, 3-4 cubes at a time, away from direct heat.
10. Wipe clean the non-stick frying pan and re-heat with a small amount of olive oil and put the monkfish back into the pan on a fairly high heat for a few minutes, turning the fish to heat both sides. Remove from the pan and cut into medallions (approximately 6 per person), and keep warm.
11. Chop the fresh chives.
12. Put the sauce back onto a low heat to keep warm, and add salt and pepper and a dash of lemon juice. Add the skinned, de-seeded and sliced plum tomatoes to the sauce at the last minute. Add the chopped chives.
13. Gently re-simmer or steam the fennel and asparagus for 2 minutes just before serving.
14. Arrange the fish on outer edge of a deep plate, around the saffron potato. Add a small amount of rock salt to the fish. Place the fennel and asparagus in the middle of the potatoes, and pour the sauce around.

SAFFRON POTATOES
1. Into a saucepan put the water, wine, saffron and thyme and simmer for 20 minutes to infuse the flavours.
2. Add the sliced potatoes and simmer for a further 10 minutes until cooked.
3. Drain and serve.

If you do not remove the sinew and membrane of the monkfish before cooking, it will tighten up giving impression of toughness.

Always rest the fish after cooking for 5 minutes, to relax the flesh.

Always cut and taste a little piece of your vegetables during cooking, for exact bite.

PRUNE AND ARMAGNAC ICE CREAM WITH SPICE BISCUITS AND A FRAGRANT TEA AND PRUNE SYRUP

Serves 4

SOAKED PRUNES

(leave for 24 hours in a fridge)
225g Adgen Prunes (cut into 8 strips per prune)
75ml Armagnac

ICE CREAM

8 Egg Yolks
30g Sugar
375ml Whipping Cream
250ml Milk
85g White Chocolate (melted)
Cut & Soaked Prunes

SPICE BISCUITS

100g Icing Sugar
33g Plain Flour
1 Good Pinch Mixed Spice
1 Good Pinch 5-Spice
1 Good Pinch Cinnamon
30g Butter (melted)
40g Milk

TEA SYRUP

185ml Water
225g Sugar
Juice ¼ Lemon
8 Dried d'Argen Prunes (cut & quartered)
2 Dessertspoons Fresh Jasmine Tea Leaves

ICE CREAM

1. Whisk the egg yolks and sugar in a bowl.
2. Put the whipping cream and milk into a thick bottom pan and simmer gently.
3. Pour the simmering mix over the eggs and sugar.
4. Return to the pan and over a moderate heat, use a spatula to continuously move the mix from the edges and bottom of the pan until a double cream or coating consistency.
5. Add the melted chocolate and stir quickly and remove from heat.
6. Sieve the mixture and allow to cool.
7. Churn in an ice cream machine (in 2 batches) until just before the ice cream is finished.
8. Add the soaked prunes (retain a few for the finished dish) and stir manually – the machine would break them up.
9. Store in a freezer for a minimum of 12 hours until set.

SPICE BISCUITS

Pre-heat oven to 220C/425F/Gas 7

1. Sieve the sugar and flour together, and add the spices.
2. Slowly whisk in the melted butter until a paste is formed.
3. Then add half of the milk and whisk until smooth.
4. Add the remaining milk and whisk until very smooth.
5. Keep in a fridge in a sealed container until required. It will keep for 1 week.
6. Remove the mix from the fridge 30 minutes before to warm to room temperature.
7. Take a plastic container lid and cut out a template stencil to the required shape (circles for this recipe).
8. Lay the template on silicon paper on a baking tray and spread the biscuit mix over the template area until smooth. Remove the template and ensure circles are formed.
9. Put in the fridge for 5 minutes.
10. Bake in the pre-heated oven for 5-7 minutes (middle shelf) until a light mahogany colour.
11. Allow to cool on the tray and remove when set.
12. Store in an airtight container – will keep for 3-4 days.

TEA SYRUP

1. Make the syrup by putting the sugar and water into a pan and simmer for a few minutes with the lemon juice.
2. Then add the prunes and jasmine tea leaves and gently simmer for 1 hour.
3. Pass the liquid through a fine sieve into a clean pan.
4. Add a little more sugar and simmer – this will remove the bitterness of the tea.
5. Cool for 12 hours and store in a pouring bottle. This will keep for 1 month in a fridge.

TO FINISH

1. Position a piece of soaked prune on the serving plate, and put a scoop of ice cream on top.
2. Drizzle the syrup around the edge of the plate.
3. Dust the biscuits with icing sugar and put into top of ice cream (1 per scoop).

If you don't own
an ice cream
machine, you
can make it
manually, but it
will mean going
to the freezer
every 10 minutes
to stir the ice
cream until set.

Only ball the
ice cream when
ready to serve
immediately, as it
will melt quickly.

The prunes can
be replaced
by figs or
dates. You can
leave out the
armagnac if
desired.

Always
difficult but
Pedro Ximenez
(PX) sweet sherry
goes well, and if
not, why not just
have a glass of
Armagnac?

THE AWARENESS LOUNGE

THE AWARENESS LOUNGE
23C NORTH STREET
EMSWORTH
PO10 7BY
T. 01243 373766

e. awarenesslounge@aol.com
www.awarenessweb.co.uk

GABRIELLE & IAIN GUILAYN,
WITH THEIR SON, GRANT

IAIN & GABRIELLE GUILAYN, RESIDENTS OF EMSWORTH, OPENED THE AWARENESS GIFT SHOP AND THERAPY CENTRE THREE YEARS AGO. THEY HAVE NOW EXPANDED THEIR BUSINESS IN RESPONSE TO LOCAL REQUESTS FOR A COFFEE SHOP IN NORTH STREET.

THE AWARENESS LOUNGE, OPENED IN MAY 2004 BY IAIN AND GABRIELLE GUILAYN, ALSO OWNERS OF THE AWARENESS SHOP ACROSS THE ROAD, IS OPEN EVERY DAY DURING THE SUMMER MONTHS (EXCLUDING SUNDAYS AT OTHER TIMES OF THE YEAR). THIS COFFEE LOUNGE SERVES HOT AND COLD FOODS AND DRINKS WITH AN EMPHASIS ON PROVIDING A HEALTHY OPTION USING ORGANIC, SOYA, WHEAT- AND GLUTEN-FREE PRODUCTS. AMBIENT MUSIC AND BOOKS ARE ALSO AVAILABLE TO PURCHASE. THE PAVEMENT TABLES AND CHAIRS GIVE CUSTOMERS THE CHOICE TO SIT OUTSIDE WHEN THE WEATHER ALLOWS.

GRANITA DI PANNA

This is a simple refreshing drink for the hot days of summer, and should be served cold in a tall glass.

1. First make some Italian espresso or other strong black coffee, and allow to cool.

2. Pour over a tall glass of crushed ice.

3. Top with panna, which is a thick Italian cream similar to crème fraîche.

4. Sprinkle grated chocolate, or cocoa powder, over the panna.

5. Serve with an almond and chocolate biscotti.

THE COAL EXCHANGE

THE COAL EXCHANGE
21 SOUTH STREET
EMSWORTH
PO10 7EG
T. 01243 375866

www.thecoalexchange.co.uk

BREWERY:
GEORGE GALE & CO LTD

PETER MCINTYRE
WITH HUMBUG

THE COAL EXCHANGE

PUBLIC HOUSE, RUN BY THE LANDLORD PETER MCINTYRE FOR THE PAST NINE YEARS, HAS LINKS WITH SELLING BEER DATING FROM 1678. EARLIEST KNOWN RECORDS SHOW THAT IT WAS ORIGINALLY A PORK BUTCHERS AND AN ALE HOUSE. ITS PRESENT NAME DATES FROM WHEN EMSWORTH WAS A BUSY HARBOUR INVOLVED WITH THE COAL TRADE FROM NEWCASTLE. THIS COSY OLD-FASHIONED PUB HAS A GARDEN TO THE REAR. FOOD IS SERVED LUNCHTIMES AND TUESDAY AND THURSDAY EVENINGS.

SEARED LOIN OF PEPPERED TUNA WITH CHARGRILLED

LEE CARTER HAS SINCE 2003 BEEN THE CHEF AT THE COAL EXCHANGE, SERVING TRADITIONAL PUB FOOD WITH A 'TWIST' AT LUNCHTIMES. HE USES FRESH INGREDIENTS FOR FLAVOUR, PRODUCING HOMEMADE PIES THROUGH TO LOCAL FISH AND SEAFOOD DISHES AND OF COURSE THE SUNDAY ROASTS, AS WELL AS THE USUAL ARRAY OF SNACKS. HE GAINED HIS EXPERIENCE WORKING IN ALL AREAS OF THE CATERING INDUSTRY, BOTH AT HOME AND ABROAD, FROM PUBS AND CLUBS TO HOTELS, BOATS AND SCHOOLS.

2 Tablespoons Balsamic Vinegar
Selection of Fresh Vegetables
1 Tablespoon Olive Oil
1 Clove Garlic (crushed)
2 x 225g (8oz) Tuna Loin Steaks
Cracked Black Pepper
Vegetable Oil

PESTO
30g (1oz) Pine Kernels
55g (2oz) Fresh Basil
30g (1oz) Fresh Grated Parmesan
100ml (4fl oz) Extra Virgin Olive Oil
1 Clove Garlic
Salt & Ground Black Pepper

PESTO

1. Toast the pine kernels in a dry pan until golden brown.

2. Put all of the ingredients into a blender (or you can use a pestle and mortar). Use quantities of olive oil and seasoning to taste.

3. Blend the mixture to your own desired consistency, either chunky or smooth.

4. Reserve the pesto.

BALSAMIC DRESSING

1. Bring the balsamic vinegar to the boil in a small saucepan.

2. Simmer and reduce by half, to a syrupy consistency.

3. Reserve at room temperature.

VEGETABLES AND PESTO AND BALSAMIC DRESSING

Serves 2

CHARGRILLED VEGETABLES AND TUNA

1. Slice the vegetables, lengthways (not too thick or thin).

2. Mix together a little olive oil and the crushed garlic, and brush onto the vegetables.

3. Cook the vegetables on a hot grill until browned on each side.

4. Meanwhile, heat a frying pan to a hot temperature.

5. Cover all sides of the tuna with cracked black pepper.

6. Drizzle a small amount of vegetable oil into the frying pan.

7. Sear the tuna on both sides in the pan until golden brown. If you like tuna served rare, sear for 30 seconds per side.

8. Serve the tuna and vegetables on a plate, and drizzle around the pesto and the balsamic dressing.

Can be cooked on a barbecue, or on a hob using a ridged grill-pan.

Grilled vegetables as desired for colour and taste – could use carrot, courgette, red onion, aubergine, fennel and peppers. You may prefer to part-cook the vegetables before grilling.

Fresh, fruity red such as Valpolicella or even a chilled full bodied, dry Rosé from the South of France.

MARK WHEELER STARTED HIS TRAINING AS A CHEF WORKING AT THE BROOKFIELD HOTEL WHEN AMANDA THOMAS WAS HEAD CHEF. HE THEN WORKED AT AMBERLEY CASTLE WHERE HE MET HIS WIFE, BEV. TOGETHER THEY NOW RUN A CATERING BUSINESS, AND AS PART OF THIS PREPARE THE FOOD FOR THE INCREDIBLY POPULAR CURRY AND INTERNATIONAL NIGHTS AT THE COAL EXCHANGE ON TUESDAYS AND THURSDAYS.

CHICKEN PASANDA A MILD AND QUICK-TO-PREPARE CURRY

Serves 4

1 Large Spanish Onion
4 Cloves Garlic
2 Teaspoons Black Onion Seed
4 Green Cardamom Pods
150ml Clarified Butter
1 Red Chilli
3 Teaspoons Garam Masala
3 Teaspoons Ground Coriander
2 Teaspoons Ground Cumin
1 Small Piece Ginger
1 Teaspoon Turmeric
Salt & Ground Black Pepper
450ml Yoghurt
1 Dessertspoon Tomato Purée
3 Dessertspoons Ground Almonds
800g Chicken Breast (diced)
3 Dessertspoons Flaked Almonds
½ Stick Cinnamon
1 Pack Mint

Pre-heat oven to 200C/400F/Gas 6

1. Fry the chopped onion, garlic, black onion seeds and green cardamom pods in the clarified butter until brown.
2. Add the roughly chopped chilli (remove the seeds for a milder taste), garam masala, ground coriander, ground cumin, peeled and chopped ginger, turmeric and seasoning.
3. After 5 minutes of gentle frying, add the yoghurt and tomato purée and gently simmer for 10 minutes.
4. Add the ground almonds, and use a hand blender or liquidizer to blend the sauce.
5. Fry the diced chicken until almost browned, then add the flaked almonds and fry until they turn brown.
6. Place the chicken and almonds into an ovenproof dish with the cinnamon stick. Pour over the sauce and cover with a lid or foil.
7. Cook in the pre-heated oven for 20 minutes.
8. Remove from the oven and stir in the chopped mint and season to taste.
9. Serve with poppadoms and rice.

CLARIFIED BUTTER

Make the clarified butter by melting a block of butter in a microwave, and leaving for 10 minutes for the fats to separate. The clarified butter is the liquid part at the top, which can be poured off.

It is always best to use clarified butter rather than oil when cooking Indian food.

The flaked almonds help to thicken the sauce.

Light unoaked whites work best, Pinot Grigio or Australian Riesling. Surprisingly, fruity Rosés can also work really well.

THE CO-OP

THE CO-OP
2 HIGH STREET
EMSWORTH
PO10 7AW
T. 01243 372663

DAVE ALLAN, STORE MANAGER

GILL GRIFFIN HAS WORKED AT THE EMSWORTH STORE FOR 13 YEARS, AND BEFORE THEN WORKED AS AN UPHOLSTERER IN CHICHESTER. SHE HAS LIVED IN EMSWORTH FOR 35 YEARS, AND IS MARRIED INTO A LONG-ESTABLISHED LOCAL FAMILY OF BUILDERS.

THE CO-OP STORE HAS BEEN IN EMSWORTH SINCE 1918, ALTHOUGH HAVING BEEN ESTABLISHED IN VARIOUS LOCATIONS THROUGHOUT THIS PERIOD. IT IS PART OF THE SOUTHERN COOPERATIVES GROUP, AN INDEPENDENT GROUP WHICH HAS TRADED FOR MORE THAN 150 YEARS. FOOD RETAILING IS ITS CORE BUSINESS, AND MORE RECENTLY IT HAS MOVED TOWARDS A POLICY OF SELLING FAIR TRADE PRODUCTS AS PART OF ITS RANGE.

SIMPLE TRIFLE

Serves 4-6

2 Chocolate Chip Muffins
290g Tin Cherries
Custard Powder
500ml (1pt) Milk
150g Fair Trade Chocolate
284ml Whipping Cream
Grated Fair Trade Chocolate to Finish

1. Cut the muffins in half and place in a glass serving dish

2. Open the tin of cherries and remove the stones, then pour over the muffins with the syrup.

3. Make up the custard with the milk, but leave out the sugar.

4. When the custard is hot, break the chocolate bar into the custard and stir until dissolved.

5. When the custard is cool, pour over the cherries and muffins.

6. Whip the cream and spoon over the custard.

7. Finish off by sprinkling grated chocolate over.

Good quaity sweet sherry seems a given here but Sauternes is also a good match.

BLACKBERRIES FROM FLOWER TO FRUIT (THREE PHASES PHOTOGRAPHED DURING JUNE AND JULY)

EMSWORTH SAILING CLUB

EMSWORTH SAILING CLUB
55 BATH ROAD
EMSWORTH
PO10 7ES
T. 01243 372850

e. secretary@emsworthsc.org.uk
www.emsworthsc.org.uk

COMMODORE: JOHN CROOKSHANK

RICHARD CLARK, WITH HIS WIFE JULIA, ARE THE CURRENT STEWARDS OF THE EMSWORTH SAILING CLUB PROVIDING LUNCH AND DINNER MENUS FOR MEMBERS OF THE CLUB, AS WELL AS FOOD FOR SPECIAL EVENT EVENINGS. RICHARD BEGAN HIS TRAINING AS A CHEF AT CASSIO COLLEGE, WATFORD IN 1973 AND HAS BEEN HEAD CHEF AT A NUMBER OF RESTAURANTS AND HOTELS BEFORE TAKING ON HIS POSITION IN EMSWORTH DURING 2001. HE IS A KEEN SAILOR AND FISHERMAN, AND WHEN THE TIME IS RIGHT, CAN OFTEN BE FOUND FISHING FOR THE LOCAL MACKEREL, WHICH HE COOKS AND SERVES FRESH FROM THE SEA.

EMSWORTH SAILING CLUB IS SITUATED AT THE END OF BATH ROAD IN THE FORMER BATHING HOUSE WHICH WAS BOUGHT IN 1919 FOR THE SUM OF £400. THE OLD HOUSE WAS IN DESPERATE NEED OF REPAIR, AND THE THREE PONDS ACQUIRED WITH THE PROPERTY HAD TO BE DEALT WITH. ONE OF THEM DISAPPEARED INTO THE MUD; ONE BECAME THE CLUB SWIMMING POOL; AND THE OTHER HAD TO BE FILLED IN. THE CLUB'S PREMISES EXPANDED GREATLY, AND A LIVE-IN STEWARD WAS EMPLOYED WHO WAS ALSO RESPONSIBLE FOR PROVIDING FOOD AND RUNNING THE BAR. DURING 1963, THE ORIGINAL SWIMMING POOL WAS FILLED AND CONCRETED OVER TO BECOME PART OF THE SLIPWAY, AND DISCUSSIONS BEGAN ON THE SITING OF THE NEW POOL. THE FIRST CLUB COMMODORE WAS MAJOR G CECIL WHITAKER. IN 1926 HE WAS SUCCEEDED BY THE EARL OF BESSBOROUGH WHO LIVED AT STANSTED, BUT PERHAPS THE MOST WELL-KNOWN TO TAKE ON THIS ROLE IN THE EARLY YEARS OF THE CLUB WAS LT CDR LORD LOUIS MOUNTBATTEN WHO WAS THEN LIVING AT ADSDEAN. A MORE RECENT FAMOUS LOCAL PERSON WHO WAS A MEMBER OF THE CLUB WAS THE LATE SIR PETER BLAKE. (FROM "THE STORY OF EMSWORTH SAILING CLUB" BY PATRICK MILLEN)

3-COURSE MENU

MEDITERRANEAN SALAD

FRESH GRILLED HARBOUR MACKEREL WITH LEMON AND LIME BUTTER

DEEP FRIED ICE CREAM WITH FRUIT COULIS

MEDITERRANEAN SALAD *Serves 4*

500g Mixed Salad Leaves
2 Beefsteak Tomatoes
½ Cucumber
200g Feta Cheese
20 Black Olives
2 Red Peppers
2 Yellow Peppers
Orange Honey & Wholegrain Mustard Dressing
Freshly Ground Black Pepper
Fresh Parsley (chopped)

1. Wash and place the salad leaves onto plates.

2. Remove the core from the tomatoes and slice them. Add to the salad leaves.

3. Slice the cucumber and arrange onto each plate.

4. Dice the feta cheese and place on top of the salad.

5. Dot each plate with the black olives.

6. Meanwhile, pan-roast the red and yellow peppers. Slice and arrange on the salad.

7. Sprinkle with the dressing, some freshly ground black pepper and finish with some chopped parsley.

Dry white or Rosé from the South of France - but watch the dressing!

FRESH GRILLED HARBOUR MACKEREL WITH LEMON AND LIME BUTTER

Serves 4

When preparing asparagus, peel the stalk end to avoid any stringy texture.

8 Fresh Mackerel (filleted & boned)
Seasoned Flour
120g Butter
2 Lemons
1 Lime
Fresh Parsley (chopped)

1. Dust the prepared mackerel fillets with seasoned flour and place on a buttered tray.

2. Take the juice of 1 lemon and the lime and put into a pan with the remaining butter, simmer to reduce for 2-3 minutes.

3. Grill the mackerel under a hot grill for 3-4 minutes. Put to one side and keep warm.

4. Add the chopped parsley to the lemon and lime butter, and coat this over the cooked mackerel.

5. Garnish with lemon wedges, and serve with new potatoes and asparagus.

Muscadet, make sure it's Sur Lie or how about a crisp, dry English white?

DEEP FRIED ICE CREAM WITH FRUIT COULIS *Serves 4*

You can use coconut or other ingredient of choice to coat the ice cream.

The oil must be very hot before immersing the coated ice cream so that it cooks immediately, otherwise you may have a messy disaster.

When finishing off the plate with the sauce, first use a pourer to blob the sauce around the edge of the plate, then use a sharp point to go through the centre of each all around the plate to form the heart shapes.

1 Frozen Arctic Roll
Flour
2 Eggs (beaten)
Cake & Biscuit Crumbs
Vegetable Oil
500g Strawberries (fresh or tin)
500g Mango (fresh or tin)
Fresh Mint
Icing Sugar

1. Cut the arctic roll into 4 portions.

2. Quickly coat in flour, then the beaten eggs and finally the cake and biscuit crumbs.

3. Put in a freezer for 10 minutes until firm and frozen.

4. Heat the clean vegetable oil in a deep pan or fryer to 180°C.

5. Purée the strawberries and mangoes into 2 separate bowls, to make the fruit coulis.

6. Deep-fry the ice cream for 1 minute. Remove and drain excess oil on kitchen paper.

7. Put the fried ice cream onto serving plates, decorated with the strawberry and mango fruit coulis sauces.

8. Garnish with mint, a fresh strawberry and dust with icing sugar.

Australian Liqueur Muscat may just cope.

FLINTSTONES TEA ROOM

FLINTSTONES TEA ROOM
THE QUAY
SOUTH STREET
EMSWORTH
PO10 7EQ

T. 01243 377577

RUPERT KERLY HAS WORKED WITHIN THE FOOD INDUSTRY FOR THE PAST TEN YEARS GAINING EXPERIENCE IN ALL ASPECTS OF CATERING MANAGEMENT PRIOR TO BECOMING OWNER OF THIS TEA ROOM.

FLINTSTONES TEA ROOM, ON THE QUAYSIDE OVERLOOKING THE HARBOUR IN EMSWORTH, SERVES A SELECTION OF HOT AND COLD DRINKS AND SNACKS, LIGHT MEALS AND AFTERNOON TEAS, AND IS PERFECTLY POSITIONED TO SIT AND ENJOY THE VIEW. THE FLINT BUILDING WAS ORIGINALLY A BARN AND IS OWNED BY THE EMSWORTH SLIPPER SAILING CLUB. RUPERT KERLY HAS OWNED AND RUN THE TEA ROOM SINCE 1996.

CHICKEN AND HAM PANCAKES

Serves 6

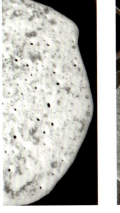

FILLING
45g Butter
45g Flour
375ml Milk
170g Cooked Ham
170g Cooked Chicken

PANCAKES
110g Plain Flour
Pinch Salt
1 Egg
250ml Milk
1 Tablespoon Oil

FILLING
1. Melt the butter in a saucepan and add the flour. Cook for 1 minute.
2. Remove the saucepan from the heat and slowly stir in the milk.
3. Return to the heat and bring to the boil, stirring constantly until the sauce thickens.
4. Add the chopped ham and chicken, and season well.

PANCAKES
1. Sieve the flour and salt together.
2. Add the egg, and gradually add half of the milk.
3. Beat the mixture well, and stir in the remaining milk and the oil.
4. Heat a small amount of oil in a frying pan.
5. Add 2 tablespoons of the batter mix, and tilt the pan to cover the base.
6. Cook until golden brown, turn and repeat.
7. Place cooked pancake on a plate, add the filling and roll the pancake.
8. Repeat for each pancake.

Lightly oaked New World Chardonnay from New Zealand or Australia.

RASPBERRY ICE CREAM   *Serves 4*

450g Raspberries
60g Icing Sugar
2 Eggs (separated)
125ml Double Cream

1. Put the fresh raspberries through a blender to purée.

2. You will need to add icing sugar to the puréed raspberries. Sweeten to taste.

3. Beat the egg yolks with 30g of icing sugar until smooth and creamy.

4. Whisk the egg whites until they form peaks, then fold in 30g of icing sugar a little at a time.

5. Gradually whisk in the egg yolk mixture to the whites, and fold in the raspberry purée and double cream.

6. Put into a freezer tray and leave in the freezer until set. This will take approximately 3 hours.

Answers on a postcard please! One to experiment with, a light Spanish Moscatel maybe?

THE GREENHOUSE CAFÉ

THE GREENHOUSE CAFÉ
9 FROBISHER GARDENS
ST PETER'S SQUARE
EMSWORTH
PO10 7AS
T. 01243 370838

SIAN & GEORGE GEORGEOU
WITH THEIR CHILDREN
ELLIS (9YRS), RUBY (6YRS) & JEM (2YRS)

GEORGE GEORGEOU HAS WORKED AS A CHEF ALL HIS WORKING LIFE, HAVING TRAINED AT A LONDON COLLEGE FOR FOUR YEARS. HE THEN GAINED EXPERIENCE WORKING FOR TRUST HOUSE FORTE HOTELS, CAVENDISH, CUMBERLAND AND ST GEORGES BEFORE JOINING THE VIDEO CAFÉ, WHERE HE WAS THE CHEF FOR THE LAUNCH OF THE VENTURE IN 1987, AND LATER BANNERS, IN LONDON. FOLLOWING THIS, GEORGE WAS CHEF AT THE CRICKETERS ARMS, DUNCTON AND THEN THE SELSEY ARMS IN WEST DEAN BEFORE BECOMING OWNER OF THE GREENHOUSE CAFÉ WITH HIS WIFE, SIAN.

THE GREENHOUSE CAFÉ, WITH ITS COURTYARD OVERLOOKING THE SQUARE, IS THE PERFECT PLACE TO SIT AND ENJOY WARM SUNNY DAYS. SITUATED IN WHAT WAS ORIGINALLY A CHAPEL AND THEN LATER A CINEMA, THE PAVILION, IT HAS BEEN A CAFÉ FOR MORE THAN FIVE YEARS. THE PRESENT OWNERS, SIAN AND GEORGE GEORGEOU, TOOK OVER THE BUSINESS IN AUTUMN 2002 HAVING ESCAPED A BUSY LIFE WORKING LONG HOURS FOR MAINSTREAM RESTAURANTS IN FAVOUR OF A MORE RELAXED LIFESTYLE. WITH CHILDREN OF THEIR OWN, THEY WELCOME FAMILIES AND CHILDREN TO THE CAFÉ AND EVEN PROVIDE FURNITURE AND CUTLERY DESIGNED FOR LITTLE ONES TO USE. FRESH HOMEMADE FOOD, CAKES, LIGHT LUNCHES, MAIN MEALS, ALLDAY BREAKFAST AND REFRESHMENTS ARE SERVED DAILY.

AVGOLEMONO SOUP

Serves approximately 10

A LIGHT TRADITIONAL SOUP FROM CYPRUS, ENJOYED ALL YEAR ROUND IN EVERY CYPRIOT HOME OR RESTAURANT

1 Chicken
100g Rice
3 Lemons
1 Egg
3 Egg Yolks
Salt & Pepper

1. First make 2½lt (5pts) of chicken stock by boiling the chicken until cooked in water. Remove and reserve the chicken, and allow the stock to cool.

2. Skim off any fat from the surface of the stock, and add the rice. Cook for 15 minutes and remove from the heat.

3. In a separate large bowl, thoroughly mix the juice of 2 lemons and all the eggs.

4. Add a tablespoon at a time of the chicken stock to the egg and lemon mixture. Keep it moving all the time, adding the stock quite quickly to prevent curdling.

5. When most of the stock has been added, return the mixture to the stock pan.

6. Heat gently, mixing constantly, allowing the egg to thicken the soup.

7. Season with salt and pepper.

8. Serve with shredded chicken and extra lemon.

Sorry, but give Cypriot wines a miss. However, there are interesting new wave whites coming out of Greece now - give them a try.

MIXED SUMMER FRUIT SMOOTHIE

Serves 1-2

6-8 Ice Cubes
2 Tablespoons Fruit Berries
   (strawberry, raspberry, blueberry,
   redcurrants etc)
250ml Apple Juice
   (other flavours if preferred)

1. Put the ice into a blender and
    blend to a snow.

2. Add the fruit and blend again.

3. Add enough juice to give a thick
    creamy consistency.

4. Pour and serve chilled.

COCONUT, PINEAPPLE AND LIME CRUSH

Serves 1-2

6-8 Ice Cubes
300ml Coconut Milk
250g Fresh Pineapple (chopped)
Juice & Grated Rind **2** Limes
Vanilla Ice Cream

1. Put the ice into a blender and blend to a snow.

2. Add the coconut milk, pineapple and juice and rind of the limes and blend again.

3. Serve with a scoop of vanilla ice cream.

HEV'N FLOWERS

HEV'N FLOWERS
39 HIGH STREET
EMSWORTH
PO10 7AL
T. 01243 375933

e. hall.leigh@ntlworld.com

LEIGH HALL WITH MEMBERS OF HER STAFF, KATE BURCH, CAROL TIPPER, REBECCA DRIDGE, ROSE HARNS & KARIN DOYLE

LEIGH HALL HAS SPENT MOST OF HER CAREER IN THE IT INDUSTRY, INITIALLY AS A COMPUTER PROGRAMMER AND LATTERLY AS A BUSINESS ANALYST AND PROJECT MANAGER. SHE HAS ALWAYS HAD A PASSION FOR FLOWERS AND WAS A KEEN AMATEUR. THE OUTCOME BEING THAT LEIGH DECIDED TO MAKE A BOLD MOVE AND LEAVE HER IT CAREER BEHIND HER TO PURSUE THIS PASSION. SHE TRAINED AS A PROFESSIONAL FLORIST BEFORE PURCHASING HEV'N FLOWERS, AND HAS USED HER DRIVE AND ENERGY TO REMODEL THE STYLE OF FLOWERS NOW OFFERED. SHE LIVES IN EMSWORTH WITH HER HUSBAND AND TWO DAUGHTERS.

HEV'N FLOWERS HAS BEEN A FLORIST SHOP SINCE 1969, TRADING AS MARIAN GIFT FLOWERS UNTIL LEIGH HALL PURCHASED THE BUSINESS IN SEPTEMBER 2003 AND RE-BRANDED WITH THE NEW NAME IN MARCH 2004. ALTHOUGH THE FLORIST CONTINUES TO SPECIALISE IN PROVIDING TRADITIONAL WEDDING, FUNERAL AND GIFT FLOWERS, LEIGH IS ESTABLISHING A DESIGN-ORI-ENTATED STYLE WHERE EACH PIECE IS CREATED WITH INDIVIDUAL FLAIR, WHETHER LARGE DISPLAYS OR SMALLER GIFT ARRANGEMENTS. THE CLIENTELE LIST IS EXPANDING, WITH A GROWING CORPORATE LIST INCLUDING PORTSMOUTH FOOTBALL CLUB. THE SHOP ALSO HAS A WIDE RANGE OF EUROPEAN VASES, SILK FLOWERS, GIFTS AND HANDMADE CARDS.

RING-O-ROSES

1

2

3

4

5

6

7

8

9

YOU WILL NEED

31cm Oasis Ring
15 White Roses
1 Large Head Hydrangea
3 Stems Viburnam
Small Bag Moss
Bunch Bear Grass
Selection Small Glass Beads
Candle
Storm Vase (optional)

1. Chamfer the edges of a 31cm (12inch) oasis ring, which has been thoroughly soaked in water.

2. Select 1 of the focal flowers and cut the stem to 5cm (2inch) in length. Cut the stem at an angle so that it enters the oasis easily and has a greater surface area from which to drink. Cluster the focal flowers in groups of 5.

3. Place another 2 groupings equidistant around the ring, so that the focal flowers are placed on the tips of an imaginary triangle.

4. Place the next flowers in a line grouping, to one side of the focal flowers – ensuring that the line is carried down either side of the oasis ring. If using hydrangea, the flower heads need to be separated into small florets and mounted onto a fine wire. This gives the stems the strength they need to allow them to be pushed securely into the oasis. Ensure that the ends of the stems are pushed into the oasis so that the flowers can drink.

5. Repeat step 4 with a third flower, and place at the opposite side of the focal flowers. In this example, viburnam has been used and this too needs mounting onto fine wire to strengthen the stem.

6. Fill in the spaces between the flower groupings with moss. This is simply placed neatly onto the surface of the oasis and pinned into place.

7. To create unity and introduce a sense of movement around the ring, stems of bear grass embellished with beads can be used to link the groups of flowers. To do this, simply thread toning glass beads onto the grass and push along the length of the stem (taking care not to cut your fingers on the sharp edge of the grass). Any burrs of grass can be pulled off.

8. Push both ends of the grass into the oasis amongst the flowers in the appropriate place. Spritz the finished arrangement with water to freshen it and provide additional moisture for the flowers.

9. Finally, place a candle in the centre of the ring, taking care that it does not burn too closely to the flowers or foliage. In this example, a glass storm candle vase has been used to keep the flames away from the arrangement.

Combinations of flowers which could be used in a 'massed' style include: gerberas, lilies, carnations, spray chrysanthemums, roses, hydrangea, viburnam, and trachelium.

White roses bruise easily and must be treated gently.

Keep roses in a chiller or cool place until the last minute.

Always first choose the best flower for the top of any arrangement.

Check that the oasis is fully covered from every viewing angle.

THEMED ARRANGEMENTS FOR THAT 'SPECIAL OCCASION'

ST JAMES' C OF E PRIMARY SCHOOL

ST JAMES' C OF E PRIMARY SCHOOL
BELLEVUE LANE
EMSWORTH
PO10 7PX
T. 01243 372715

www.stjamescecprimaryemsworth.ik.org

HEAD: SEAN MCARDLE

LAWRENCE MURPHY WITH CHILDREN AT THE SCHOOL

ST JAMES' C OF E PRIMARY SCHOOL DATES BACK TO 1863, AND WAS UNTIL APPROXIMATELY 30 YEARS AGO BASED CLOSE BY THE CHURCH, IN A BUILDING WHICH IS NOW THE COMMUNITY CENTRE FOR THE VILLAGE. HOWEVER, A LARGER SITE WAS NECESSARY, AND THE SCHOOL RELOCATED TO ITS PRESENT ADDRESS IN BELLEVUE LANE. THE SCHOOL ENROLES CHILDREN FROM THE AGE OF 4 TO 11 YEARS, AND MORE THAN 140 YEARS AFTER ITS BEGINNING, CONTINUES TO ENJOY A GOOD REPUTATION IN THE AREA AND IS PROUD OF ITS STRONG LINKS WITH ST JAMES' CHURCH AND THE WHOLE EMSWORTH COMMUNITY.

LAWRENCE MURPHY, OWNER AND CHEF OF FAT OLIVES, WITH YEAR 6 CHILDREN: LAWRENCE WARREN-WEST, LUKE SLADE, SARAH VINCENT, EMMA DURHAM, TIA HARDING, ELEANOR AYLING, ALEX MOTHERSELE AND ANDREW MEREDITH, PLUS SEAN MCARDLE, HEAD AND MARIE BARKER, TEACHING ASSISTANT

SEA BASS ON COUSCOUS WITH GARLIC, LIME AND CHILLI DRESSING

Serves 4

THE FRENCH NAME FOR SEA BASS TRANSLATES AS 'WOLF OF THE SEA'. IT HAS LONG SPINES WHICH IT USES FOR DEFENCE WHEN ATTACKED, AND WILL EAT OTHER FISH, SMALL CRABS AND EVEN OTHER SEA BASS.

DRESSING

1 Shallot
4 Cloves Garlic (sliced)
6ml Olive Oil
2 Limes (juice & zest)
½ Chilli (seeds removed)

MAIN DISH

Tomatoes & Red Peppers
 (to make 1½ cups juice)
2 Shallots
Olive Oil
1½ Cups Couscous
2 Knobs Butter
4 Fillets Sea Bass (pin-boned & scaled)

DRESSING

1. To make the dressing, sauté the chopped shallot and garlic gently in a little olive oil.

2. Add the zest of the limes and the chopped chilli pepper.

3. Add the olive oil and lime juice and stir thoroughly.

4. Remove from the heat and put to one side. Keep warm.

MAIN DISH

1. Juice the tomatoes and red peppers in a centrifugal juicer to make 1½ cups of juice. Or, buy juice from a health food shop.

2. Sauté the chopped shallots in a little olive oil.

3. Add the juice of the tomatoes and peppers, and heat the mixture.

4. Add the couscous and stir. (This will cook the couscous.)

5. Add the butter and season to taste.

6. Leave to simmer for 3 minutes.

7. Meanwhile, pan fry the prepared sea bass in a little olive oil.

8. Spoon the couscous into the middle of the plates, and then lay the fish on top. Finally, pour the dressing around.

Ask your fishmonger to prepare the sea bass fillets.

Score the skin of fish before frying, to give a larger surface area which will help it to crisp during cooking.

Scrape to remove all scales from the skin of the fish – this also removes moisture and allows the fish to fry in the oil rather than boil.

Lawrence recommends Isle of Wight garlic for best flavour available.

On the assumption this has been cooked for mum and dad, new world Sauvignon Blanc from Chile or South Africa. Add some water for the kids and let them try.

For the school's recipe in this book, Lawrence Murphy met with and set 8 children from year 6 (aged 11 years) a task to develop a main course dish for the summer, using seasonal ingredients of their choice. They worked in pairs and put forward their suggestions of: lamb steak with cucumber and tomato salad; pasta with onion, bacon, tomatoes and garlic; sea bass with couscous, spring onions and tomatoes; and bbq chicken breast with lime and garlic. Lawrence chose from this to do a sea bass dish with the children, introducing some ingredients from other ideas put forward. In the kitchen at his restaurant, he demonstrated and fully explained how to prepare and present their dish in a restaurant-style, before they all sat down to taste the finished product.

SPENCERS RESTAURANT & BRASSERIE

SPENCERS RESTAURANT & BRASSERIE
36/38 NORTH STREET
EMSWORTH
PO10 7DG
T. 01243 372744/379017

www.spencersrestaurant.co.uk

LESLEY & DENIS SPENCER

DENIS SPENCER TRAINED AT THE LOCAL HIGHBURY COLLEGE BEFORE WORKING AT THE SAVOY HOTEL, LONDON AND THE PALM BEACH CASINO AND THEN BECAME HEAD CHEF AT EQUITIES RESTAURANT, ALSO IN LONDON. DURING 1988, ALONG WITH HIS WIFE LESLEY, HE STARTED HIS OWN BUSINESS WITH SPENCERS RESTAURANT WHERE HE CONTINUES TO WORK IN THE KITCHEN WHILST LESLEY HAS RESPONSIBILITY FOR THE FRONT OF HOUSE. THE FOOD SERVED IS MODERN ENGLISH, AND INCLUDES A WIDE CHOICE OF FISH DISHES. WHEN NOT WORKING AT THE RESTAURANT, DENIS CAN BE FOUND SAILING HIS BOAT IN THE HARBOUR AT EMSWORTH.

SPENCERS RESTAURANT & BRASSERIE BUILDING WAS ORIGINALLY TWO COTTAGES DATING BACK TO 1850. ONE OF THESE COTTAGES BECAME A HARDWARE STORE AND LATER WAS USED BY A YACHT ARCHITECT AS A DESIGN OFFICE. THE UPSTAIRS RESTAURANT HAS BEEN OWNED BY DENIS AND LESLEY SPENCER SINCE 1988. IN 1994, THEY BOUGHT THE GROUND FLOOR BAKERY AND RAN IT AS A FRENCH BAKERY AND PATISSERIE UNTIL 1996, WHEN IT BECAME SPENCERS BRASSERIE. THE RESTAURANT STILL USES GAS LIGHTING IN BOTH THE DOWNSTAIRS AND UPSTAIRS. PERHAPS IT IS BECAUSE OF THIS REMINDER OF TIMES GONE BY THAT IT IS RUMOURED TO BE INHABITED BY A GHOST.

DENIS SPENCER MESSING AROUND IN HIS BOAT

BAKED ENGLISH ASPARAGUS SPEARS WRAPPED IN PARMA HAM WITH LEMON SCENTED BEURRE BLANC

Serves 4

3-COURSE MENU

BAKED ENGLISH ASPARAGUS SPEARS WRAPPED IN PARMA HAM WITH LEMON SCENTED BEURRE BLANC

LOBSTER SALAD WITH BASIL AIOLI AND SMOKED PAPRIKA AND LIME MAYONNAISE

CARAMELISED STRAWBERRIES WITH VANILLA ICE CREAM IN BRANDY SNAP BASKET

24 English Asparagus Spears
12 Slices Parma Ham (rind removed)
Salt
Freshly Ground Black Pepper
4 Tablespoons Parmesan Cheese
  (freshly grated)
Extra Virgin Olive Oil
50ml Double Cream
Zest of ¼ Lemon
125g Butter
Flat Leaf Parsley (to garnish)

Pre-heat oven to 180C/350F/Gas 4

1. Prepare the asparagus by peeling the bottom of the stem where it is mauve coloured, and trim off the side leaves.

2. Wash in running cold water and tie in bundles of 8 with white string (not blue).

3. Cook in salted boiling water for 3-4 minutes, until when squeezed there is give in the flesh.

4. When cooked, plunge into ice-cold water to arrest the cooking.

5. Lay out the Parma ham slices.

6. Place 2 spears, cut in half, across the Parma ham.

7. Sprinkle with salt, pepper and parmesan cheese, and wrap the Parma ham around the spears.

8. Place the rolls on a baking tray, drizzle with olive oil and bake in the pre-heated oven for 8 minutes.

9. Arrange the cooked asparagus onto 4 plates.

10. Boil the cream with the lemon zest, and when bubbling whisk in the butter until fully emulsified.

11. Spoon the sauce over the asparagus and serve garnished with flat leaf parsley.

Must be top quality South African Sauvignon Blanc or Pouilly Fumé from the Loire Valley.

LOBSTER SALAD WITH BASIL AÏOLI AND SMOKED PAPRIKA AND LIME MAYONNAISE

Serves 4

SIMON HAYNES, CHEF

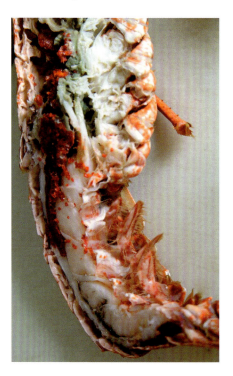

4 x 500g Live Lobsters
2 Eggs
Salt
White Pepper
50ml White Wine Vinegar
400ml Olive Oil
1 Teaspoon Smoked Paprika
Juice 1 Lime
2 Cloves Garlic (puréed)
1 Bunch Fresh Basil Leaves
1 Bag Mixed Salad Leaves
1 Lemon
500g Jersey Royal Potatoes
Butter
Fresh Mint

PREPARING THE LOBSTERS
1. Cook the lobsters by inserting in a large pot of salted, boiling water for 15 minutes. They will die as they hit the boiling water.
2. Remove and chill.
3. When cold, remove the claws and trim off the legs.
4. With a large chopping knife, chop the lobsters in half lengthways.
5. Remove the tail flesh and clean out the dirt track along the top edge.
6. Clean out the head of the shell, and any stomach.
7. Slice the lobster tail meat, and replace into the opposite shell from that which it came, so that the red colour is uppermost.
8. With the back of a chopping knife, crack open the claws and remove the flesh. Divide evenly between the 2 halves.
9. Place all in a fridge.

MAYONNAISE
1. Place the eggs into a food processor, season with salt and pepper and add the vinegar.
2. With the processor running, drizzle in the oil until the mayonnaise is thick.
3. Remove and split into 2 halves.
4. In the first, add the teaspoon of smoked paprika and the lime juice.
5. In the other, add the garlic purée and finely shredded basil leaves.

TO SERVE
1. Place the lobster halves in the shells on a plate, and arrange salad leaves tossed in olive oil and white wine vinegar.
2. Place a spoonful of each mayonnaise on the side and garnish with a wedge of lemon.
3. Serve with hot, buttered, minted, boiled, jersey royal potatoes.

The best white Burgundy you can afford or a top notch but not over oaked New World Chardonnay.

CARAMELISED STRAWBERRIES WITH VANILLA ICE CREAM
IN BRANDY SNAP BASKET

Serves 4

JORGE MORRISON, CHEF

BRANDY SNAP BASKETS
50g Butter (unsalted)
55g Caster Sugar
60g Golden Syrup
1 Teaspoon Vanilla Extract
1 Tablespoon Brandy
1 Teaspoon Lemon Zest
55g Plain Flour
½ Teaspoon Ground Ginger

CARAMELISED STRAWBERRIES
250g Caster Sugar
500g Strawberries

Real Vanilla Ice cream

BRANDY SNAP BASKETS
Pre-heat oven to 180C/350F/Gas 4
1. Place the butter, caster sugar and golden syrup in a saucepan and place over a moderate heat.
2. Stir regularly with a wooden spoon until the butter and syrup have melted and the sugar has dissolved.
3. Leave to simmer for 2 minutes and remove from the heat.
4. Stir in the vanilla essence, brandy and lemon zest.
5. Then gradually mix in the flour and ground ginger, until well incorporated.
6. Set the mixture aside for 15 minutes to cool and become firmer.
7. Place the mixture onto a non-stick baking tray 1 dessertspoonful at a time – with enough room between each to allow for them to spread as they cook. Make 6 to allow for breakages.
8. Bake in the pre-heated oven for 10-15 minutes until rich golden brown in colour.
9. Remove from the oven and allow to cool for 1 minute.
10. Place 6 small teacups upside down on a work surface.
11. Carefully remove the brandy snaps from the tray whilst still pliable.
12. Place each one over a teacup and shape into baskets.
13. Leave to harden.
14. Once set, remove from the moulds and store in an airtight container until ready to use.

CARAMELISED STRAWBERRIES
1. Put the caster sugar in a saucepan and cover with water.
2. Bring to the boil and simmer.
3. As the water evaporates, use a wet kitchen paper towel to wipe away the sugar crystals from around the pan above the water line. This reduces the chance of the sugar crystallizing.
4. Keep simmering until the syrup turns a dark caramel colour.
5. To stop the sugar going any darker, remove from the heat, put the pan in the sink and carefully tip in 75ml of cold water. This will spit violently, so do it slowly and carefully.
6. When all the water has been added, return the pan to the stove to re-boil. The caramel is now ready and can be put aside until required.
7. Place 2 ladles of caramel into a frying-pan, bring to the boil and add the washed and dried strawberries and toss until fully coated.

TO SERVE
1. Place a scoop of vanilla ice cream in each basket.
2. Spoon the strawberries onto the plates and cover with caramel sauce.

If you do not wish to make the brandy snap baskets, you can buy ready-made ones.

You have got this far, so push the boat out and go for demi-sec Champagne - absolutely delicious!

VILLAGE FRUIT & VEG

THEIR DAUGHTER, HANNA AT THE 2003 FOOD FESTIVAL STALL.
PHOTO BY TREVOR BURDETT

VILLAGE FRUIT & VEG
6 HIGH STREET
EMSWORTH
PO10 7AW

CLARE & KEV DOSWELL

KEV DOSWELL DECIDED TO GIVE UP HIS CAREER IN ELECTRONICS FOR THE MOD, TO BEGIN TRADING IN FRESH FRUIT AND VEGETABLES WHEN HE STARTED HIS BUSINESS IN EMSWORTH. HE IS PASSIONATE ABOUT USING FRESH PRODUCE IN OUR DAILY DIETS, AND THE IMPORTANCE THAT YOUNG CHILDREN UNDERSTAND WHAT VEGETABLES LOOK LIKE BEFORE THEY ARE CUT-UP AND COOKED. MUCH OF WHAT HE SELLS HAS THAT DAY COME FROM THE FIELDS DIRECT TO THE SHOP. KEV LOVES MEETING PEOPLE, AND IS HAPPIEST WHEN OUT AND ABOUT IN HIS VAN MAKING HIS REGULAR DELIVERIES.

VILLAGE FRUIT & VEG WAS ESTABLISHED AS A GREENGROCER IN THE VILLAGE FROM 1993 UNTIL EARLY 2004, WHEN IT TEMPORARILY RELOCATED TO HAVANT DUE TO PROPERTY DEVELOPMENT IN THE ORIGINAL LOCATION. KEV DOSWELL IS OVERJOYED TO BE BACK IN THE VILLAGE, HAVING FOUND ALTERNATIVE PREMISES TO RUN HIS BUSINESS WHERE HE FEELS HE BELONGS. HE PROVIDES A RETAIL AND WHOLESALE SERVICE DELIVERING PRODUCE TO THE ELDERLY RESIDENTS AND RESTAURANTS OF THIS VILLAGE. MUCH OF THE FRESH DAILY PRODUCE IS SOURCED LOCALLY DIRECT FROM FARMERS.

TOMATO AND AUBERGINE TARTLET

Makes 1 (large) or 4 (individual)

PASTRY CASE
75g (2½oz) Butter
110g (4oz) Flour
Pinch Salt
2 Tablespoons Cold Water

FILLING
8 Plum Tomatoes
4 Shallots
2 Cloves Garlic
Butter
½ Glass White Wine
Freshly Ground Black Pepper
Salt
1 Aubergine
Olive Oil

PASTRY CASE

Pre-heat oven to 160C/325F/Gas 3
1. Rub together the butter, flour and salt to form breadcrumbs.
2. Add the water and combine to form a dough.
3. Refrigerate for 20 minutes.
4. Roll out on a floured surface.
5. Line the pastry case and bake blind in the pre-heated oven for 15 minutes, until lightly golden.

FILLING

Pre-heat oven to 180C/350F/Gas 4
1. Blanch the plum tomatoes in hot water for 15 seconds, then plunge into cold water.
2. Peel and chop the tomatoes.
3. Finely chop the shallots and garlic and sauté in butter until soft.
4. Add the white wine and the chopped tomatoes with the pepper and salt,
5. Simmer until thickened.
6. Cut the aubergine into thin slices, and lay on a tray. Sprinkle liberally with salt and leave for 20 minutes.
7. Wash the sliced aubergine in cold water, and dry using kitchen paper.
8. Heat a frying pan with olive oil and fry the aubergine slices on both sides until light brown in colour.
9. Put the tomato mixture into the pastry case until half filled.
10. Top with the cooked aubergine slices.
11. Put into the pre-heated oven for 20-25 minutes.

Add asparagus for extra interest and flavour.

You can use any combination of vegetables to your liking.

You can use ready-made pastry for the case.

You can make individual tartlets or a large tart.

Serve as a starter with fresh salad leaves, or as a main course dish.

Alsace or Australian dry Riesling would be perfect here.

BBQ PINEAPPLE *Serves 4*

1 Pineapple
2 Tablespoons Runny Honey
3 Tablespoons Malibu or Cointreau
1 Level Teaspoon Ground Cinnamon
Crème Fraîche or Ice Cream

1. Remove the top and bottom of the pineapple and cut into quarters.

2. Remove the core.

3. Then remove the flesh of the fruit from the skin and cut into chunks.

4. Cut squares of foil, and place pineapple onto the foil.

5. Mix together the honey, Malibu and cinnamon, and spoon over the pineapple.

6. Fold the foil into parcels and put onto a hot bbq to cook until warm.

7. Remove from the foil and serve with crème fraîche or ice cream.

Hopefully the pineapple will slightly caramelise so a new world "sticky" should work well here – Australian Botrytised Semillon sounds good.

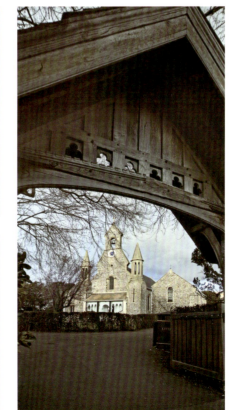

INTER-DENOMINATIONAL SERVICE IN SQUARE　　*CARRYING THE CROSS, GOOD FRIDAY*　　*ST. JAMES' CHURCH AND THE 'CONCERT OF CELEBRATION' FOLLOWING INTERNAL RENOVATION*

WESTBOURNE

LUMLEY

HERMITAGE

WARBLINGTON

EMSWORTH

Emsworth
Marina

PRINSTED

SOUTHBOURNE

Thornham
Marina

THORNEY ISLAND

IN AND AROUND EMSWORTH

EMSWORTH MAY HAVE NO MOUNTAINS TO CLIMB, BUT IT OFFERS A GREAT STARTING POINT FOR MANY EXCELLENT WALKS. BOTH IN-LAND AND AROUND THE COASTAL PATHS, IT CAN PROVIDE BOTH DEMANDING AND EASY WALKS FOR YOUNG AND OLD.

LATER IN THIS BOOK, WE HAVE GIVEN JUST THREE EXAMPLES WITH WALKS OUT OF THE VILLAGE IN EACH DIRECTION (ALAS NOT SOUTH, AS THIS REQUIRES A BOAT).

THE FIRST IS AROUND THORNEY ISLAND TO PRINSTED. AS WELL AS GREAT VIEWS ACROSS THE CHICHESTER HARBOUR, YOU WILL SEE A WIDE VARIETY OF WILDLIFE, PARTICULARLY IN THE WINTER AND SPRING. IT'S FAIRLY DEMANDING AT ABOUT SEVEN OR EIGHT MILES (DEPENDING ON ROUTE), BUT WELL WORTH THE EFFORT. IT ALSO REQUIRES ACCESS TO MOD LAND AND YOU SHOULD KEEP TO THE DESIGNATED PATHS IN THIS SECTION.

OUR SECOND WALK TO WARBLINGTON IS MUCH LESS DEMANDING, BUT IS BEST TAKEN IN THE SUMMER MONTHS AND NOT AT HIGH TIDES. THIS ONLY APPLIES TO ONE SECTION AND YOU WILL BE EASILY ABLE TO JUDGE WHETHER TO CONTINUE ON THIS FORESHORE SECTION, OR TAKE IN 'IN-LAND' ROUTES IN BOTH DIRECTIONS.

OUR THIRD WALK IS NORTH TO WESTBOURNE AND IT COVERS SOME GREAT SCENIC SECTIONS WITH THE CHANCE TO VISIT A PUB AT HALF-WAY. THE WALK SHOULD NOT TAKE MORE THAN TWO HOURS UNLESS YOU SPEND TIME IN THE VILLAGE AND VISIT THE HOSTELRIES.

WESTBOURNE

PRINSTED

WARBLINGTON

THORNEY ISLAND

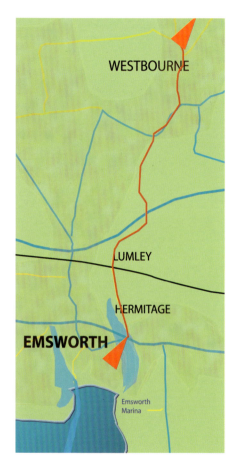

The bridlepath route from Emsworth to Westbourne is popular with cyclists young and old. Many continue up to the South Downs for a more demanding ride, while families can return after a look around the village and perhaps some refreshment. This route also forms part of the Westbourne walk detailed later in this book.

PHOTOGRAPH BY MIKE AUSTEN

PHOTO BY MIKE AUSTEN, LOCAL EMSWORTH PHOTOGRAPHER

THE ROUTE OUT OF EMSWORTH AND HERMITAGE

THE FINAL SECTION LEADING INTO WESTBOURNE

BROOK MEADOW

BY BRIAN FELLOWS, CHAIRMAN, BROOK MEADOW CONSERVATION GROUP

Brook Meadow is a lovely open space near the centre of Emsworth, owned by Havant Borough Council and managed on their behalf by the Brook Meadow Conservation Group. The site is approximately 6 acres, and consists of a large area of wet grassland flanked by the River Ems and the Lumley Stream and two areas of woodland. There are a number of good footpaths through the site, with access for all. Information boards with up-to-date news and photographs are sited at each of the three entrances, plus two interpretation boards displaying the superb artwork commissioned from local wildlife artist, Marian Forster. Brook Meadow has been formally designated a Site of Importance for Nature Conservation in recognition of its ecological value.

The most important wildlife on Brook Meadow is the Water Voles, delightful creatures that live on the banks of the River Ems. They eat only vegetation and are quite different in their habits from Brown Rats with which they are sometimes confused. The Water Vole is the most highly endangered mammal in Great Britain and is protected by law. The occasional Roe Deer passes through, and Moles are very common. In the summer, several species of bats feed over the streams. Brown Trout are an attraction in the river, where large Eels can also be seen. Impressive shoals of Grey Mullet come up the Lumley Stream from the harbour, at high tide.

Birds are always present, particularly in the wooded areas. Breeding residents include Robin, Wren, Dunnock, Blackbird, Song Thrush, Blue Tit, Great Tit, Chaffinch, Greenfinch and Wood Pigeon. In winter Goldcrest, Goldfinch, Long-tailed Tit and Great Spotted Woodpecker are common, while Chiffchaff, Whitethroat and Blackcap are regular summer visitors. Little Egret, Grey Heron, Grey Wagtail and Kingfisher are regularly seen on the waterways. Over 20 species of butterfly are found on Brook meadow, including Small Tortoiseshell, Painted Lady, Comma, Red Admiral, Peacock, Speckled Wood, Gatekeeper, Meadow Brown and Ringlet. The waterways also attract a range of damselflies and dragonflies, including the Banded Demoiselle with dark bands on its wings, and the bright green Southern Hawker which may fly low to inspect you.

Over the past few years, a complete survey of all the plants growing on Brook Meadow has been conducted in collaboration with local naturalists. Currently, the list is approaching 280 plants with more than 170 wild flowers, 40 trees and shrubs, 50 grasses, sedges and rushes, plus many mosses and liverworts. There are seven old meadow indicators. In winter, the river banks are covered with the sweet smelling Winter Heliotrope, while spring is heralded by the bright yellow flowers of Lesser Celandine (a favourite flower of Wordsworth). The pink flower spikes of Butterbur are distinctive on the river banks in early spring; in summer, this plant grows huge leaves which traditionally were used for keeping butter cool. In summer, the meadow is full of wild flowers such as, Ragged Robin, Cuckooflower, Meadowsweet and Strawberry Clover among others. In late summer, the meadow is ablaze with the yellow flowers of Fleabane. Brook Meadow has a wonderful variety of grasses, but botanically the most important plants are the sedges, of which some like Divided Sedge are nationally scarce. Greater and Lesser Pond Sedge grow on the banks of the streams.

Although basically a grassland, Brook Meadow has a large number of trees which are very important for wildlife. There are two areas of dense woodland on either side of the meadow, plus more than 100 mature Crack Willows along the banks of the River Ems. In early spring, Hazel and Alder provide a fine show of hanging catkins, while later in the spring Pussy Willows are covered with catkins. Alder, Buckthorn and Hawthorn have been planted for their wildlife value. Despite its wetness, Brook Meadow does not have many fungi although what it lacks in quantity it makes up for in quality, for the rare and very tasty Agrocybe Cylindracea grows on certain old willow stumps.

The Brook Meadow Conservation Group was formed in September 2000 by a number of local residents to help restore, protect and conserve the natural environment of Brook Meadow and its wildlife for the benefit and quiet enjoyment of the people of Emsworth. For their £3 subscription, members receive bi-monthly newsletters or weekly news updates via e-mail. The group's website is regularly updated with all the news from Brook Meadow plus wildlife photographs. Workdays, walks, surveys and other special events, such as Nature Hunts, are held throughout the year, and school visits are also organised.

For further information:
Brian Fellows, Chairman, Brook Meadow Conservation Group,
11 Bridge Road, Emsworth, PO10 7QU (T. 01243 375548)

e. brianfellows@tiscali.co.uk
www.hants.org.uk/brook-meadow

WILDLIFE IN BROOK MEADOW

PHOTOGRAPHS ON THIS PAGE BY BRIAN FELLOWS

COCK CHAFER IN MAY

SMALL TORTOISESHELL FLEABANE

SPECKLED WOOD IN BROOK MEADOW

WATER VOLE IN MARCH

LITTLE EGRET VISITS DOLPHIN QUAY BUT OFTEN FOUND IN BROOK MEADOW

WATER VOLE PHOTOGRAPHED BY THE RIVER EMS DURING APRIL

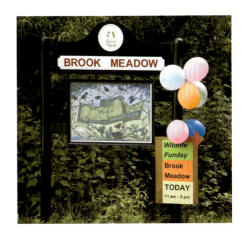

PUSSY WILLOWS - FEMALE (APRIL)

PUSSY WILLOW - MALE

HEDGEROW CRANESBILL MARINS

CUCKOO FLOWER

CHICHESTER HARBOUR

BY CHICHESTER HARBOUR CONSERVANCY

Not only one of the few remaining undeveloped coastal areas in Southern England, but rarer still, Chichester Harbour remains relatively wild. Its bright wide expanses and intricate creeks are at the same time a major wildlife haven and among some of Britain's most popular boating waters.

Backed by the South Downs, the harbour is a series of tidal inlets, with a narrow mouth to the sea, punctuating areas of fertile farmland. Fringed by a narrow margin of wind-sculptured oaks and hawthorn, the fields in turn give way to salt-marsh and intertidal mud-lands, broken by a maze of creeks and rithes.

The rich diversity of the area is enhanced by the patterns of sea and land changing with the tides and seasons. In this flat landscape, the vertical elements of church spires and old mills are an important part of its character, as are the colour-washed, red-roofed villages.

The massive stretch of tidal flats and saltings are of outstanding ecological significance. Very large populations of wildfowl and waders use the mudflats feeding on the rich plant life and the huge populations of intertidal invertebrates. More than 7,500 Brent geese overwinter on the intertidal mud-land and adjacent farmland and more than 50,000 birds reside in or visit the Harbour throughout the year.

Picturesque creekside villages encircle the shoreline, which straddles the boundary of West Sussex and Hampshire counties. These range from the vibrant village of Emsworth, to the beautifully quiet hamlet of Prinsted. The harbour lowlands contain high quality arable farmland and boatyards; marinas and commercial fishing are important elements of the local economy.

This is one of the south coast's most popular sailing waters with as many as 12,500 craft regularly using the harbour, with competitive racing taking place among the 14 sailing clubs of the Chichester Harbour Federation.

The villages, sea walls and footpaths are a popular leisure area for residents and tourists alike.

Set up by Act of Parliament in 1971, Chichester Harbour Conservancy has the duty to conserve, maintain and improve the harbour and amenity area for recreation, natural conservation and natural beauty. As well as being the statutory harbour authority, the Conservancy manages the Area of Outstanding Natural Beauty (AONB).

Chichester Harbour Conservancy consists of 15 members informed by an Advisory Committee including representatives of all harbour users. The Harbour Office operates from Itchenor, with a small sub-office at Emsworth.

Following a grant from the Heritage Lottery Fund in 2003, the Rhythms of the Tide project will see the implementation of around 40 projects throughout the AONB. These include improvements to disabled facilities, the purchase of a solar powered boat for informative and educational trips around the Harbour, archaeological research and habitat enhancements. One of the projects will see the restoration of the last working oyster boat in Chichester Harbour, the 'Terror'. 'Terror' was based at Emsworth, she will be fully restored and then put into public use.

For more information on Chichester Harbour Conservancy:
www.conservancy.co.uk
Harbour Master: Lt Col JQ Davis, Royal Marines   T. 01243 512301

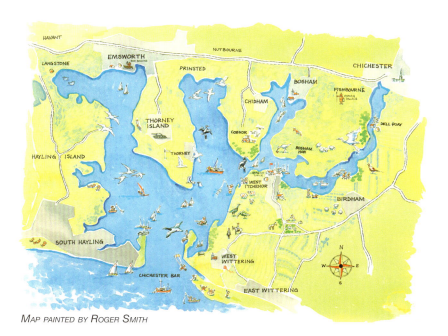

MAP PAINTED BY ROGER SMITH

THE TERROR

PHOTOGRAPH COURTESY OF EMSWORTH MARINA

EMSWORTH BETWEEN THE WARS SHOWING THE BOATYARDS

Chichester Harbour Conservancy and Emsworth Maritime and Historical Society have hatched an ambitious plan to restore the only surviving Chichester Harbour working boat, the 'Terror'. Subject to Heritage Lottery Funding, it is intended to become a centrepiece of a heritage experience, aimed at re-telling the story of the Emsworth Oyster Fleet, based in Emsworth. The Terror will be able to carry up to 8 people for a sail past the relics of the oyster ponds, layings and boatyards of Emsworth. In addition, the restored boat will be used to give less able-bodied people a sailing experience in the harbour. The restoration work will be undertaken at a local Emsworth boat builder, Dolphin Quay Boatyard who will employ an apprentice to do some of the work involved.

The Terror, an open sailing boat, was built around 1890 and used for conveying oysters around Chichester Harbour. It is believed that it was constructed by Foster's boat yard in Emsworth, and owned by Mr Kennett, an Emsworth oyster, winkle and cockle merchant as well as a trader in sand and gravel. The fortunes of the boat declined when the oyster industry of Emsworth was destroyed by a now notorious food poisoning incident in 1902. She has since had a number of owners, but is now in desperate need of restoration.

THE TERROR BEFORE RESTORATION AND A MODEL SHOWING HOW IT LOOKED

TERROR'S SISTER SHIP, THE GRAMPUS

A DAY IN THE LIFE OF SYD KENNETT, HARBOUR HAND, EMSWORTH

CHICHESTER HARBOUR CONSERVANCY 'SOLAR HERITAGE'

RIBBON CUT BY LADY PIPPA BLAKE OF EMSWORTH ABOVE TWO PHOTOS BY MATT SIMMONS

THE SOLAR BOAT MAKES A NUMBER OF TRIPS FROM EMSWORTH. CONTACT THE HARBOUR MASTER ON 01243 512301 FOR DETAILS

THE EMSWORTH FOOD FESTIVAL

I still have to pinch myself when I think about the Emsworth Food Festival, a really quite extraordinary event in an even more extraordinary village. I have lost count of the number of people from outside Emsworth who have said to me that they wish they either lived in a village like Emsworth or had a village like it near them. What started out as an idea based around Emsworth's food heritage has turned into the most wonderful example of a community working together to showcase their village. Old fashioned values? Village pride? I don't really know the answer to that, but I do know in this my last year as Chairman, that it has been an absolute honour to be involved, it has changed the way I view things and I am eternally grateful for being given the opportunity to be part of it.

As with many things in life, you cannot dwell on the past, you have to move forward and I have no doubt that the Festival will continue to build on its success. Food is a wonderful theme, it appeals to us all, we are now I believe a nation who 'live to eat', no longer do we merely 'eat to live'. By encouraging people who are passionate about food, whether they are shopkeepers (sounds so much nicer then retailers doesn't it?) or producers, the Festival will ensure that it offers visitors a wealth of both quality and diverse products. For the Festival quality is the key word - from the stallholders, to the entertainment, to the cookery and wine demonstrations, to the new initiatives such as the Young Chef of the Year competition – because it should never be forgotten that it is Emsworth and its residents who lend their village to the Festival for a weekend every September.

Which in a round about way brings me to this book. I actually hesitate to use the word 'book' as it is so much more than that. The dictionary definition of book is " a set of blank, printed or written sheets of paper bound together along one edge and enclosed within protective covers to form a volume". Nowhere does it mention heart, soul, pride or commitment, which are just some of the ingredients you will find in this - and I use the word deliberately - unique document of Emsworth. From award winning chefs to school children and every part of village life in between, it is perhaps the reason why this village is so special and why the first Cookbook sold out so quickly. I must take this opportunity to thank John and Elaine - your commitment has never ceased to amaze me - and to everyone who appears in the book, you have all created something quite extraordinary.

ALISTAIR GIBSON, CHAIRMAN, EMSWORTH FOOD FESTIVAL

I have no doubt you will treasure this book and I also have no doubt you will continue to enjoy the Emsworth Food Festival. But also please remember that it is not just about those three days in every September. Emsworth is a wonderful and beautiful place, full of passionate shopkeepers, restaurateurs and publicans all year round.

Lastly may I raise my glass - from the Wine Village of course - to this great village and all its residents, special doesn't even barely cover it!

Alistair Gibson
Chairman, Emsworth Food Festival

www.emsworthfoodfestival.co.uk

PHOTOGRAPH BY TREVOR BURDETT

LOWER THREE PHOTOS BY TREVOR BURDETT

DURING 2003 I WAS ASKED BY MY NEIGHBOURS, GRAHAME AND MURIEL DRYDEN, TO PRODUCE A DRESSING TO ACCOMPANY THE OYSTERS THAT CHARLIE READING TRADITIONALLY SERVES AT THE EMSWORTH FOOD FESTIVAL. THEY WANTED SOMETHING DIFFERENT, AN EXOTIC MALAYSIAN SAUCE PERHAPS? I AGREED HESITANTLY AS MANY WOULD SAY OYSTERS ARE A FEAST IN THEMSELVES AND NEED NO ADDITIONAL FLAVOURS TO ENHANCE THEIR TASTE. WE DECIDED THAT I WOULD TRY TO COME UP WITH A FEW OPTIONS AND HOLD A TASTING SESSION TO SEE IF ANY WERE WORTHY OF ACCOMPANYING THE OYSTERS AT THE FESTIVAL.

THE TASTING DAY DULY ARRIVED, AND WE TRIED OUT VARIOUS DRESSINGS INCLUDING THE TRADITIONAL SHALLOT, VINEGAR AND TOMATO WITH WORCESTER SAUCE. OTHER COMBINATIONS INCLUDED POSSIBLY MY FAVOURITE, A VARIATION OF THE FIJIAN COCONUT BASED KOKONDA. THE TOMATO CORIANDER RECIPE PRINTED HERE GOT THE MAJORITY VOTE AND HOPEFULLY IT IS SIMPLE AND LIGHT ENOUGH NOT TO OVER-WHELM THE TASTE OF THE OYSTERS. IF YOU HAVEN'T ANY OYSTERS TO HAND, TRY THIS AS AN ACCOMPANIMENT TO GRILLED PRAWNS OR FISH.

MARGUERITA TAPLIN

JALANAGONG

A DRESSING TO ACCOMPANY FRESH OYSTERS

450g Ripe Red Tomatoes
Large Bunch Fresh Coriander
3 Spring Onions
4 Tablespoons Fresh Lemon Juice
Salt

1. Blanch the tomatoes by immersing them in a bowl of boiling water for approximately 4 minutes. Discard the water and allow the tomatoes to cool slightly before peeling off the skin and then liquidising the tomatoes.

2. Chop off the stalks and thoroughly wash the coriander. Drain off excess water and chop a cupful of the leaves extremely finely (using a food processor if possible).

3. Discard the outer skin of the spring onions and the greenish leaves. Use a food processor to chop up the stalks very finely.

4. In a bowl, combine 12 tablespoons of the tomato pulp with 3 tablespoons of the chopped coriander. Add 2.5 tablespoons of the chopped spring onions, 4 tablespoons of lemon juice and a pinch of salt. Mix thoroughly, and if possible refrigerate for 15 minutes before use.

5. To serve, add a teaspoon of the dressing to each half shell containing shucked oysters (or grilled fish or prawns). If you prefer a slightly stronger flavour, add an additional tablespoon of chopped coriander and half a tablespoon of spring onions to the mixture.

Any excuse to talk wine with oysters - Champagne if you want to push the boat out, if not Chablis or Muscadet and finally there's always Guinness!

HOLLYBANK WOODS

BY ANDREW BROOK FOR THE FRIENDS OF HOLLYBANK WOODS

Hollybank Woods (still shown on many maps as the southern part of Southleigh Forest), is an area of woodland to the north of Emsworth (OS Grid Ref SU7408), and to the south of Emsworth Common Road.

Acquired in 1996 by Havant Borough Council from the Southleigh Estate on a 999 year lease, as part of a deal involving the granting of permission to build houses on Locks Farm at Denvilles, the woodland covers approximately 150.7 acres (61 hectares) and is designated as an area of Special Interest for Nature Conservation (SINC).

Hollybank Woods has a diverse structure of trees and habitat that support a rich biodiversity of plants, insects and mammals. Deer are a common sight in the woodland: Fallow, Roe and Muntjac are all resident breeders. Bird life is also abundant with Tawny and Little Owls, Buzzard, Thrush, Treecreeper and Nuthatch to name but a few of the year-round residents. In winter, Redwing and Fieldfare visit and in summer the woods echo to the song of visiting Willow Warbler and Chiffchaff.

Oak, Beech, Holly, Yew and Birch jostle for position. In autumn the Chestnut trees reward the walker with bountiful supplies of chestnuts to roast on winter evenings. Whilst there is a young conifer plantation to the central eastern area of Hollybank Woods, about 30 years old, there are also fine examples of Douglas Fir to be found throughout the wood. On the southern boundary there are also two 150-year-old Scots Pine. Windblown trees are also a common sight where the soil is shallow and drainage has been impeded, and these offer many insects a tailor-made micro habitat in which to prosper.

Fungus, mosses, grasses and wild flowers are abundant throughout the year, and provide rich pickings for many insects. Brambles and Honeysuckle predominate in many areas and the woodland is lucky to have a population of White Admiral butterfly that have increased in numbers here over the past few decades. Back in 1972-3, when the last recorded survey was carried out by Peter Craddock, it was thought that they had been wiped out from these woods, so their return in significant numbers has been encouraging.

Whilst Havant Borough Council carries out the overall management of Hollybank Woods, the need for regular conservation activity and to encourage and promote the use of the wood for local residents, led locals to form a conservation group. The Friends of Hollybank Woods formed in the spring of 2001, and is fully supported by Havant Borough Council. The friends organise workdays throughout the winter months, carrying out much needed path repair and clearing. Regular guided walks are arranged from spring through to late summer, during which time work ceases in the woods to allow the resident and visiting wildlife to breed and raise their young.

There are two main entrances to the woods, located at the top of Hollybank Lane (off Southleigh Road), and in a layby on the Emsworth Common Road.

For more information about the woodland: a leaflet is available from the Emsworth Library that also includes details on joining the Friends of Hollybank Woods and becoming more involved in the conservation of this ancient woodland.

www.hants.gov.uk/hollybank-woods

PHOTO BY ANDREW BROOK

ELEPHANT HAWK MOTH

Marking the 60th anniversary of D-Day on 6th June 2004 at the foundations of a Nissen hut. Hollybank Woods were used throughout World War II for training and as part of a military encampment.

LUMLEY MILL

Although the original Georgian house stands today, the mill itself was burnt down during an enormous fire that engulfed the building and mill works in the early hours of Tuesday 25 May 1915, just after the Lumley estate with its farmland as well as the mill had been sold by the then owner, James Terry. Although damaged, the house survived the fire, but the mill was totally destroyed and never re-built.

It is thought that the old mill was one of four mentioned in the Doomsday Book, there having been a working mill at Lumley well before Lumley House was built. Throughout its time, the mill has had a chequered history of ups and downs with prosperity and a grand lifestyle as well as being almost derelict at times. It had strong links with the navy in Portsmouth, providing ships biscuits (baked next to the mill stones), salt pork and flour to Nelson's fleet. In fact, Napoleonic prisoners of war were employed to build some of the structure of the house. And, it is rumoured that Lady Hamilton was a guest at a ball held there.

The name Lumley comes from Lord Lumley, later Earl of Scarborough, Lord of the manors of Stansted, Westbourne and Prinsted when the residence was built.

INFORMATION AND PHOTOGRAPHS REPRODUCED BY KIND PERMISSION OF THE PRESENT OWNERS.

LUMLEY TERRACE (THE WHITE BUILDING) WAS BUILT AT THE SAME TIME AS LUMLEY MILL. VICTORIA TERRACE WAS BUILT LATER USING THE BRICKS OF THE MALTINGS SOME TIME AFTER THE FIRE

NORE BARN WOODS

BY ROY EWING, SECRETARY, FRIENDS OF NORE BARN WOODS

Nore Barn Woods is special. At times it can be busy, at times deserted. Changing its character with the season, time of day and the tide, you will always find something new. Walking from a dark woodland area, you will suddenly be in a clearing, surrounded by shafts of sunlight, butterflies and birds. A place to find solitude and nature.

Nore Barn Woods is the only open space in south west Emsworth. It may have originated as part of the Forest of Bere, but it is more likely to be semi-natural woodland.

To find it, follow the Wayfarers' Walk from the end of Warblington Road, heading west. At high tide you may get your feet wet!

The Wayfarers' Walk continues along the northern perimeter of the wood, bordered by farmland. The western edge has fine views across the fields to Warblington Castle and the Church. The southern border is formed by Chichester Harbour, an Area of Natural Beauty, with open views across to Hayling Island and Thorney Island.

The woods cover an area of 6 acres and is owned by Havant Borough Council. There are several species of tree, with Hawthorn, Oak, Ash and Elder being dominant. The canopy is dense in the central and western areas and there is little ground flora as a result. A few Field Maple, Spindle and Beech saplings are present. In the understorey there are a number of young Holly bushes, a few Yew saplings and also Butcher's Broom.

Many species of flower are represented; Bluebells, Violets and Honesty are widespread. In spring, May blossom covers the trees.

More than 40 species of birds have been recorded, from cuckoo to woodpecker, and squirrels too are abundant.

The woods provide a quiet and enjoyable environment, and are used extensively by ramblers, dog walkers and horse riders.

A conservation group, 'Friends of Nore Barn Woods' (FONBW) was established in 2002 to allow local volunteers to work with official bodies to improve the management of the woods. The group is affiliated to the British Trust for Conservation Volunteers.

The aim of FONBW is to maintain the character of the woods, whilst improving sympathetically some of the dereliction. To support this aim, regular workdays are held. Much of the work is directed towards regeneration of the woods. Many of the trees are over-mature, and to improve this some of the trees have been coppiced to allow re-growth. In the meantime, light reaching the forest floor will stimulate the growth of flowers, which in turn will support an increase in butterflies and insects. In addition, more than 200 saplings and gorse have been planted to thicken the hedging and edges of the woodland.

FONBW has also worked with Havant Borough Council to improve the paths through the woods, and to provide a bridleway around the southern perimeter of the woods for horses. The improved paths have also made access easier for the disabled.

According to FONBW, Nore Barn Woods is one of the jewels in Emsworth's crown. Bringing together the three "w"s of woodland, wildlife and water, its existence is now more secure than it has been for many a year.

For further information:
Bruce Darby, Chairman, Friends of Nore Barn Woods (T. 01243 372905)
www.norebarnwoods.org.uk

Photo by David Linington

PRINSTED

BY THE VILLAGERS OF PRINSTED

PRINSTED IS A BEAUTIFUL VILLAGE,
BUT MOSTLY, PRINSTED IS ABOUT ITS PEOPLE.

PEREN STEDE (A PLACE WHERE PEARS GROW) OLD ENGLISH
PERNESTEDE: CIRCA 1253
PRYNSTED: CIRCA 1587
PRINSTED: MODERN USAGE
(FROM THE PLACE NAMES OF SUSSEX (1775) BY J GLOVER)

PHOTOGRAPHS ON THESE TWO PAGES BY JEANNIE SUTHERLAND

Prinsted, a small hamlet on the edge of Chichester Harbour, is part of the Parish of Southbourne. It is in an area of outstanding natural beauty and has the best of many worlds. Picturesque, quiet, and unspoilt, it is just far enough off the beaten track to make the life of its inhabitants most agreeable. Made the more so by a caring, yet not intrusive concern that its villagers have for one another. The abiding wish of everyone in the village is that none of this should change.

First mentioned in 1066, and part of all that, the name Prinsted emerged from the old English description for 'a place where pears grow'. Originally part of the Manor of Westbourne, it was owned by Roger de Montgomery, a relative of King William. The Montgomery family continued to own it until the middle of the sixteenth century. It then passed to John Lord Lumley, son-in-law of the Earl of Arundel.

By the early 1800s despite land reforms and the policy of enclosure, ownership of the land around Prinsted still remained in the hands of a few wealthy individuals. In 1829, a Mr William Padwick bought the village. At the time it had about forty dwellings. Since then Prinsted has grown by 'in-filling' to the present day total of over one hundred and sixty dwellings - and rising.

This extended period of development has provided a wealth of diverse and attractive architecture, giving simple pleasure to people as they walk through the village. Cold the heart that cannot warm to the serenity oozing from thatched roofs - and there are quite a number of them in Prinsted.

In the early days, Prinsted families came from very similar backgrounds. Generation after generation centred their working lives in and around the village. Farming and market gardening, and allied cottage industries, together with a few shops and pubs, provided employment for most inhabitants.

There have been colourful characters along

the way. In the late nineteenth century, a William Terry built a sea-going tricycle fitted with floats, paddles and wheels, about four feet in diameter. He tested and demonstrated the contraption on the Millpond at Emsworth. All went well, and for reasons not recorded other than it was there, he decided to cross the English Channel. He set off, and legend has it that many hours later he reached France and was promptly arrested by a local gendarme as a spy, probably because he had forgotten to take his passport.

Judy Baldwin was a member of the Fabian Society and a Prinsted political activist. Canvassing in the early 1930s she must have been quite a sight with a shock of unkempt red hair, men's breeches, and an old mac. She kept to her schedule using a wind-up alarm clock. She promised local children a reward for supporting her election campaign, with the beating of drums, shouting and rattling tins. The 'children' are still waiting for the reward. She received few votes.

More recently the village has lost one of its most beloved inhabitants. Bill Rogers was born in Prinsted 93 years ago. Bill grew up, worked and raised his large family in the village, and was a fount of kindly and sound advice on life in Prinsted, and the way to deal with anything that grows in the soil. His life was never rushed. Everything he did was at the same gentle pace, from driving his beloved Ferguson Tractor to wielding his felling axe for the daily supply of logs for the fire. He was still doing this at the age of 93. He was truly a Prinsted stalwart.

Since the end of the Second World War gradual changes have taken place. There are no longer any pubs or shops, and the villagers now come from a much wider background, to share the pleasures of living in Prinsted. For a time it was thought that the name ought to be changed to 'HMS Prinsted'. More recently however - 'Is there a doctor in the house' - would get at least fifteen positive replies. But, none of these changes really matter since with only 160

families or so, most villagers know and enjoy their neighbours for what they are, rather than for what they do!

In 1998 following an initiative by Bob Marshall, another long-standing family name in Prinsted, the Prinsted Village History Group was formed. Its aim was to research and produce a light hearted history of Prinsted to celebrate the Millennium. With help from an extensive team of villagers, Dennis Barry, the author produced 'PRINSTED - a place where pears grow'. The book was launched on 28th November 1999 at the Scout Hut, and over 400 copies were sold within two hours.

Following the success of the book, a village meeting was held to discuss how the profit from its sales should be spent. The general consensus was that it should be used to improve access to the foreshore, particularly for the disabled. The village arranged fund-raising events and investigated how the foreshore could be improved. The discovery that improvements would cost a good deal more than was anticipated coincided with the Harbour Conservancy bid for Lottery Funds, which the Prinsted Foreshore Project was invited to join. Happily, thanks to the Harbour Conservancy, the project to improve the Prinsted Foreshore, without altering its present natural appearance, is now a reality.

The general tranquillity of the foreshore is a priceless asset for everyone in Prinsted. Villagers enjoy moments of peace and quiet strolling round Chichester Harbour with all the benefits of wildlife conservation. In the summer villagers of all ages enjoy wind- surfing, and dinghy sailing. Equally, there are a number of such an age that they just prefer to watch from the foreshore.

The foreshore and harbour also provide a backdrop for the thriving activities of the 1st Southbourne Sea Scouts Group. The Group was established by Mr Charles Brundrett, gentleman farmer, in the outbuildings of his property Walnut Tree Farm in May 1933. The present headquarters is on the site of the old village pond, and was constructed in

1962/63 entirely by parents and ex-Scouts. The principal farm building, vacated by the Scouts in 1973, was subsequently dismantled and reconstructed at the Weald and Downland Museum, Singleton. Mr Brundrett and his wife, Sheila, now live in retirement in the Welsh Marches. He is in his 95th year.

In village life, size does matter. Celebrations such as the Millennium and Golden Jubilee events have been successful because Prinsted is big enough to make them worthwhile yet small enough to make them truly family occasions. This village spirit and support is always there for other events, not least of which is the Carol Singing on Christmas Eve, held in the village square and always a great village and family occasion.

PEAR AND WINE SORBET   *Serves 4*

1.8kg Very Ripe Pears (peeled & cored)
2 Tablespoons Caster Sugar
2 Vanilla Pods (split lengthways)
200ml (8fl oz) Water
125ml (5fl oz) White Wine
Juice 2 Lemons

1. Cook the pears slowly over a low heat with the sugar, vanilla pods and water, until soft.

2. Drain and add the wine and lemon juice.

3. Push through a fine sieve and leave to cool.

4. Put into an ice cream machine and churn until frozen. If you do not have a machine, freeze in an appropriate container.

5. The sorbet will keep in the freezer for up to 2 months.

6. Allow the sorbet to stand at room temperature for a few minutes to serve, otherwise it will be too hard to scoop.

AMANDA THOMAS, A RESIDENT SINCE 1990 OF THE LOVELY HAMLET OF PRINSTED, IS ALSO MANAGER OF THE BROOKFIELD HOTEL IN EMSWORTH. HER CAREER STARTED IN THE KITCHENS WHERE SHE WORKED AS A CHEF, AND WAS INITIALLY HEAD CHEF AT THE BROOKFIELD BEFORE DECIDING TO STEP AWAY FROM THIS TO RUN THE HOTEL. HER LINKS WITH PRINSTED DATE BACK TO 1964 WHEN HER FAMILY MOVED FROM HERTFORDSHIRE TO EMSWORTH, AND AMANDA ATTENDED LONGMEADOW SCHOOL, PRINSTED UNTIL 1969. SADLY THE SCHOOL NO LONGER EXISTS AND IS NOW A PRIVATE HOUSE IN PRINSTED LANE. AMANDA HAS CHOSEN HER RECIPE BASED ON THE OLD NAME FOR THE HAMLET, PEREN STEDE, A PLACE WHERE PEARS ARE GROWN.

Never easy, but Muscat de Beaumes de Venise works as well as anything.

'LITTLE ORCHARD' ON THE CORNER OF HAM LANE WAS ALSO A CORNER SHOP AT THE BEGINNING OF THE 20TH CENTURY. THE OLD DOOR HAS NOW BEEN BRICKED UP TO WINDOW HEIGHT.

'LITTLE ORCHARD', AND BARN IN 1920S

THORNEY ISLAND AND THE SALT-MARSH CATTLE SCHEME

THORNEY ISLAND WAS FIRST USED BY THE ROYAL AIR FORCE IN 1935 AND WAS A FIGHTER STATION AND BASE FOR COASTAL COMMAND DURING THE SECOND WORLD WAR. IN 1984, IT WAS TAKEN OVER BY THE ARMY AND IS NOW THE HOME BASE FOR AN ARTILLERY REGIMENT.

IT IS NO LONGER TECHNICALLY AN ISLAND, HAVING BEEN JOINED TO THE MAINLAND DURING 1870 AFTER THE RECLAMATION OF 72 HECTARES OF TIDAL MUDFLATS. THE MIXTURE OF OPEN GRASSLAND WITH A VARIETY OF MEADOW PLANTS, SCRUB AND REED-BEDS PROVIDE AN IDEAL HABITAT FOR A NUMBER OF SPECIES, INCLUDING BRENT GEESE, OYSTERCATCHERS, LAPWINGS, CURLEWS, SKYLARKS AND SHELDUCK.

BECAUSE THE ISLAND IS PART OF MOD PROPERTY, ACCESS BY ROAD IS RESTRICTED. HOWEVER, THE SITES OF SPECIAL INTEREST MAKE IT A POPULAR PLACE FOR RAMBLERS WHO CAN USE THE PUBLIC FOOTPATHS. WITHIN THE ARMY BUILDINGS AND THE RUNWAY, CAN BE FOUND A LITTLE OASIS WITH AN OLD FARMHOUSE WHICH HAS BEEN IN THE SPRACKLING FAMILY FOR GENERATIONS. THE TWO BROTHERS HAVE A THRIVING HERD OF ABERDEEN ANGUS CATTLE, AND HAVE BECOME INVOLVED WITH THE THREE HARBOURS GRAZING MARSH BEEF SCHEME WHEREBY THE CATTLE SPEND THE SPRING AND SUMMER MONTHS GRAZING ON THE SALT MARSHES ON THORNEY — A TRADITION DATING BACK IN TIME, WHICH VASTLY IMPROVES THE FLAVOUR OF THE MEAT.

SHON AND SIMON SPRACKLING, LOCAL ORGANIC BEEF FARMERS, HAVE SET UP ROTHER VALLEY ORGANICS TO SELL ORGANIC MEAT DIRECT TO CUSTOMERS' DOORS — HANDLING THE ENTIRE PROCESS LITERALLY FROM PASTURE TO PLATE. THE BROTHERS ARE SELLING THEIR OWN ORGANIC ABERDEEN ANGUS BEEF, AND ARE ALSO WORKING WITH OTHER LOCAL FARMERS TO OFFER A WIDE CHOICE OF ORGANIC MEATS SUCH AS LAMB AND PORK. ALL OF THE MEAT IS FULLY TRACEABLE, AND THE SPRACKLINGS HAVE THEIR OWN BUTCHERY WHERE THE MEAT IS HUNG FOR AT LEAST 21 DAYS AND THEN CUT BY MASTER BUTCHERS TO THE HIGHEST STANDARDS.

THE BROTHERS NOW HAVE MORE THAN 400 ABERDEEN ANGUS CATTLE WHICH ARE FED ON A VARIETY OF ORGANIC GRAZING LAND FROM ROGATE, NORTH OF THE SOUTH DOWNS TO THORNEY ISLAND. THE HERD LIVES OUTSIDE ALL YEAR ROUND, AND IS MOVED AROUND THE FARM TO BENEFIT FROM THE BEST SEASONAL GRAZING — CLOVER RICH ON THE HILLS IN THE WINTER TO RIVER BOTTOM PASTURE AND SEA FRONTAGE MARSHLAND IN THE SPRING AND SUMMER. A DIET RICH IN WILD PLANTS AND HERBS HELPS TO GIVE THE MEAT EXCEPTIONAL FLAVOUR.

SHON & SIMON SPRACKLING
ROTHER VALLEY ORGANICS
SANDILANDS FARM
ROGATE
PETERSFIELD
HANTS
GU31 5HU
T. 01730 821062

e. shon@rothervalleyorganics.com
www.rothervalleyorganics.co.uk

SHON & SIMON SPRACKLING ON THORNEY ISLAND

ROTHER VALLEY ORGANICS AIMS TO HELP PRESERVE THE ENVIRONMENT,
AND MUCH OF THE GRAZING LAND IS EITHER AN SSSI (SITE OF SPECIAL SCIENTIFIC INTEREST) OR AN ESA (ENVIRONMENTALLY SENSITIVE AREA). THE BROTHERS HAVE JOINED FORCES WITH THE THREE HARBOURS GRAZING MARSH BEEF SCHEME, A NEW FOOD INITIATIVE BETWEEN THE CHICHESTER HARBOUR CONSERVANCY AND THE FARMING AND WILDLIFE ADVISORY GROUP (FWAG) AIMED AT SECURING THE SURVIVAL OF THE COASTAL GRAZING MARSHES. AS PART OF THIS, ABERDEEN ANGUS SUCKLERS ARE GRAZED ON THORNEY ISLAND, WHICH NOT ONLY IMPROVES THE MEAT BUT ALSO HELPS PRESERVE THE ENVIRONMENT AND MAINTAIN IT AS A HABITAT FOR RARE PLANTS, WILDLIFE AND BIRDS.

SHON AND SIMON SPRACKLING DEVELOPED THE IDEA FOR ROTHER VALLEY ORGANICS DURING 2003 TO ALLOW CUSTOMERS TO BUY FRESH ORGANIC MEAT (WHICH HAS NOT BEEN FROZEN) LOCALLY KNOWING THAT THE ANIMALS HAVE BEEN KEPT IN THE HIGHEST WELFARE CONDITIONS AND TREATED HUMANELY. BY DEALING DIRECT WITH LOCAL FARMERS, LOCAL MONEY IS BEING PLOUGHED BACK INTO THE LOCAL ECONOMY.

ORGANIC BRAISED BEEF

Serves 4

1 Medium Onion (sliced)
Knob Butter
Pinch Caster Sugar
750g Organic Diced Braising Steak
Plain Flour
1 Clove Garlic (crushed)
½ Glass Red Wine
Salt & Pepper
1 Tablespoon Tomato Ketchup

Pre-heat oven to 190C/375F/Gas 5

1. Cut the onion in half and slice lengthways, and place into a frying pan with the butter and sugar.

2. Cook until the onions start to brown.

3. Set the onions aside, leaving the liquid in the pan.

4. Toss the braising steak in the flour and brown the meat in the frying pan.

5. Return the cooked onions to the pan and add the garlic and wine. Simmer for a few minutes.

6. Season to taste and add the tomato ketchup.

7. Transfer the mixture to a casserole dish and add half a glass of water.

8. Cook in the pre-heated oven for 90 minutes.

9. Serve with creamed potatoes, seasoned with freshly grated nutmeg, baby carrots and green broccoli.

VIC MAY INITIALLY TRAINED AS A BUTCHER BEFORE GOING TO CATERING COLLEGE TO TRAIN AS A CHEF. HE THEN COMBINED BOTH SKILLS, OPENING A BUTCHER SHOP WITH A DELI WHERE HE PREPARED ALL OF HIS OWN PRODUCTS. AS WELL AS NOW HAVING HIS OWN CATERING BUSINESS HANDLING DINNERS, PARTIES AND WEDDINGS HE ALSO WORKS FOR SHON AND SIMON ADVISING THEM ABOUT THE BUTCHERING SIDE OF THEIR NEW COMPANY AND ACTING AS CONCEPT CHEF WITH RECIPE IDEAS FOR THE MEATS SOLD.

A red from the Rhone Valley or Southern French red, both areas have many organic or even bio-dynamic wines.

ORGANIC ROLLED LAMB CUSHION

Serves approximately 8

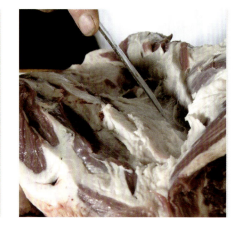

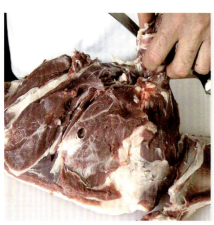

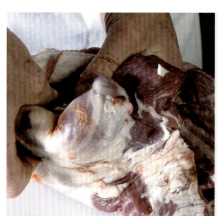

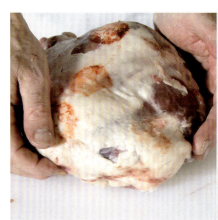
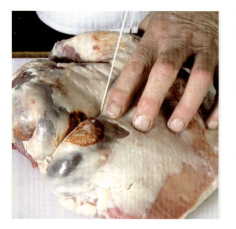

1500g Organic Lamb Cushion
Fresh Mint (chopped)
Redcurrant Jelly
White Wine
2 Tablespoons Double Cream

Pre-heat oven to 190C/375F/Gas 5

1. Roast the cushion of lamb in the pre-heated oven for approximately 2 hours.

2. When cooked, set the lamb aside.

3. Put the roasting tin on the hob with moderate heat.

4. Stir in a little mint and redcurrant jelly with a good splash of white wine and a little water.

5. When it has reduced by half, add 2 tablespoons of double cream.

6. To serve, cut the meat into segments or carve and drizzle the sauce over the lamb.

Lamb cushion is prepared from the shoulder cut of meat. Ask the Rother Valley Organics butcher (or any other butcher) to prepare a lamb cushion for you.

Again something organic, but go for a Cabernet Sauvignon from Bordeaux or South Africa.

ORGANIC BURRITOS

Makes 6

Vegetable Oil
250g Organic Diced Shoulder Pork
250g Organic Diced Braising Steak
1 Small Onion (chopped)
1 Clove Garlic (finely chopped)
1 Level Teaspoon Salt
2 Green Chillies
   (seeded & finely chopped)
425g Red Kidney Beans (drained)
25g Cheddar Cheese (grated)
6 Small Mexican Tortillas or Fajitas

1. Heat the oil in a large saucepan, add the pieces of pork and beef (a few at a time) and brown them well – removing them from the pan as they brown.

2. Return all of the meat to the pan, and add the onion, garlic, salt, chillies and 350ml of water.

3. Bring to the boil, reduce the heat, cover and simmer for 2 hours or until the meat is tender.

4. When the meat is cooked, flake it with a fork.

5. Continue to simmer, uncovered, until the liquid has reduced and the mixture has thickened.

6. Meanwhile, mix together the beans and cheese in a small saucepan and stir over a gentle heat until the cheese melts.

7. To make up a burrito, spread 2 tablespoons of the bean and cheese mixture over the tortilla or fajita with the same amount of the pork and beef mixture.

8. If required, add finely shredded crisp iceberg lettuce.

9. Fold and eat while hot.

Browning the meat in small amounts helps the meat to fry rather than boil.

When preparing garlic, split the clove and remove the green inner part which can be bitter to taste.

Surprisingly, perhaps, Mexico does produce particularly tasty reds, try a Petite Syrah, and if you can find an organic one let me know.

ABERDEEN ANGUS CATTLE ON THORNEY ISLAND

PHOTO BY MIKE AUSTEN

MICHAEL AUSTEN PHOTOGRAPHY, 671A FULHAM ROAD, LONDON, SW6 5PZ   T. 020 7384 3907
e. michael@michaelausten.co.uk   www.michaelausten.co.uk

PHOTO BY MIKE AUSTEN

PHOTO BY MIKE AUSTEN

SIR PELHAM GRENVILLE WODEHOUSE (1881-1975)

THREEPWOOD, RECORD ROAD, EMSWORTH WHERE WODEHOUSE LIVED

PG WODEHOUSE LIVED IN RECORD ROAD, EMSWORTH FROM 1904-1914. DURING THIS TIME HE WROTE NUMEROUS ARTICLES, AND HIS NOVEL, DAMSEL IN DISTRESS, WAS BASED IN EMSWORTH. IT COULD BE SURMISED THAT ONE OF HIS CHARACTERS, LORD EMSWORTH RESULTED FROM TIME SPENT LIVING IN THIS VILLAGE.

HE WROTE MORE THAN 70 NOVELS AND 300 SHORT STORIES DURING HIS LIFETIME, AS WELL AS BEING A LYRICIST, PLAYWRIGHT AND JOURNALIST.

THE PG WODEHOUSE SOCIETY (UK) HAS KINDLY PROVIDED THE RECIPE TO BE FOUND ON THE NEXT PAGE. ALBERT ROUX, ONE OF THE FOREMOST CHEFS OF HIS GENERATION, ON BEHALF OF THE SOCIETY TOOK UP THE CHALLENGE TO RECREATE RECIPES FOR FOUR OF ANATOLE'S MOST FREQUENTLY REMEMBERED DISHES. THESE WERE PUBLISHED IN THE SOCIETY'S NEWSLETTER 'WOOSTER SAUCE'. THE ONE PRINTED HERE IS REPRODUCED BY KIND PERMISSION OF NORMAN MURPHY, CHAIRMAN, ON BEHALF OF THE UK SOCIETY, FROM THE MARCH 1999 ISSUE. THE DISH WAS MENTIONED IN FOUR OF THE NOVELS.

THE PG WODEHOUSE SOCIETY (UK) HAS MORE THAN 1,000 MEMBERS

FOR FURTHER INFORMATION ABOUT THE SOCIETY:

www.eclipse.co.uk/wodehouse

MEMBERSHIP SECRETARY: CHRISTINE HEWITT, 26 RADCLIFFE ROAD, CROYDON CR0 5QE

MIGNONETTE DE POULET PETIT DUC, BY ALBERT ROUX   *Serves 4*

4 Breasts of Chicken (skin removed)
200g Butter
2 Large Shallots (finely chopped)
1 Decilitre Madeira
300ml Veal Stock (reduced)
300g Fresh Morrels (preferably small,
      black and with stalks removed)
1 Small Bunch Asparagus Tips
1 Small Truffle
Salt & Pepper, to taste

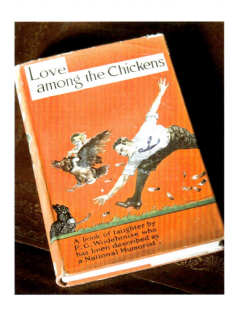

THE CHICKEN

Slice each breast into thin slices to form a scallop shape. Gently pound them on a flat surface. Keep refrigerated.

THE MORRELS

Split the morrel in half and wash thoroughly in cold water. Drain and dry the morrel on a tea-towel.

THE ASPARAGUS

Peel the asparagus up to the head, leaving the tips as they are. Cut the stalks away and keep for another use. Blanch the asparagus tip in boiling, salted water. Drain and refresh.

TO COOK AND ASSEMBLE THE DISH

1. In a large sauté pan, heat up 80g of butter until just bubbling.

2. Season the pieces of chicken and cook a little at a time to a light brown colour, 1-2 minutes on each side. Repeat the process until all the pieces are cooked. Keep the chicken warm.

3. Reduce the heat and add the chopped shallots to the pan. Cook for a few minutes.

4. Deglaze the pan with the Madeira and reduce by two-thirds.

5. Add the reduced veal stock, bring to a simmer and cook until the sauce is slightly syrupy. Strain the sauce through a fine sieve and return to a pan.

6. Meanwhile, sauté the morrels with butter.

7. Add the morrels to the sauce with the sliced truffle.

8. Gently, bring the sauce to a simmer, add a little knob of butter to the sauce and mix well.

9. Add the mignonettes of chicken to the sauce with the asparagus tips.

10. Heat up for a few seconds and check seasoning.

TO PRESENT

Arrange the mignonettes of chicken on to each plate, and spoon the sauce over.
Serve with fresh pasta.

I have the feeling that PG Wodehouse would prefer something more traditional with this dish, mature Claret or red Burgundy would work.

A WALK TO THORNEY ISLAND AND PRINSTED

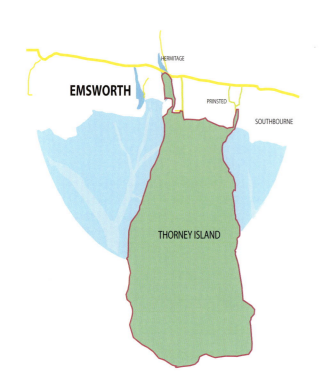

OUR FIRST WALK IS THE MOST DEMANDING - YOU SHOULD PLAN TO SPEND HALF A DAY TO COMPLETE IT.

THE BEST PLACE TO START IT IS THE EAST SIDE OF THE VILLAGE, AND THE LORD RAGLAN WOULD PROVIDE THE PERFECT PLACE.

WALKING AROUND THORNEY REQUIRES YOU TO ENTER AN ARMY CONTROLLED AREA AND YOU WILL BE REQUIRED TO PROVIDE YOUR NAME, ADDRESS AND A PHONE NUMBER. DON'T BE PUT OFF BY THIS - IT'S WELL WORTH THE EFFORT.

We start on the left side of The Lord Raglan and take the signed footpath marked by the paving stones on the left of this photograph. After passing under the building, go through the gate onto the causeway.

Walking through the Marina you will see a row of rectangular houses raised from the ground (right of this photo). Head towards these and look for the footpath signs that take you back towards the sea.

On your left is the Slipper Mill Pond (home to the ducks on the Raglan's pages of this book). To the right is Dolphin Quay and straight ahead where the houses are, was the site of Fosters Boat Yard.

When you arrive by the water look to your left and take the path which heads south. At this point you will find an excellent board with map and details of wildlife and other useful information.

Following the route of the causeway, you will arrive at the old Mill building which is now converted to housing (turn right as you go through the gate). Follow the pathway in this photo to the Emsworth Marina.

Follow the path until you arrive at the 'guard post' gate which is locked. Press the buzzer and answer the questions to be allowed access. You must keep to the footpaths on this section of the walk.

For most of our route you follow a path very close to the sea, but remember that during the war this was a vital airfield protecting the South of England. Although the RAF no longer uses the base, the runway and hangers can be seen in the distance as you walk round Thorney.

At the far south of the Island the path is not too well maintained and you may need to follow the old 'Peretrack' until the coastal path becomes more 'usable'. Many weekends the local model aircarft enthusiasts will be seen (and heard) at the end of the old runway.

We continue on our way from history back to nature and we carry on down our shoreline walk. Remember that during the summer you may have to divert round nettles and other natural barriers!

During summer and when the tide is high, the club boats can be seen to your right.

The only good stretch of sand in the Emsworth area can be found here. On a good day it provides a great spot to stop for refreshments (as long as you brought them with you). Most of the time, you will see very few people on this walk.

At the southern extreme of Thorney Island you can find a paradise for wildlife (particularly in the winter).

You may even find an old pillbox (war time concrete sentry box) which has now been converted into a bird observation shelter.

In the distance you will see the entrance to Chichester Harbour and Pilsey Island which is leased by the RSPB.

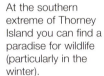

Just over half way through our walk we arrive at the old Thorney village and the parish church. The first main building you will see is the Sailing Club, closely followed by the old parish church. Remember that before the war this was just a small country village.

Saint Nicholas Church dates back to the 1100's.

You are now going North and during the Autumn and Winter months it's a great spot to watch thousands of birds such as waiders and wildfowl.

We now arrive at the other end of the military controlled part of Thorney. Press the buzzer, give you name etc. and you will be a free person again.

The cemetery is not only for the local folk who lived in the village, but also the military personnel who died during World War II. This photograph shows the graves of the German pilots shot down during the "Battle of Britain", sharing a common resting place with the Allied forces who died protecting England.

You will now arrive at the end of the raised embankment at Thornham Point on Thorney Island. Although it's called an 'Island' it has been joined to the mainland for more than a hundred years. Again you will find excellent information on the display board about your walk.

We now reach two boat yards, Thornham Marina and Paynes. Our path passes through both. 'Boaters Café' is one of only two refreshment stops (the other is only available on summer weekends).

Alas the village pub is long gone, so after a good look around this wonderful place, head back to the coastal path.

Heading West, do not be put off by the signs, this is our route back to Emsworth.

Continue down the road until you see the footpath on the right and shown in this photograph.

It leads over fields (past perhaps some grazing ponies) to the Emsworth Marina.

We now arrive in Prinsted which is well worth a visit.

First mentioned in 1066, and part of all that, the name Prinsted emerged from the old English description for 'a place where pears grow'.

Follow the narrow road, watching out for any car that may try to end your walk before you expected. Most people are considerate!

Continue for about half a mile and turn right into the road at the next T junction.

Back to those houses we saw at the beginning of our walk. The well maintained track leads back to the entrance to the Marina and the other facilities.

In Summer months the local Sea Scouts Hall offers light refreshments over the weekend. I can assure you it was a welcome break for the author of this walk!!

After a short distance you will come to another junction - turn right.

This road heads North and affords a pavement. It's the main road onto Thorney Island, and mainly used by the personnel on the base.

Backtracking to the old Mill building we can either carry straight on towards the 'Sussex Brewery' or turn left down the causeway to the 'Lord Raglan'.

A WALK TO WARBLINGTON

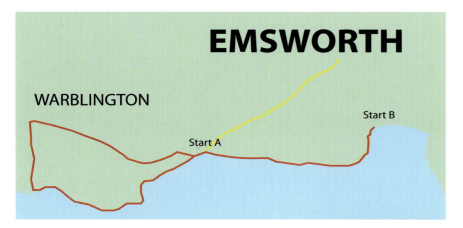

By now you should see Langstone in the distance ahead of you. Carry on until you find the wooden steps that take you up to a field south of Warblington. Go up these and through the field and through the gate into the cemetery.

A nice and easy walk - best at low tide.

You can start this walk from the village or drive to the end of Warblington Road where there is parking for about 5 cars (A). If you start in Emsworth, walk up Bath Road on the west side of the Mill Pond and turn right at the Sailing Club (B) and it's about half a mile to Start A.

From the foreshore at the end of Warblington Road turn right (west) and take the footpath to the left of Nore Barn Woods. (Seen in this photo.)

There are a number of tracks running through the woods which you can explore. As Nore Barn is not very large, you should be able to get back to the coast side easily when you get to the far (western end).

Make your way to the north east corner of the church yard where you will see a brick building (toilets). Leave the churchyard by the gate which brings you out by St Thomas à Becket church.

Parts of the church date back to Saxon times, with other building work in the 12th and 13th centuries. This was once the centre of a village which was deserted after the Black Death. You may see a small brick and flint hut which was used by gravewatchers who prevented body snatching.

Follow the coast route south then round the point heading west again. You should go no further if it's high tide, but otherwise follow the tide line for well over half a mile.

This leads to a second gate and then follow the path over fields. Behind, you will get a good view of the remains of Warblington Castle, which is now on private land. Also in the fields you may find cattle from the local dairy which is based next to the church.

After a good look round take the path to the right of the church using the path with a gate (see photo).

The track to the right is used by farm tractors and the cattle going for milking.

Nore Barn Woods is special. At times it can be busy, at times deserted. Changing its character with the season, time of day and the tide, you will always find something new. Walking from a dark woodland area, you will suddenly be in a clearing, surrounded by shafts of sunlight, butterflies and birds. You can find out more about it on its own pages in this book.

Eventually you will come to a small crystal-clear stream which is home to watercress and brookweed. In winter it can get a little muddy here, but should be nothing more than a pair of boots can deal with.

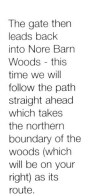

The gate then leads back into Nore Barn Woods - this time we will follow the path straight ahead which takes the northern boundary of the woods (which will be on your right) as its route.

Back to the end of Warblington Road and your car or carry on along the coastal route towards Emsworth.

THE PARISH OF WARBLINGTON WITH EMSWORTH

Now divided into two by the main road, the northern half of Warblington is much changed from former times. However, as you travel south to the shore, you pass the old Georgian rectory and the ruined castle turret before coming upon the church. The farm and its lands have been worked since Saxon times.

On the south side of the churchyard of St Thomas à Becket is a yew tree that is at least 1,000 years old, and mentioned in the Domesday Book.

Warblington has always been an attractive place, close by the sea and also having fresh water supplies combined with woodland and rich soil. It is reputed that a Roman villa was sited in the grounds of what is now Castle Farm.

During Saxon times a settlement, 'Weorbling's Ton' was established where the castle and church are today situated. The Domesday Book of 1086 recorded about 120 people living at Warblington, with an absentee landlord, Robert Montgomery, Earl of Shrewsbury.

During the 12th century the creek at Warblington became too shallow for fishing, however springs at the end of South Street in Emsworth were uncovered and so Emsworth became more habitable. The beginning of the decline of Warblington, and the rise of Emsworth. Nevertheless, the Manor of Warblington retained its importance as a useful gift at the disposal of the Crown.

During the early 13th century, the Warblington manorial rights were usurped and Isabella Bardolph was evicted from the Manor House. Later in that century, Herbert Fitzherbert was granted a charter to hold weekly markets at Emsworth. Havant already had its own market, so the importance of Warblington declined further. The population reduced, and during the 15th century those remaining were forced out when the fields around the church became a private deer park for Warwick the Kingmaker, then Lord of the Manor.

The church, the earliest building being Saxon and built of flint and stone, retained its importance for the villagers of Emsworth who did not have their own church in which to worship. During 1789 the Chapel of Ease of St Peter was built in the square in Emsworth, but it was not licensed for weddings and funerals so these still had to take place across the fields at Warblington. With a growing population, the church building was extended throughout the following centuries, culminating in work in the 19th century to build the top stage of the tower, extend the chancel and uncover the Saxon arched openings. If you look at the church today, the 14th century doorway with its intricately carved barge boards is thought to have been constructed from ship's timbers. In the churchyard are two Gothic-style flint buildings, originally grave watchers' huts built in 1828-9 to guard the graves from body snatchers. The graveyard contains many memorials dating from the early 18th century, and continued to be used, although St James' Church was opened in Emsworth in 1840 with its own graveyard.

Warblington Castle was built between 1515 and 1525, by Margaret Pole, Countess of Salisbury. All that remains today of what was a great building and courtyard surrounded by a moat, is a single turreted tower. Margaret was the granddaughter of Richard Neville, Earl of Warwick, known as the 'king maker' because his wealth and land ownership made him a powerful figure between the Yorkists and Lancastrians. Henry VIII apparently stayed in Warblington Castle in 1526 and entrusted his daughter Mary to the Countess for her early upbringing. However, because she did not support the king in his wish to re-marry, the family lost favour and she was beheaded in the Tower.

Richard Cotton became Lord Of the Manor of Warblington in 1552 whilst a member of Edward VI's Privy Council, and was there visited by the king who hunted in the park. Henry, Richard's youngest son and godson of Queen Elizabeth I, became Rector of Havant and Bishop of Salisbury. The family supported the Crown in the Civil War, and in 1644 the castle was razed to the ground by Parliament.

Source: 'The Church of St Thomas à Becket' booklet.

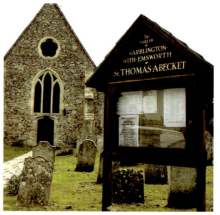

A WALK TO WESTBOURNE

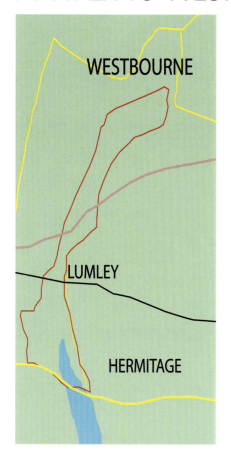

Start at the car park just off North Street, which will always (except during the Food Festival!) offer a place to park. Plan on paying for three hours parking if it's during a period when charges are due. We take the path at the southern end of the car park, shown in the first photo, and head directly east until we come to Peter Pond. On passing that turn north and make your way up Lumley Road. On your left after you pass Brook Meadow (see their section in this book for more details), you will see some charming cottages reached by little footbridges over the river. This leads to Mill Lane, where Lumley Mill used to be located. Part of the buildings are still there, but the main buildings were destroyed by fire many years ago.

The bridleway continues north and is also used by cyclists heading off towards the South Downs. The path is clear, and easy to follow. On the left is the River Ems - on the right farm land. You really do feel that you are in the country.

After about half a mile you come to a cross-road (no cars though) and take a left crossing over the A27 bypass. It's not difficult to miss as the concrete road produces a lot of noise. Hopefully one day it will be re-surfaced and peace will reign again!

For this walk we will head north to the village of Westbourne. In fact, part of ths route was used by smugglers to take the contraband from their boats to bases that straddled the counties and were therefore difficult to police.

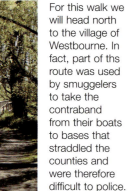

Carry on with a bend to the right and then straight on towards Westbourne. You will know you are close, when the dirt track changes to a 'macadam' surface. You will also see that you are still following the river route.

You now arrive in Westbourne with the church directly over the road in front of you. You must spend a little time looking round the church and its grounds. The Yew trees (pictured on the next page) were planted in the 15th century and it is now the oldest Yew avenue in England.

Spend some time looking round the village and enjoy it. If you time it right for a meal, there is a selection of good pubs, a restaurant, a fish and chip shop, and café.

Back-track past the church and its hall (on the left). Head straight on west out of the village until you come to the scouts hut, and you will find a footpath to your left The pathway will lead to a field where there is a right of way south.

This really is one of my favourite places. The fields are used by a local farmer for his bullocks, but they are very friendly and, in my ten years of walking here, I have never had a problem. The grass is lush and the stream is crystal clear. You can even find mushrooms at the right time of year.

Going south you will come to a pillbox in the narrow part of the west-most field. This is a real reminder of the area's important role in defending against invasion in WWII. You can almost see the Home Guard making their way there to defend King and country.

A few hundred yards on, past some magnificent trees, is the gate through to a path running under the A27 again.

From here a path takes a route that directly follows the boundary between West Sussex and Hampshire. Although close to Emsworth there is still a sense of being away from civilisation.

At the end of the path you will see a sign for Brook Meadow on your left. Take this route over the stile into the meadow. More details about this conservation area are in its section of the book. Take the path all the way through and you will find your way back to the car-park.

The Village of Westbourne

by The Westbourne Local History Group

Westbourne has been in existence for at least 1000 years. It was once owned by Earl Godwin, the father of the ill-fated Harold of '1066 and All That'. After the Norman Conquest ownership passed to Roger de Montgomery, the first Earl of Arundel who, had the right to hold a fair on the Feast of the Beheading of St. John the Baptist (August 29th). The fair was held annually up to the 1880's before falling into disuse, however the Church Fete is still held on or near that date. None of the buildings from those earliest days survive. The oldest dated domestic buildings are the thatched cottage opposite the War Memorial and Box Cottage in East Street, dated 1585 and 1548 respectively.

Westbourne was once an important market town centred on the Square. The area between the Church and the North Street/East Street junction was open in medieval time; the buildings only began to encroach on this space in the 16th century. One building bears the date 1631 and the initials JHA, and is reputedly the Market House that once had a projecting balcony at first floor level overlooking the Market Square. Norman House in North Street may have been a medieval house and a beam carved with the date 1639 was discovered during extensive alterations carried out in 1885. The Victorian appearance of the house dates from that time. Between White Chimney Row and Mill Lane lies the supposed site of the ancient Manor House that once provided hospitality to mediaeval Kings.

Until late Victorian times the job of Rector of Westbourne was something of a plum - highly paid with next to no duties. This is reflected in Westbourne Court, a former rectory, which suffered at the whim of an incumbent who gave it considerable Victorian embellishment, including an observatory, all of which has now been removed.

There is no known evidence of Saxon work and only slight indication of Norman work in the fabric of the church, but with the granting in 1071 of the right to hold the fair and this date being also the dedication of the church, the indication is that a church of some form has been here for some 1000 years. Domesday Book is unclear on the matter quoting Warblington as being part of the Manor of Westbourne and having, among other facilities, two churches. This could refer to sites in the two named settlements. The church has been altered many times in its life. A tower was added to the south-west corner in the 14th Century; the present tower dates from the 16th century, and to this, in 1770, a very ornate spire in the Gothic/Chinese style was added. All decoration was removed in 1860 and in 1865 a major restoration took place, leaving the building much as we see it today.

By 1858 the graveyard was full and a potential health hazard, so a new site on church owned land was selected. The new cemetery was opened in 1860 and was complete with its own chapel. Before the days of Parish Councils, the business of the Parish was conducted by the Parish Vestry, an unelected group of worthy ratepayers who met at the Vestry, hence their name! However the first item of business usually ensured that they all adjourned to the Lamb Inn, no doubt feeling this to be a more congenial setting. The Lamb is the symbol of St. John the Baptist to whom the Church is dedicated so use by the Vestry can be argued to be appropriate. Lamb Buildings is all that remains of the Lamb Inn.

Another public house of long standing is the White Horse, the badge of the Earls of Arundel, which is the origin of the name. From here the business of the market was regulated by the Earl's stewards. Across the Square is the George and Dragon, the name still faintly discernible between the upper windows. This building now ministers to man's needs again as a Doctors' Surgery.

Of the other Inns the Good Intent, in North Street displays a small naval ship, probably a cutter operated by the Revenue men. The Stags Head in the Square probably alludes to the hunting that used to take place in this part of the Forest of Bere long before there were any buildings on the market place. The last beer house to be established as a Public house is the Cricketers, on Commonside overlooking the cricket field it is appropriately named.

The Baptist chapel was built in 1867 to accommodate the congregation that had outgrown the 18th Century building next door, Old Chapel Cottage which had served as a place of worship for Nonconformists in the 1840's.

Also at Commonside are the last remaining fragments of the Workhouse. It was built in the 18th century to serve the Parish and had to be much enlarged to cater for the dozen parishes that made up the Westbourne Poor Law Union from 1835 to 1929.

Formal education for the village children began in 1819 when a school was set up in the Poor House. 27 years later a purpose built school appeared in School Lane. Segregation of boys from girls took place in 1876 when the girls were moved to Church Road. These two schools did duty until 1913 when the present school was built in River Street. Next to the school is the Westbourne Club, given to the village in 1899 as a gymnasium and boxing club, by George Wilder, a sporting Squire of Stansted.

The River Ems, only a stream today, has powered many water mills in its short run to the sea. The last surviving mill building is in River Street and may stand on the site of a mill of Domesday times. It continued working up to the 1920's. Another mill stood at the end of King Street. Lumley Mill as seen today is more correctly the mill house. The Mill burned down in the early 1900's and all that remains to be seen is the brickwork of the steps to the mill, now part buried in the undergrowth.

THIS BRIEF OVERVIEW OF WESTBOURNE HAS BEEN TAKEN FROM 'AROUND WESTBOURNE', A BOOKLET PUBLISHED BY THE WESTBOURNE LOCAL HISTORY GROUP.

ONE YEAR IN EMSWORTH AT A GLANCE

OCTOBER

NOVEMBER

DECEMBER

JANUARY

MAY

JULY

SEPTEMBER

OCTOBER

JULY

JANUARY

FEBRUARY

OUR RESIDENT WINE EXPERT

As has been said before, and indeed was said in the first Emsworth Cookbook, the pairing of good food with wine is by no means an exact science. Whatever else you do when choosing a wine to go with a dish, first and foremost drink what you enjoy.

The wine recommendations in this cookbook are meant as nothing more than a guide. They range from traditional pairings, through to some that are slightly more offbeat. I have increasingly noticed that as dishes evolve and we eat simpler, less rich food, that more and more of the recommendations have turned to dry, clean, less oaky white wines such as Pinot Grigio and Australian Rieslings.

Red wines seem to be going the other way with an almost bigger is best style. It will be interesting in ten years to look back, no doubt it will go full circle once again.

Lastly, many dishes are incredibly difficult to match wines with, and this year the chefs in this book seem to have conspired together to ensure that one of the most difficult crops up with regularity. Ice cream is the wine matcher's nemesis! All I can suggest is enjoy experimenting; you never know, you may find the ultimate wine to go with raspberry ripple with toffee chunks and a chocolate sauce. If you do ... be sure to let me know!

Alistair Gibson
Hermitage Cellars
T. 01243 373363

As well as the many businesses and organisations that have prepared the recipes and floral arrangements contained in this book, we should like to express our thanks to the following for their help and assistance. With so many individuals and groups volunteering material required, if we have forgotten to list your name here, then please accept our apologies.

Michael Austen, photographer
The Brook Meadow Conservation Group & Brian Fellows
Trevor Burdett, photographer
Chichester Harbour Conservancy
Countryside Agency & Terry Heathcote
Chris Collins, historical photographs
Emsworth Marina
Emsworth Maritime & Historical Society
Marian Forster, artist
Alistair Gibson, Hermitage Cellars (wine recommendations)
Bernard Gudge, photographer & historical photographs
Tim & Maggie Hart
Havant Tourist Information Office
Jenny Henderson, historical photographs
Friends of Hollybank Woods & Andrew Brook
Beryl Jobling
Alan Lambert, historical photographs & history
David Linington, photographs
Barry Mapley, historical photographs
Linda Newell, history of food
Friends of Nore Barn Woods & Roy Ewing
Prinsted Villagers & John Southgate
St Aubin-Emsworth Twinning Association
Matt Simmons, photographer
Monika Smith, photographer
Roger Smith, painted map of Chichester Harbour
Jeannie Sutherland, photographer
Sarah & Nigel Turner
The Westbourne Historical Group & Peter Barge & John Veltom
The PG Wodehouse Society (UK) & Norman Murphy

CONVERSION CHARTS

OVEN TEMPERATURES
FOR FAN OVENS, ADJUST ACCORDING TO MANUFACTURER'S INSTRUCTIONS

°Celsius	°Fahrenheit	Gas	
50C	100F	-	
75C	150F	-	
100C	200F	¼	cool
110C	225F	¼	cool
130C	250F	½	cool
140C	275F	1	very low
150C	300F	2	very low
160C	325F	3	low
180C	350F	4	moderate
190C	375F	5	moderate/hot
200C	400F	6	hot
220C	425F	7	hot
230C	450F	8	very hot
250C	475-500F	9	very hot

LIQUID MEASURES

Approx Metric	Imperial
25ml	1fl oz
50ml	2fl oz
75ml	3fl oz
100ml	4fl oz
125ml	5fl oz (¼pt)
250ml	10fl oz (½pt)
375ml	15fl oz (¾pt)
500ml (½ lt)	20fl oz (1pt)
1000ml (1lt)	40fl oz (2pts)

(if you wish to be more specific, the actual conversion is 1lt = 1.76pts)

METRIC WEIGHTS

Metric equivalent	Imperial weights
30g	1oz
45g	1½oz
55g	2oz
85g	3oz
110g	4oz
140g	5oz
170g	6oz
200g	7oz
225g	8oz
255g	9oz
285g	10oz
310g	11oz
340g	12oz
370g	13oz
400g	14oz
425g	15oz
450g	16oz (1lb)
560g	1¼lb
675g	1½lb
790g	1¾lb
900g	2lb
1kg	2lb 3oz

SPOON MEASUREMENTS

1 Teaspoon	5ml
1 Dessertspoon	10ml
1 Tablespoon	15ml

(Using measuring spoons not domestic spoons)